T0000516

# I AM ONIR, & I AM GAY

# I AM ONIR, & I AM GAY

ONIR *with* IRENE DHAR MALIK

**PENGUIN**
**VIKING**

An imprint of Penguin Random House

VIKING

USA | Canada | UK | Ireland | Australia
New Zealand | India | South Africa | China

Viking is part of the Penguin Random House group of companies
whose addresses can be found at global.penguinrandomhouse.com

Published by Penguin Random House India Pvt. Ltd
4th Floor, Capital Tower 1, MG Road,
Gurugram 122 002, Haryana, India

Penguin
Random House
India

First published in Viking by Penguin Random House India 2022

Copyright: © Onir and Irene Dhar Malik 2022

All rights reserved

10 9 8 7 6 5 4 3 2

The views and opinions expressed in this book are the author's own and the facts
are as reported by him which have been verified to the extent possible, and the
publishers are not in any way liable for the same.

ISBN 9780670094738

Typeset in Adobe Caslon Pro by Manipal Technologies Limited, Manipal
Printed at Replika Press Pvt. Ltd, India

This book is sold subject to the condition that it shall not, by way of trade
or otherwise, be lent, resold, hired out, or otherwise circulated without the
publisher's prior consent in any form of binding or cover other than that in
which it is published and without a similar condition including this condition
being imposed on the subsequent purchaser.

www.penguin.co.in

*To Ma, Baba,*
*Didi, Tabu, Trisha*
*and my friend Sanjay Suri*

*Equality is non-negotiable.*

# Contents

# NEW RHYTHMS

# 1

# First Crush

I met him in 1984, when I came to Calcutta (now Kolkata) for my higher secondary studies. There's a lot about those two years that I try to forget—the disillusionment of the young boy coming from a Himalayan small town to a big city, whose excitement had quickly transformed to disappointment and anxiety—but I will always remember him. In this city that I used to visit every year during the winter vacation and that had seemed full of welcoming relatives, I now desperately searched for accommodation and ended up in many scary or awkward living arrangements.

We didn't even have television in Bhutan at the time a fifteen-year-old me moved to Calcutta. The protectionist policies of the Bhutanese government ensured that it was the last country in the world to allow television, which was as late as 1999. Calcutta was overwhelming and, in many ways, I was the proverbial small-town boy experiencing big-city blues. I quickly realized that I wasn't going to get admission in any of the well-known schools as my ICSE marks were abysmally low by Calcutta standards. Anything above 60 per cent was considered first division and therefore something to celebrate back home in Thimphu, but my marks were woefully inadequate here. Those were not yet the days when students scored 99.9 per cent, but a 90 per cent didn't hurt anybody, as we found out the following year when my brother easily secured admission into La Martinière for Boys. As for me, I finally got admitted to St Augustine's in the rather dingy Ripon Street neighbourhood of Calcutta. It was a tiny and somewhat cramped school at the time. The stairs were grimy, the classrooms small and windowless.

I think we were about ten or twelve students. Though they must have, like me, not been academically brilliant, my classmates were all very kind and generous, and that made all the difference. Of the teachers I don't have many memories, except that I was so enamoured by my biology teacher Miss Mukherjee that biology quickly became my favourite subject. I still haven't forgotten her gentle voice and kind smile.

I also remember my Bangla teacher, even though his name escapes me. I remember him because I was terrified of him. My Bangla was atrocious, having started learning the alphabet only when I was in Class 9, and it was by some miracle that I passed my ICSE Bangla paper. At St. Augustine's, I used to hate my Bangla teacher and his classes. After I cleared my Class 12 Bangla paper, the man I had been so terrified of wore a broad grin as he patted me on the shoulder and said, 'I never thought a *gadha* (donkey) like you would pass, I'm so relieved.' I realized that he was perhaps actually fond of me and had been so severe with me only because he hadn't wanted me to fail.

It was during those years that I had what I can call my first crush. He was tall and dusky, with thoughtful eyes and sensuous lips, and he had somehow decided to take me under his protective wing. He not only made sure no one bullied me, but also helped me cross roads and board buses. I couldn't manage to cross the busy Calcutta streets on my own, nor board the crowded buses or trams before and after school. Very often, I used to walk long distances just to avoid getting into a crowded bus.

So yes, he was the one who would hold my hand or navigate me through the streets of Calcutta, his arm around my shoulder. I had no idea then what being gay meant. But unlike my Bhutan schooldays, I did not fall in love with any girl in my Calcutta school. There was an element of physical attraction with one of my classmates, but there was no emotional involvement at all with that boy. Stolen moments of touching and kissing in cinema halls, classrooms, deserted parks. There was no shame or sense of wrong in me, just the acknowledgement that sex was supposed to be something hush-hush; and we were discreet, like most boys and girls were those days.

I was aware that what I felt for my tall and dusky friend was different, but I didn't give much thought to that difference. Life went on, and we sat for our ISC exams. We knew that we would soon go our diverse ways, our paths dictated by education and career choices.

One afternoon, it was just the two of us in his flat. We sat on the floor in his room, next to each other, our backs resting against the bed, talking about many, many things, as teenagers tend to do during languid Calcutta afternoons. I don't really recall the exact flow of events, but I remember his white vest and the lungi he wore, and I can still remember his smell. At some point he put his arms around me, drawing me close to him, and asked me if I would like to touch him. This was not my first sexual experience, but I was nervous that afternoon, maybe because I had felt that unspoken and as yet unexplored feeling of love. This wasn't the first time I had kissed someone, but whenever the reference to the 'first kiss' happens, it's him that I think of. Of that sweaty afternoon and my limbs intertwined with his long limbs. When I walked back home that evening, everything had seemed pleasantly hazy. Yes, I know it sounds like a cliché, but maybe that one time in my life, I did experience that cliché of being blissfully in love.

Much like in the falling-in-love sequences of the Hindi films that I'd grown up watching, his image was omnipresent for the rest of the day, superimposed over all details of my mundane existence.

At 7 a.m. the next morning, there was a knock on my door. When I opened the door, I was surprised to see him standing there. He didn't want to come in but asked me to step out so that we could talk for five minutes.

Standing in the narrow lane outside the tiny Calcutta flat I then shared with my siblings, surrounded by the din of morning chores being executed in the surrounding middle-class households, I heard what he had to say. 'Look, I thought about it, and whatever happened yesterday shouldn't have happened. It was wrong, and what we did is a sin. I want you to erase that memory and so will I. And since that alone is not enough, I think it's best that we don't meet for the next ten years.'

He walked away. I was so numb that I didn't utter a word as I watched him turn around and leave. No parting hug, not even a wave . . . he just walked away.

It was not then, but a couple of days later, when I was walking near Dhakuria Lake, that the truth suddenly hit me, and I could not stop the tears. The year was 1986, and I was seventeen. I realized for the first time that my love was not acceptable to the world I lived in and that something that was priceless to me was considered sinful by others. I didn't understand why, but I was filled with a sense of emptiness, a great sadness, because I knew that this was not fair.

A couple of years later, I happened to pass by the building where he lived. Perhaps it was by design, but I don't think so. After a lot of hesitation, I went up to the building watchman and asked about him. The entire family had emigrated to the US.

We never met again.

I discover you once again,
Like countless other times,
In another body,
In another land,
In another century,
And make love to you in another tongue.

And I know,
In lives to come,
In different forms,
I will find you.
So I rest reassured,
As the paths diverge,
And silence conquers your heartbeat,
That I will travel centuries,
To another universe,
And I will find you again.

# 2

# Antigonus and Dadabhai

I have a long history of names. When I was born, my Dadabhai (maternal grandfather) named me Antigonus (Greek for 'worthy of his father'). I have no idea why he named me after a Greek hero who was the Macedonian general under Alexander the Great or if my parents and Dadabhai were really aware of the meaning. But then, Dadabhai had a penchant for giving his grandchildren foreign names—my sister was named Irene, my younger brother Antony. Only my sister still carries the burden of having to explain why she is called Irene—Antigonus and Antony metamorphosed into Anirban and Abhishek.

Dadabhai was the perfect, doting, affectionate, indulgent grandfather one hears of in stories, and we loved our holidays at his home. My memories of those holidays start with Baba and Ma beginning to pack the trunk, hold-all and suitcases in preparation for the three-month-long winter vacation that we would spend in India, largely at the maternal grandparents' home in Odisha. We travelled by bus from Bhutan to the Indian border, then by train to Calcutta where we would stop for a few days in what now seems like a really run-down hotel, and then again take a bus to Baripada, Odisha. As children, I don't think we really cared about how run-down the Calcutta hotel was because we spent our waking hours in the balcony, amazed at the sea of traffic and humans. Of special interest were the tramcars and how the trolley pole sliding over the overhead cable created sparks at some points of contact—Didi, Bhai and I would make up games counting the number of times we spotted these sparks—or double-decker buses or maybe even a completely yellow cab! Everything was an adventure then, right from watching the hotel cook toast bread on a coal oven, spread butter on it and then sprinkle some sugar on top, to the shops that sold so much amazing stuff and the pavement hawkers—we looked at everything in the big city with wide-eyed amazement. But the real holidays awaited us in Baripada, where Dadabhai lived in a sprawling bungalow at the Hamilton Gardens, being trustee of the Sir Daniel Hamilton Estate in Baripada.

After the bus reached Baripada, the luggage and the humans would get divided across a few cycle rickshaws, and our excitement would grow as the journey neared its end. Dadabhai, Didibhai (maternal grandmother), the uncles and aunts, the household staff—everybody would surround us as we got off the rickshaws, and there was much talking in loud voices, much laughter, appraisal of the kids' growth as well of the *shondesh* one had got along from Calcutta. So much excitement and shared bonhomie . . .

A distinct memory I have of one such trip is when we travelled from Thimphu with our pet rabbit, Tony. Tony was a rabbit from Kashmir, gifted to us by a family friend. Every morning we would open the kitchen door and he would scurry across to the garden, nibble to his fill and return home. At night, when we sat around the *bukhari* (fireplace) studying, he would sit by our side. If we ever tripped on him accidentally, he would hide in a corner and sulk. We would then have to beg before he agreed to come out. Tony quickly became an inseparable part of our family, and when we travelled to India for our winter vacation, Tony came along in a cardboard box with strategically punched holes. During this trip, we had lots of luggage like always, and the porter had placed, among other stuff, the rabbit box on his head. At some point, liquid trickled down his face. He was worried that something was broken, and we maintained a guilty silence.

Being big fans of Phantom and Tarzan comics, we tried to get Tony to make friends with Dadabhai's Alsatians. In a panic, Tony scratched us and fled for cover under a bed. We didn't try it again.

When we were back in Bhutan, one night a bear took him away from the rabbit house outside.

Dadabhai's bungalow stood in the middle of a huge mango orchard, surrounded by a large variety of trees, shrubs, flowering plants and a well from which water was drawn for watering the plants as well as to serve the entire household's needs. I think one of the house helps would draw water from the well all day long, filling two huge tin containers. He would then hang these on two ends of a bamboo pole and sling the contraption across his shoulder. He would probably begin his day by watering the plants, then filling the various water containers in the house, which he would keep replenishing all day long, and end his day with another round of watering the plants. Dadabhai loved gardening—I think I inherited my love of plants from him. Dadabhai used to wake up early and pluck flowers for Didabhai's puja every morning. Didi, also an early riser, loved accompanying Dadabhai on these flower-plucking trips. The plucking had to be done really early in the morning as the flower thieves would arrive early too, and we had to beat them and get the best flowers for Didabhai's deities!

The *thakur ghar*, as we called the prayer room, had framed pictures of many gods and goddesses and a few venerated ancestors. Didabhai would not allow us kids into this space, but we entered anyway, as Dadabhai allowed his grandchildren to break every rule that Didabhai set! So, right from sneaking into the *thakur ghar* to jumping on the thick mattresses and stealing pickles directly from the jars, to following no regimen about meals and bathing, to eating paan—we did it all, and Dadabhai was thus our absolute favourite person.

Maybe I also wanted to enter the *thakur ghar* as I thought of myself as religious when I was a child. For me, religion was about imitating Dadabhai, and I would love to do what I saw him do—adorn the deities with flowers and sandalwood paste, shut my eyes and pray ardently. Back home in Bhutan, Baba and Ma were not really religious. Baba, being a leftist, was almost an atheist, and Ma had never cared much for ceremonial rituals. As for every Bengali, Durga Puja was an important festival for my parents, but it wasn't really about religiosity but just a time for good food, new clothes and festivities. Having grown up in Bhutan, I don't really have the associations with Durga Puja that most Bengalis do. And my religious associations are only via my grandparents.

Come to think of it, Ma had a quirky relationship with God. She had a small wooden mandir in her bedroom where a few deities were installed, and these would keep changing regularly. Unlike Didabhai, who would offer her gods a bit of sugar or *batasa* in individual brass plates every day, Ma only offered the resident gods *payesh* (rice pudding) when she knew her children were longing for some, and it was strictly a token offering! If something bad happened to anyone close to her, she would banish the gods for months, loudly proclaiming through her tears that God didn't exist.

~

I used to have very bad nightmares as a child, sweating in my sleep and waking up traumatized. The dreams were very visual, and I still remember some of them, especially the ones about losing my Ma.

It's a grey day and Ma and I are inside a forest. Maybe we're there for a picnic, I don't know. I am chasing her as she runs into an oval clearing in the forest. The grass is almost like a soft, silky carpet. As she runs to the middle of the clearing, suddenly the grass carpet becomes the surface of a lake and Ma starts to sink into the water. I would wake up with a start and make up a happy ending for the dream, telling myself that I would jump into the water after her, pull her out and save her. This was a recurrent and much-dreaded dream.

Maybe this dream came from a constant childhood fear of losing Ma. Many years later in Calcutta, while watching Andrei Tarkovsky's *Ivan's Childhood*, Ivan's dream about his mother reminded me of my childhood nightmares. When I made *I Am*, Abhimanyu's dream sequence, where he sees himself as a girl, was inspired by a dream of mine.

I also dreamt of climbing mountains where us children would get lost and not manage to get back home for three days. I have those dreams even today, and they feel as tangible as reality. Only now, I have become a pro and I see myself negotiate steep ice glaciers, gorges and climb the Everest. Yes, I have scaled the Everest in my dreams! I have no idea where such vivid details come from.

Apart from these recurrent nightmares, I would dream of the villain from any horror or murder mystery film that I had recently watched and get really scared. Till date, I can't watch horror. I remember being chased by the hairy murderer from *Jaani Dushman* (1979) in a chilling dream. I would wake up frightened, leave the kids' room and slip in between Baba and Ma and hug Baba tightly. I remember his vest would be wet with my sweat.

Dadabhai came to my rescue in dealing with nightmares. He told me that every night before going to sleep, I should write 'Ram Ram Ram' on the pillow with my finger, and all my bad dreams would stay away. And it did work most of the time. On scarier nights, I would hide under the blanket with my nose sticking out so that I could breathe and start chanting 'Ram, Ram'. Then I would doubt if Ram was strong enough to take on all the demons and start chanting 'Krishna, Krishna', then move on to Buddha, Jesus, Shiva and end with Durga and Kali . . . By the time the powerful female forms were invoked, I would be so exhausted that I would fall asleep. The truth is that even now at fifty-two, after watching anything of the horror genre, I take shelter under the blanket and recite those names to feel brave.

I wasn't the only one at home who had recurrent nightmares—Didi used to have nightmares about me being stuck to the floor or some sticky surface, and the harder she pulled to free me, the tougher the task became. And as she pulled, I would become smaller, and she would wake up scared that I would disappear, that she would lose me. I think Didi always felt very protective about me—when we were children, and even now.

At some point, Ma and Baba decided that Antony and Antigonus would henceforth be known as Subhashish and Santoshish. I am not sure if the second one actually exists as a name, but it was chosen for me as I was this gentle kid and the Bengali word *shanto* means calm!

Winter evenings with Dadabhai meant us sitting in the verandah, huddled in the warmth of his all-encompassing shawl. It must have been really big because all three of us would be wrapped in its folds along with him while he told us the most amazing stories. They were mostly ghost stories, but there were also some stories about how he and Didabhai had trained in stick fighting (*lathi khela*), a traditional Bengali martial art form, so as to fight against the British, stories about the freedom fighter Master-da (Surya Sen), and of Partition. Now when I think of it, I cannot recall the man who lost so much during Partition—when he shifted from Rangpur in East Pakistan (now Bangladesh) to West Bengal—ever, and I repeat ever, say anything against the Muslim community. In fact, one of our favourite stories was about how his Muslim friend helped him dress up like one of them so that he could escape from Bangladesh. There was something in the escape story about jumping into a river at night, staying still and later swimming away, but I don't remember more.

While reading Jhumpa Lahiri's novel *The Namesake*, I was reminded of our lives back in Bhutan. Throughout the year, Ma would knit sweaters, caps and mufflers for her father, mother and siblings and also for my Bawropishi (Baba's eldest sister), who was our favourite person from Baba's family. Ma loved and respected her like the mother-in-law she never had. The trunk that travelled with us would be full of gifts—Ma always loved giving gifts as much as she loved receiving them. She was a good daughter who cared for and took responsibility for her parents, like the eldest child of the family is supposed to in India. She was the big boss when it came to her family, and there was no negotiation about the fact that we would spend at least 70 per cent of vacation time with Dadabhai.

I also remember the phone calls that came from the telegraph office in Thimphu when they thought the news was very urgent and needed to be conveyed at once. This usually meant bad news. The day my father heard of his young brother-in-law's death a thousand kilometres away, the last bus for the day had already left—the buses from Thimphu to the border town Phuentsholing would all leave in the morning so that the treacherous mountain road could be covered in daylight. He didn't tell Ma the news till late afternoon, putting off that awful moment for as long as he could. Only Didi knew, and she and Baba were both spooked when Ma came running from the kitchen and told us that she had felt a strange presence, as though someone was standing behind her as she cooked. Baba, who would normally laugh at this, stayed in the kitchen with her that day. After lunch, when she settled in bed for her afternoon siesta, Baba broke the news. I still remember the shrill cry that escaped her lips when she learnt that her younger brother had died. She cried for hours. Bhai and I tried to comfort her while Baba and Didi made preparations for the trip the next day. It was a long trip—eight hours by bus from Thimphu to Phuentsholing, where we would stay overnight, then four hours on another bus to New Jalpaiguri, an overnight train to Calcutta, and then a seven-hour bus ride to Baripada. This time we did not halt overnight in Calcutta as usual but travelled continuously, Ma's enormous grief making our exhaustion seem insignificant.

When our cycle rickshaws rolled into the driveway outside Dadabhai's house, Ma leapt off the rickshaw and went running to her parents, wailing inconsolably. It was a solemn moment, and unlike other occasions, our arrival didn't herald any joy. We were acutely aware of the fact that Mejomama had become a garlanded photo and would no longer be able to play cards with us or regale us with dialogues of his favourite Hindi movie villains. Yes, this brother of Ma's had a great love for masala Hindi films and their villains, knowing many dialogues by heart. He would watch the films first day first show, preserve tickets and write down the film names along with dates in a slim notebook. I guess the love for films began in that generation—my mother and at least two of her three brothers were crazy about films—and I took the love story a little further. Mejomama had some mental health issues and also had a weak heart. I'm not sure what killed him, but his memorial still stands somewhere among the many mango trees.

# 3

# East and West

In Bengal too, we have an 'east is east, west is west, and never the twain shall meet' situation. Beyond the political partition, there also exists a sociocultural divide in how the *epar Bangali* (Bengalis from *this* side) and *opar Bangali* (Bengalis from *that* side) react to situations and live their lives. Baba was the outsider, the one from *opar*, the *bangal* from the east, and Ma was the *epar ghoti* with roots in the west—their families differed in how they ate, spoke, lived their lives and even in how they reacted to any tragedy. Baba would become uncommunicative, maybe skip a meal and lie down quietly in his room. I have seen the same sort of response in most of my relatives from his side. On the other hand, Ma and her relatives didn't hesitate to display their emotions in a pretty full-blooded manner.

My paternal grandfather, originally from Sylhet, had shifted to Ramkrishnanagar in Assam after the Partition, but Baba and Sejopishi (an elder sister Baba was very close to) had stayed back in Sylhet (Bangladesh). They were both politically active, Sejopishi having been a part of the Nankar Andolan, a peasant movement that took place in Bangladesh from 1937 to 1950, and Baba in the Bhasa Andolan (the Bangla language movement), protesting against the imposition of Urdu over the native Bangla as national language. Both of them were also members of the then-banned Communist Party. Baba was arrested and remained in jail as a political prisoner from 1948 to 1955 in East Pakistan. He came to India in 1955, when his professor in Dhaka alerted him that he might get arrested again after his release and that it would be safer for him in India. Sejopishi was tortured heavily in jail—in fact, given up for dead by her family. Her spinal cord was permanently damaged and she miscarried her first child because of the beatings.

When Baba and Sejopishi came to Calcutta, they were survivors. Resilient, hardworking, with the dream of setting up a new life, Baba became a private tutor to earn his board and lodging while he got himself an education. Much later, while watching the films of Ritwik Ghatak, I caught glimpses of what my father's life must have been like as a young refugee in Calcutta. I would cry buckets while watching *Meghe Dhaka Tara*, *Komal Gandhar* or *Subarnarekha*, as those films gave me a sense of the quiet dignity of this community that had lived through so much pain and loss.

The pain of losing home is something that moves me deeply. I experienced it personally when we, in a sense, had to leave Bhutan when the Bhutanese government suddenly changed its policies towards Indians. My father resigned from his job in 1989, and I think he felt an immense sadness that he was treated thus by a country to which he had dedicated his life. For me, home still conjures an image of our house in Bhutan, even after all these years. Maybe the experience of losing one's home is also what led me, subconsciously, to find my best friend in Sanjay Suri—a Kashmiri Hindu who was made homeless in 1990 when his father was shot dead by militants.

I remember revisiting Thimphu in 1993, six years after we had left the city for Shemgang in 1987 and four years after Baba permanently shifted back to India in 1989. I was taking my friend and teacher Hanno Baethe to my homeland. I remember how difficult it was to stop the tears when we landed in Paro. In Thimphu, I was howling outside the school that Baba had literally built from scratch—Moothithang High School—and I don't know if I was sadder for Baba or myself. Going back to our old house was overwhelming—there was a hole in the ceiling where the *bukhari* chimney used to be, the flowerbeds now turned into a vegetable garden. Only the willow tree still stood outside the house, preserving our memories. No image can ever replace this one for me as home.

I have never been back since. It's kind of strange that I will always think of Bhutan as home, and that I will always be considered an outsider in the country of my birth—an Indian. What really makes home home? Is it race, language, religion? Or is it the bond that one has with the soil where one has planted seeds, grown saplings and watched the flowers bloom? I think I will forever remain an outsider everywhere. I was never considered Bengali enough in Calcutta, and in Berlin, as a student of cinema, I was, of course, a brown outsider, looked upon with suspicion. Even in Bombay (now Mumbai), the city I love so much for having given wings to my dreams, even in the place where I have lived for the longest period, I am occasionally reminded that I am an outsider. Maybe the feeling of being an outsider is also deeply ingrained in me because of my sexuality. Perhaps subconsciously, that too is why I have felt like an outsider. To be honest, I've never felt at home in these crowded cities the way I did in the mountains.

In 2019, I visited the now-deserted Pandit refugee camps from the 1990s in Mutthi, Jammu. I felt the same pang of homelessness. How could these hot plains and tiny concrete huts replace the lush green Himalayas and the spacious houses these people had to leave behind? And how cruel is the narrative that claims that 'they fled for better lives in Jammu'!

Dadabhai and Didabhai, along with Ma and her younger brother, weren't really refugees, even though they were living in what became East Pakistan before the Partition. For them, it was coming back home as they had ancestral property and family on this side of the border. In fact, Dadabhai had already sent his family to India before the Partition so that it was he alone who had to travel during those dangerous times. Once in India, Dadabhai soon started working with the Hamilton Estate. Ma grew up in Odisha in a household that functioned in a rather zamindari fashion. Meanwhile, Baba was sleeping in garages, teaching kids, attending political meetings and trying to complete his education. Ma and her family were much more comfortable—Ma was into music, dance, singing and theatre. Of course, her otherwise lenient father did not encourage the actress in the daughter, nor her love for a then-struggling actor.

Perhaps because they had experienced the upheavals of Partition, Baba's family was a little less traditional than Ma's in some matters. I remember women from Ma's family wearing white and turning vegetarian when they were widowed. Bordida (my Dadabhai's elder brother's wife) would come to live with Didi, Bhai and me at times when we were staying in a rented apartment in Calcutta as students. She would take over running our tiny household while she was there, and I think she enjoyed living with us because she could freely eat fish and egg there without being judged. Didibhai liked to eat mutton once in a while, apart from fish every day, after she became a widow.

It breaks my heart now to think how Bordida was always desperate to please everyone, being childless and dependent on her relatives after her husband's death. She was tall, strong and very lonely. Joint family politics are strange, and though I don't remember the details clearly, I had heard stories of how she seemed to always need more money. But imagine not having any money of your own—she might have wanted to buy a gift for someone or just something for herself. Imagine having to ask someone else for every bit of money you spend, for every single need.

Awareness about mental health wasn't very prevalent in those days, and as kids, I think we always remained a little distant from Didabhai because we had heard tales of her being possessed or even mad. Apparently, she collapsed when she heard the news of her mother's death, and when she regained her senses, she was raging mad. I've heard it whispered that she had tried to kill Ma and her brother, that it would take a few people to restrain her when she was 'possessed'. She was sent to a *pagla garad* (an institution for the mentally disturbed) a couple of times, where she was given electric shock therapy. But it was an *ojha* (exorcist) who finally cured her. The *ojha* (exorcist) performed some puja, at the end of which he asked Didabhai to pick a *kalash* with her teeth and run. Didabhai did as asked, and while running with the *kalash* (large vessel) between her teeth, she collapsed under a tree. A branch of the same tree snapped at that moment—the spirit had finally left her!

Later, when I read the works of Gabriel García Márquez, the tales would often transport me back to the world of those childhood stories.

Growing up, we saw Dadabhai's world slowly crumble. He was never good with money and had hardly any savings. There were some complications with the estate that led to endless court cases, which took a toll on his physical and mental health. He was a strong man who still had bulging biceps and stood erect till the end, but he had multiple ailments in the last years of his life. He used to smoke a lot and eventually got throat cancer. He was treated in Calcutta, and I remember how, when he came home after radiation therapy, we—his grandchildren—would apply ointment on the area marked by purple lines. It would slowly turn black and, later, the skin would peel. It was horrible to see our Dadabhai suffer so much, but the treatment did give him some more years. Then the cancer came back, this time quickly spreading its tentacles all over, and we knew that this was a battle that he would probably not win. But he did fight till the end, and Ma was there by his side throughout.

# 4

# The Dancing Boy

I used to love singing and dancing when I was in school. I was also very good at athletics. At the school's annual sports event, I would win a lot of prizes, and Bhai always created a ruckus afterwards because he did not get as many prizes as me. Bhai was always throwing tantrums in those days—I would be happy with a reasonably priced doll, but he would howl because he wanted a big toy car that was beyond our parents' budget. He would throw such a tantrum, sometimes in the middle of a marketplace, that it was almost embarrassing for our parents. Similarly, he always created a scene whenever we were to go for a film. He wouldn't want to come along but couldn't be left home alone either. So he would be bribed to watch movies, mostly with sweets. When we went to watch *Umrao Jaan* in Calcutta's Metro Theatre, he kept his head down and sobbed throughout the film, opening his eyes only when there was a horse riding sequence! Afterwards, he had to be bribed with a digital wristwatch before normalcy could be restored in the household. The pampered, bratty younger sibling grew up to become one of India's top physicists.

In school in Bhutan, I mostly danced to Nepali songs and the bhangra. The two Nepali songs I still remember having danced to are '*Hera na kancha yoh khola, bogero kahan jane ho*' (Look at the stream, young man. Where is it flowing to?) and '*Himalay chareo chauri gai*' (The mountain goat climbed the Himalaya). Like all the boys, I too wanted to dance with the prettiest girl in the class. But I would never be paired with the girl I had a crush on as she was taller than me.

I think the first person to teach me to dance to Nepali songs was Aruna 'Miss', and some of the fondest memories of Bhutan centre around 'Miss' Aruna and her family. I write 'Miss' because when we first met her in Geylegphug, she wasn't yet married to AK Uncle and was our teacher and Ma's best friend. Even after she got married, had children and now grandchildren, the 'Miss' keeps slipping in, and one has to make an extra effort to call her 'auntie'.

Very often, on the first night of our stay at Dadabhai's home, there would be a performance by us kids. I remember I used to look forward to the evening when my maternal aunts (Mitamashi and Khukumashi) would dress me up in a ghagra and apply make-up to my face. I would wear a veil and dance to Hindi film songs with total abandon. Sometimes I would dance like Helen, sometimes Bindu . . . and no, I didn't identify myself as a girl; I think I just wasn't conscious of gender boundaries. Until one evening when I was a student of class eight and must have been around twelve years old. Ma and Baba had a talk with me after the performance, telling me that I was too old to be dancing like a girl and that it was very embarrassing for them to watch me dance in such a shameless way. It was one of those rare occasions that Ma and Baba disapproved so strongly of something I did. That night, my dreams of being a dancer were shattered, and I wept a lot.

I remember a night in Calcutta a few years later, when Didi and I were staying as paying guests at Ramgarh. Load-shedding was common in those days, and I had gone up to the terrace to escape from our stuffy little room. It was dark on the terrace.

As faint moonlight shone down, I could magically hear ballet music, and I started happily jumping around the terrace, a ballet dancer to an imaginary 'Swan Lake' theme being played. And then I heard people giggling—the family with whom we were staying had sneaked in and was watching my performance with great amusement.

Lead me within you,
Dark, wet, cold and magical.
I sink,
Drawn by the primal force,
Voices beseech me
Not to take the path.
But I can hear another voice singing softly,
The Lotus-eater beckons me.

My steps no longer subject to my command,
Take flight,
Intoxicated I step into the clouds,
To be one with the Lotus-eater.

# 5

# Not Good Enough

As a child, I used to also love combing my mother's hair, applying make-up to her face, approving how she looked before she went for a party. Till today, she appreciates my taste when it comes to choosing her clothes.

When we were growing up, Ma would often talk of leaving us when we were a little older and going to live with the person she was in love with from before her marriage. She never told us this directly, but she would discuss this with her friends at night when she assumed we were asleep. That was probably the reason I always dreamt of losing her. I think imagining that future probably gave her the strength to continue with the life she was living. They were such different people, my parents—Ma is a romantic at heart to this day; she loves art, music, dance, good clothes, travelling and socializing. Baba is a pragmatic, matter-of-fact introvert. He had very few close friends, and family mattered to him the most. What was amazing about him was that he shared all the housework with Ma—cooking, raising us, washing clothes, shopping, teaching us. In everything, he was an equal partner. When he started teaching in Bhutan, he encouraged her to take up teaching too, making her more independent, but the truth still is that she stepped into his world. He never really learned to appreciate or understand her world and her dreams. So Ma would often get angry and scream at Baba. He would stay quiet and not talk for a day or two. We kids hated it when this happened, and it happened pretty regularly in our home as we were growing up.

I had a major complex about my skin colour. Didi was fair. When we went to Baripada for our winter vacations, everyone would call her 'Toma' (from tomato) because of her pink cheeks. Bhai was fair too. Because I was dark, I was often questioned thus by relatives, 'Your Ma, Baba are so good-looking, Toma and Tabu are fair, why are you the way you are?' Being called 'Kalia' (blackie) or 'Kele' (black) was common, and the politer people would say that I was nice-looking in spite of being dark. I would wonder why God had made me so ugly. At times like these, Didi was always there to fight for me and comfort me. I don't remember details, but I know her presence always protected me from these assaults by relatives.

My inferiority complex also came from the fact that of the three of us, I was the weakest when it came to academics. Didi was good, especially in humanities, and Bhai was just brilliant. I struggled to pass in subjects like maths, physics, chemistry and Bengali. I was all right with history, English, geography and biology, but my scores were nothing to feel proud about. I used to also believe that Baba secretly loved Didi the most and Ma loved Bhai, so I felt left out here too.

I used the image of a protective Didi for the character of Anu in *My Brother Nikhil*. When I was writing the script, I thought about whom I would choose to tell my story if I was dead. It would be Didi, and so all through the scripting process, I would imagine her voice and her presence as Anu. It was kind of prophetic, for when in 2011 I was falsely accused of molesting a guy, Didi again took up the same, fiercely protective role. Like Anu, she too campaigned for me.

I used to pray a lot as a child, and one of my fervent prayers would be that I would wake up and find that God had listened to my prayers and made me fair. When I had a healing abrasion, I loved the lighter-than-normal shade, and I would try to peel off a little bit more of the surrounding skin. I remember reading Somerset Maugham's *Of Human Bondage* and then starting to meditate on that one wish—a wish to be fair. I would sit in a dark room with a candle and focus and keep waiting for the magic to happen. It did not. By the time I was in Class 10, I decided that I needed to overcome this feeling of inadequacy, this dependence on a deaf God. I wanted to stop believing in God, but that wasn't an easy process. That's when I did something that I am not proud of, but it liberated me—I stepped on the image of one of the gods Ma worshipped. I was terrified that I would be a cripple by the next day. But as months passed, I felt free, and I learnt to accept myself as I was. I no longer prayed to ask someone else to make my life better—it was my life, and the entire responsibility of finding happiness was mine. I also reasoned that if there was a God, She/He/They would forgive me as I was leading a good and honest life. Maybe God would be relieved that one less human was reaching out, seeking forgiveness for their sins or—as is the case more often—to ask for a favour. My gratitude would henceforth be for the friends and family members who stood by me and helped me to be myself.

~

My tumultuous relationship with gods notwithstanding, I'm sure Didabhai must have thanked them over and over the night I came into this world. It was a stormy night when I had made my appearance in a government hospital in Samchi, Bhutan and

Didabhai, who had come to help Ma during the childbirth, had been ecstatic at the birth of her first grandson. She immediately started calling me '*Amar Krishna Thakur*' (my Lord Krishna)! I believe my birth brought my parents much happiness too, also because they had been transferred to a small town with a hospital due to Ma's pregnancy. This was an improvement on their first posting in Bhutan—Chargharey, a place with no civic facilities. I was therefore called a harbinger of good fortune. I don't have a birth certificate, probably because birth certificates weren't so common then. So, when I was in Class 9 and Bhai in Class 8, our parents decided it was time to rename us (again) so that the school-leaving certificate would have our final, official names. Ma was never too happy about Santoshish and Subhashish, names suggested by our family doctor, I believe. Ma was a big fan of Amitabh Bachchan, and so Bhai was named Abhishek. I don't remember why I was named Anirban. I do remember that I would at times add Ma's surname to mine, writing Anirban Bose Dhar, and the teacher would always cut out the 'Bose'. I wanted 'Bose' for various reasons. Firstly, 'Anirban Dhar' sounded like 'Anir Bandhar' (monkey) and contributed to my getting bullied and being called not just '*kalia*' but also '*bandhar*'. 'Bose' would serve as a buffer. Secondly, I was closer to Ma's family and always wondered why Ma's surname wasn't a part of my name. During my college days in Calcutta, I had got an affidavit made, changing my name from Anirban Dhar to Anirban, but it did not work for most official documents those days. The father's name and/or surname was required while filling all forms. The funny part was that Ma was more upset than Baba about me choosing to lose the 'Dhar'!

When I started working in Bombay, I got terribly sick of people mispronouncing my name: 'Anir Bhan', 'Amir Bhan', 'Amir Bhai', 'Anil Ban' . . . everything but 'Anirban'. I remember one assistant director credited Didi as 'Irene Ban' for a TV show she had edited as she was 'Anil Ban's' sister, after all! When I made my first film, I decided to create an artist identity for myself . . . just 'Onir'. Maybe I was also leaving behind a lot of baggage, as I started a new journey as a film-maker.

# 6

# Luger Theatre

The journey to becoming a film-maker has been a long and very empowering one. When did it all begin? It's not as if there was this one day or moment when I decided I wanted to be a film-maker; it was a long love story. In Thimphu, a new Hindi film was released every week at the town's only cinema hall, the Luger Theatre. Since Ma was passionate about films, we ended up watching all the watchable ones . . . and a few of the really unwatchable ones as well! The theatre was about an hour's walk from our home in Mootithang, and although walking downhill was easy enough in the pre-car days, we would always end up being late. This was because Ma took hours to get ready—she was never happy about the sari she wore or how she wore it, or maybe it was the blouse, which would in any case get covered with a cardigan and shawl, that wouldn't be the right shade. The manager's son was a student of the high school at Mootithang, so Baba would call up the manager and request that he wait till we reached. Arriving 15–20 minutes late was common, and the audience was probably subjected to reruns of trailers and slides till then. The crowd would give us dirty looks when we finally entered the usually packed hall.

I used to watch those films with such involvement, going through a total emotional roller coaster. I wept buckets while watching *Deewaar, Haathi mere Saathi, Mili, Anand and Sholay*. I used to get especially emotional about the all-sacrificing, much-nurturing 'Ma' characters. Dev Anand was Ma's all-time favourite actor, so when he came to Thimphu for the fourth king HM Jigme Singye Wangchuck's coronation in 1974, her excitement knew no bounds. She went with Baba to Bhutan Hotel to have breakfast with him and also recorded the conversation on a cassette recorder till the point when he requested Ma to switch it off. That audio cassette must have been played a record number of times for all our friends and family till it was so damaged that it was finally truly beyond repair. She has a photo with him that she displays with pride to this day. She would also brag about the fact that no one at the coronation recognized Vijay Anand apart from her. Although Dev Anand was the heartthrob, she thought it was Vijay Anand who was the real talent. Ma was actually quite a versatile cinema watcher. So, along with the mainstream fare, we also started watching films like *Bhumika, Aakrosh, Junoon, Albert Pinto Ko Gussa Kyon Aata Hain, Manthan, Mandi* and *Arth*. These films weren't meant for kids, and I didn't always understand everything, but something definitely seeped through, and I always got this feeling that these films were special. *Chakra* was the only film I remember our parents watching without us.

There had been a screening of *Pather Panchali* in our school, and us Indian students had felt so embarrassed by the poverty depicted. How come the Indian government granted aid to Bhutan while we had so many poor people at home? It had really confused me. Once, *Bhumika* was to be screened in our school, and as I had heard Ma rave about how beautiful Smita Patil was, I told everyone that we would get to watch this most amazingly beautiful actress. When the film started, I quickly realized that she wasn't what everyone considered beautiful. Being dark, she was immediately rejected by my Bhutanese friends.

Some of the films I watched in those childhood years remained with me forever. I was in Class 6 when I watched Shyam Benegal's *Junoon*. I watched it just once, but the visuals overwhelmed me—the colours and the scale—it felt like no other film. I would keep dreaming of the scene where Shashi Kapoor, on horseback, turns to go away and Nafisa Ali comes running out of the house and screams, 'Don't go.' That was the only dialogue she had in the film, and the understated nature of their relationship and the looks they exchanged stole my heart. I fell deeply in love with cinema that evening. I also fell in love with the dashing Shashi Kapoor and the gorgeous Nafisa Ali—I don't remember who among them stole more of my heart.

Another film was *David Copperfield*. I think I was in Class 5 when I watched it, probably the 1974 version. What has remained with me forever is the image of David sitting on a rocking chair, rocking the very ill Dora. When he wakes up, she is dead. When I shot Jimmy Shergill and Juhi Chawla on a rocking chair in *Bas Ek Pal* (2006), it was a tribute to that image.

~

As a child, I always wanted to fly—as in, actually have wings and soar in the sky. In my dreams, I would be leaping across buildings in pursuit of bad guys. I really believed that it was possible to fly. I would stand at a slight height behind our house and jump, believing that one day I would be able to just take off and soar. The gods were unkind to me yet again, just like they were about my complexion, which they refused to lighten—my wings never appeared. Then, I decided to be a pilot but quickly gave up on that ambition once it was proven that I was terrible in science.

I next decided that it was the merchant navy for me, and I loved the idea of sailing the world. I failed the entrance exam for marine engineering, and I also didn't know how to swim. Someone had apparently predicted my death by water, and so I was never encouraged to learn swimming as a child. In fact, I developed an acute aquaphobia thanks to my parents. I tried to learn swimming in Calcutta (with no success) and only got rid of the fear much later in Bombay.

My dream to travel for a year on board a ship is still alive. Someone please grant me that dream. My first trip by ship was in 1995, when I crossed the English Channel as I travelled from Calais to Dover. The approaching cliffs of Dover, engulfed in mist, appeared magical. I kept thinking of another favourite film of mine, *The French Lieutenant's Woman*. Of course, the trip ended much too soon.

Our parents had wanted me to be a doctor, Bhai an engineer and Didi a professor of English literature. When Didi completed her MA in English and cleared the UGC MPhil entrance exam, it looked like she was nearing her destination. Bhai was brilliant at science and cleared the JEE, taking admission in the department of mechanical engineering of Jadavpur University. But then, he quit engineering and joined Presidency College, pursuing a BSc (Physics Honours). Didi turned her back on academics and went off to FTII, Pune, to study film editing. I quit science after ISC and initially joined the Asutosh College English department and then shifted to Jadavpur University to study comparative literature. So, all three of us sort of dashed our parents' dreams and chose to follow what we felt was our calling.

I started getting ideas for stories around the time I was in Class 9, but I would never really get down to writing them because I hated my handwriting. I remember Shibaji da, one of my favourite professors at Jadavpur University, had once said that if one dipped a cockroach in ink and set it free on paper, the cockroach would leave imprints that looked like my handwriting. Honestly, my handwriting was that terrible.

When I was in Class 10, Didi was already studying in Calcutta. I remember her taking me to what used to be an ice skating rink for a film festival, and we watched Satyajit Ray's *Charulata* and Karel Reisz's *The French Lieutenant's Woman*. My world turned topsy-turvy and I realized that I was now utterly enamoured by this art form and wanted to pursue it at some point in life. By then, Didi had already started thinking about FTII, something Baba wasn't very happy about. I also wondered if I suffered from a 'copycat syndrome'. But Madhabi Mukherjee, Meryl Steep and cinema had absolutely captivated me.

You have taught me how
To annihilate myself,
To slowly stop waiting,
To slowly stop expecting,
To deny yesterday,
To dismiss tomorrow,
To be free
Of you.

# 7

# Homeless in Calcutta

Most students from Bhutan used to go to schools in Darjeeling after completing their tenth grade, but I refused to go to Darjeeling, giving up a chance to study in a well-known school, as I wanted to be closer to Didi. I knew that I would get to experience more of the world of cinema if I stayed in Calcutta. But the higher secondary years were such a struggle that films hardly ever figured in the scheme of things. I was struggling with finding a place to live, struggling with the power cuts of Calcutta, the oppressive heat, the mosquitoes, the crowd, the dust and Bangla.

In my first year in Calcutta, I think I shifted places around thirteen times in a never-ending quest for shelter. I remember staying at a relative's place in the Bowbazar area of Calcutta when power cuts were a regular feature, and I would feel too shy to ask for a lantern so that I could read. So, while the son of the house studied with a lantern, I stood at the balcony and read by the light of the street lamps at the crossing nearby. None of my relatives were too keen to host me; maybe they didn't want the responsibility, or perhaps they were worried that I was into drugs. The polluted Calcutta air did not suit me, and not only had I become thin, but my eyes would be perpetually red. I have been called a druggie and abused—people just assumed that I was one.

I had a strange sleeping arrangement at a paying guest accommodation, where I was to share the room with the daughter of the house. This was a house in College Street where, apart from the young daughter, there also lived a son, a maid and the rather formidable landlady. It was a four-storey building from the British era with a courtyard in the centre. We were staying on the second floor and the bathroom was on the ground floor, though the problem was not the location as much as the fact that the bathroom didn't have a roof. To this day, I don't understand how it was acceptable for all the inhabitants of the building to be bathing in what was almost full view of the people from the higher floors, even if they were bathing half-clothed! I used to be very shy, so I found the only possible solution—I would wake up really early and bathe before anyone else woke up.

This brings back memories from a few years earlier when I was in Class 8 and Bhai in Class 7. Our parents had thought it would be a good idea to put us in a boarding school in Calcutta, especially since Didi was already studying in the same city. We were admitted to St. Thomas' Boys' School, Kidderpore. The school had sprawling grounds, and Bhai and I were excited about this new adventure. A set of six new shirts, three pairs of trousers, three shorts, jackets, a trunk full of sundry other stuff for each of us—ah, it had all seemed so promising! Once in the hostel, it was quickly obvious that the reality of hostel life wasn't going to match up to what we had imagined, based probably on some Enid Blytons that we had read. The toilets were filthy and the bathrooms open. Both Bhai and I were shy, so we would wake up at unearthly hours to bathe before the others and also use the toilets before they became unusable. Bhai's classes had already begun, but for some reason, mine hadn't yet. I remember us at breakfast—we were slow eaters, believing in chewing each mouthful meticulously, and the bell that signalled end of mealtime always rang before we were halfway through. I suppose they never meant it when they taught in class that you should chew your food properly. The biggest shock was post dinner, when some boys came up to us, pretended to be pally, and started showing us their private parts, asking us to show ours and touch theirs. That was when a tall and kind-looking senior intervened. He asked the other boys to leave us alone and kind of took us under his wing. No one troubled us after that. Ma and Baba hadn't yet left Calcutta and came to meet us three days later to see how we were settling in. Before we could start complaining, Ma took one look at us and broke down. She cried and cried, and finally Baba spoke with the school authorities and we left the same day, glad to be heading back home to Thimphu.

I forgot to mention that although I was better than Bhai at athletics, he always beat me at table tennis. And when we paired up, we would always win the doubles. I remember the two of us walking to the Development Club every evening for practice, a good forty-five minutes away. It was a long walk but so much fun to go there and play. Bhai and I had been junior runners-up and champions many times in the annual competitions held at that club. I still remember our first Chinese racquets—they were so much lighter and more comfortable than the ones we had used so far. They were expensive, but Baba and Ma always encouraged us to play. It wasn't only table tennis—late afternoons and early evenings were meant for playing or gardening. You wouldn't find us indoors until we absolutely had to be inside and face the horrible, horrible reality of homework time! Going to the school where your father was the principal and mother the history teacher meant that you always had to do your homework.

Our growing up years were mostly fun. Birthday parties were big events in Thimphu. During the day, the entire class would land up at home, and I would be waiting for everyone to leave to be able to open my gifts. In the evenings, family friends would come over. Food would often come from Bhutan Hotel or Moothithang Hotel. My mouth waters just thinking of those chicken sandwiches and finger chips. And, of course, a lot of *ema datshi*, apart from the regular chicken and mutton. Very often, us kids would pour a little bit of whiskey or rum into a bottle cap and take a quick sip. Baba and Ma hated to go to parties without us, and when they returned home a little tipsy, they would wake us up and hand out cashew nuts and any savouries that they had stashed for us in their pockets or purse. We would wake up and nibble on those while they imitated how people were dancing in the party!

Calcutta was thus a big transition from Bhutan. In the College Street PG, I was supposed to get a room to myself, and that is how it was when I moved in. But the arrangement soon changed, and one day I returned from school to find that they had moved another single bed into the room, and I was told that the daughter would move in and the maid would sleep on the floor between the beds! The son was to share the other bedroom with the mother. I didn't complain to my parents as they had just left for Bhutan, and I was afraid that they might suggest that I drop a year till my accommodation problem was solved.

A month later, when I returned from school, I was told that my bed had collapsed and I would have to sleep on the floor till I bought a new bed. Obviously, I didn't have the money to buy a bed. The next day, Didi was visiting me, and when she saw how I was being harassed, she spoke to some of her friends and immediately shifted me to the Salvation Army hostel on Ripon Street.

Debashish da was the one who got me into the Salvation Army hostel. The room I stayed in had two beds and usually anywhere between four to six people crashing there for the night. All of them were five to eight years older than me, but everyone treated me with a lot of love and care, as if I was a little brother they had to take care of. But the problems started soon enough. My school was early in the morning before the canteen opened, so I would store bread and eggs for breakfast. The guys I was sharing the room with would very often smoke up and then feel very hungry. I would feel bad for them and end up giving them my breakfast. I was missing breakfast on most days and becoming weaker by the day, but I didn't initially tell Didi anything since I had started feeling that the problem perhaps lay with me. Things got worse when a couple of them started borrowing small amounts of money from me, and I would end up having no money to buy my lunch and dinner.

Once, I had no food for two days as they hadn't returned my money and I was too shy to ask or tell anyone. Didi, my saviour, visited on the weekend and realized what was happening. She decided that she would give up her hostel so that both of us could stay together as paying guests somewhere—it would be easier to find a nice place for a brother-sister duo rather than for a single red-eyed young lad. A friend of Didi's connected us with a lovely family who lived in Ramgarh, and for a few months, that was home for us.

And then it was time for Bhai to come to Calcutta. He got admitted to La Martinière for Boys, and Ma and Baba decided that the best thing to do was to rent a flat for the three of us. It was nice for the three of us to be together again and good to have Bhai back in my life. Though we were like chalk and cheese, we were also inseparable as he was just a year younger. We fought a lot as kids but always came together as a team when it came to a third party. We started living in a two-room flat on Salimpur Road, and even though we had to cook our own meals, this was a wonderful phase of our Calcutta lives.

From 1984 to 1987, each time I had my vacations, the mountains would be calling. Going back home to Bhutan was like getting a detox. Little did we know that there would soon come a day when those clear blue skies would not belong to us and we would no longer call Bhutan home. The Bhutan government policies that rightly wanted to empower the native Bhutanese were very unfair to many Indian nationals who had been a part of the nation's development. Baba, who had helped in building schools and gone house to house to convince parents to send their children to school, was suddenly told that the schools could no longer be headed by non-Bhutanese. He had been working since 1965, teaching in some of Bhutan's first schools, in areas so remote that there were no motorable roads, electricity or running water. This strange new policy of the Bhutan government didn't recognize years of dedication and hard work and expected a school principal to be willing to work as an assistant teacher. As a special favour to Baba, who was much loved, he wasn't immediately demoted but transferred to a remote place called Shemgang, where an Indian heading a school would attract less attention.

This was also the time when the problems with the Nepalese section of the population began and I believe were dealt with a very firm hand. The Nepalese are very proud of their language and culture, and Bhutan was a small kingdom that needed to preserve its own identity. The clear casualties of this strategy were the Indians and the Nepalese. We had to conform, transform or leave. Maybe this is what one calls collateral damage, and that is why I hate the term so much.

For me, leaving Thimphu has forever meant the loss of my home. When Baba and Ma were transferred to Shemgang High School in 1987, it felt like a punishment posting. Baba, who was in his fifties, was being asked to go away from the school he had helped build—Motithang High School. None of us could stop crying as we went ahead with the process of dismantling and packing up our home and saying various goodbyes. I was to head back to Calcutta while Bhai, Didi, Baba and Ma drove to the new destination. I will always remember the house receding from my line of vision, never to be my home again.

It was lovely—the three of us living together, learning to be responsible young adults. Though Didi did most of the actual running of the household, I want to believe that it wasn't because of any gender stereotype but as she was the eldest and also the bossiest. Bhai and I helped with the cooking, and one of us made breakfast for sure. Bordida came to live with us sometimes, and we were so happy when she took over the kitchen. She made the best rotis in the world and the most amazing *khichuri*.

The Salimpur Road house was right next to a small mosque, and we used to wake up every morning to the sound of the azan. There were no intrusive loudspeakers in those days, and it always sounded beautiful and felt like a gentle nudge to wake up. It never bothered our parents that we were living next to a masjid, and I sometimes wonder whether it would have been the same in today's polarized India. I wonder now about the naming of the road—about the story behind Salimpur Road—but I never had these questions then.

Baba's eldest sister, our favourite aunt, Bawropishi, also lived on Salimpur Road, a short distance away. Her husband, whom we called Pishemoshai, was a tall, kind and godly man. Pishemoshai would mostly be in the puja room, and he spoke so softly that you had to focus on what he was saying to understand him. Right from childhood, one of the main attractions of coming to Calcutta was meeting Bawropishi. She was more like the paternal grandmother we had never known and the one person whom everyone in Baba's family loved and respected. She had the same kind and gentle smile as Baba, and Ma has told us stories about how Bawropishi used to be protective towards her when she was a new bride and always helped Ma whenever Ma reached out to her. Bawropishi was a terrific cook, and we always looked forward to eating at her place. She is one person I miss meeting whenever I go to Calcutta nowadays.

The Salimpur Road flat was where my first boy crush walked out on me. I think we stayed in this flat for about three years, and then we moved into our own house on Jheel Road, Bank Plot just a ten-minute walk away. Our parents hadn't considered it safe for us to be living there by ourselves, but we had by now proved how capable we were. I was now a second-year student of Comparative Literature at Jadavpur University, a space that had so huge a role in shaping me into who I am. Our house became a favourite place for friends to hang around. There were no adults monitoring us, and I had also discovered that I loved to cook for my friends.

# FRAME BY FRAME

# 8

# Jadavpur University

Whenever I go back to Jadavpur University (JU) now, I start talking about how the atmosphere has changed, how it's no longer like it was during our times, that it has lost its charm . . . and I'm sure the generation before us used to say the same things while revisiting the university.

For the longest time, whenever I went back to Calcutta, I would take a stroll inside our campus. Enter through the main gate from the direction of the Jadavpur 8B bus stand and walk past the engineering department, past the huge green field we had right in the middle of the campus, the basketball courts which always brought back memories of my beautiful half-Armenian, half-Bengali friend Aznive Joakim. Aznive and I were really close. She loved to play basketball, and I would very often accompany her to the court. All the engineering faculty boys would hang around just to watch her and many made me their friend. I felt flattered by all the attention till I understood that all they actually wanted was an introduction to my gorgeous friend. Aznive was a strong and brave girl; she would give it back to men in crowded buses if they misbehaved. Another dear friend who had the same quality of fearlessness was Jhuma Basak.

Jhuma was a stunner—an extremely talented dancer, a Bengali beauty who had the courage to do as she pleased. She was a year junior to me and came to college dressed in vibrant colours and big colourful bindis. I think all the boys in the university were besotted with her. I was initially a little intimidated by her, and all the girls in my class would tease me, saying that I too was smitten. I finally gathered the courage one day to tell her how stunning she looked with her blue eyeliner and bindi. I remember she was wearing a bright blue kurta, her hair tied up in a ponytail. The smile in her eyes told me that she knew that my heart had skipped a beat. It's been over thirty years now that we've been friends, and we've promised each other that if we are still single when we are in our sixties we will get married. I think both of us have a history of multiple, passionate and failed relationships.

Jhuma used to ride a Scooty at one point and she would carry an umbrella with her. Anyone misbehaving from buses or cars would get a taste of the umbrella's fury. Both Aznive and Jhuma also kept large safety pins with them while boarding public buses and used them liberally on men who couldn't keep their hands to themselves. One of my biggest disillusionments with this so-called cultured city was how it treated its women. While there was this superficial culture of calling everyone 'didi' (elder sister) or 'boudi' (elder brother's wife) and a tradition of worshipping goddesses, the reality was different. I remember how angry and helpless Didi, Bhai and I would feel as we were from Bhutan, where eve-teasing was not common at all. Boys and girls grew up together, treating each other as friends and respecting each other. I don't remember hearing about crimes against women in Thimphu while growing up, but in Calcutta, it was almost an everyday occurrence that women were supposed to learn to live with. While walking through Gariahat Market, inside a cinema hall or in a bus, men would touch, stalk and harass women. And like Jhuma and Aznive, Didi was also fiery and would often hit back. Bhai and I started practising boxing and eating more rotis so that we could protect Didi. Of course it was stupid, but we were young.

I'll never forget one incident when, around 8 p.m. one evening, Didi and I were returning from Sejopishi's house in Tollygunge. The metro construction was happening those days, and the area around the bus stop was somewhat dark, but there were people around. Suddenly, a lot of things happened very quickly—Didi slapped a man, and now eight guys surrounded her, with one of them holding her hand and asking how she dared to slap him. The guy had intentionally fallen on her in an empty bus stop and the slap had been a reflex action. I now started trying desperately to make him let go of her hand, but he wanted Didi to apologize. A few people watched from across the road, but no one came to help us. Didi was trying to put up a brave front and saying that if he had fallen on her by mistake, she was sorry, but he was still not letting go of her hand. At this point, one young man appeared from somewhere and asked the bunch what the hell was going on. They were a little disconcerted and let go of her hand, and luckily for us, we could now see a bus approaching. The young man waited till the bus stopped, and we quickly boarded the bus. It was only then that Didi broke down. That was the first time that I realized how unfair it all was, how messed up as society we were if a girl could not walk around as freely as a boy. I never had to worry about my safety the way she had to. I didn't have to worry if I was wearing shorts, but she would be judged. Years later, when Didi had shifted to Bombay and I came to meet her, I was happy for her. Yes, bad things do happen in Bombay, but it's a far more women-friendly city.

Yes, I was much safer than my sister was, but when I was a school student in Calcutta, there were many times when people have tried to touch me inappropriately. I used to get terrified and just change buses or walk. And NO, I did not feel good about being touched by random men. I can only imagine how it must be for women to be surrounded by so many men who want to feel them up or undress them with their eyes.

Calcutta also gave me many memories that I'll always cherish, mostly from my JU days. I always say that my soul belongs to Thimphu, JU shaped my imagination, Berlin gifted me discipline and craft and Bombay combined all those elements and gave me wings to fly. Our B.A. in Comparative Literature had four boys and seventeen girls. I was one of the youngest and also looked very young, so somehow, instead of ragging me, my seniors decided to be protective of me. Most of the classmates soon became close friends, though I wasn't that close to the boys. It was a strange coincidence to find out later that Suman Mukherjee (Lal) too had become a film-maker. While doing our M.A., we had Badal Sarkar in our class. So, while we were learning from his books and all of us looked up to him, he was sitting with us as a fellow student. Yes, learning has no age. He must have been nearly sixty years old at that time, and while he used to try and be pally with us, it's rather unfortunate that we didn't really manage to cross the age barrier.

I think we were in our third year of B.A. when Hanif Kureishi visited our department and we watched *My Beautiful Laundrette*. I immediately had a huge crush on him because his whole personality was so charming and chilled out! Also, maybe because for the first time I was seeing a film where I was present. I mean as a queer person—I had no opportunity earlier to watch any film that represented us.

JU had a very active film club, and somewhat coincidentally, the seniors who had taken me under their wing were very actively involved with it. My favourite three were Arup da, Chitra di and Malay da, and I started hanging around with them as much as possible. I remember going to the Archives to collect film reels— we would bring films of Roman Polanski, Andrei Tarkovsky, Luis Buñuel, Jean-Luc Godard, Andrzej Wazda, Satyajit Ray, Ritwik Ghatak, François Truffaut, Pier Paolo Pasolini, Federico

Fellini, Robert Bresson, Wim Wenders, Ingmar Bergman, Akira Kurosawa, Krzysztof Kieślowski—suddenly there was this exciting new world opening up for me, sucking me in. The magic of the projection room, carrying the reels, the endless talks over weed about all these amazing film-makers, reading books on them—we were living cinema and dreaming cinema.

When I look back, I feel that four film-makers had a very strong impact on my growth as a film-maker: Andrei Tarkovsky, Luis Buñuel, Ritwik Ghatak and Krzysztof Kieślowski. I do not have the audacity to compare my work with any of these masters, but while watching films like *Belle de Jour*, I learnt how to portray characters with different shades, not confining them to black, white or grey. I loved how Buñuel's films always challenged social norms, and I admired that ability to subvert. Tarkovsky meant poetry, magic, emotions—I think the presence of water bodies in my films is somewhere connected with my observations on how he used water. When I make films, colours are important for me, and I feel that learning came to me from the fascination I felt watching every frame of the *Three Colours* trilogy, *Red*, *Blue* and *White*. And finally, Ritwik Ghatak—that man had soul. I think when choosing the narrative voice of *My Brother Nikhil*, I was constantly thinking of the brother–sister relationship in *Meghe Dhaka Tara*. I will be forever grateful to those evenings at Gandhi Bhavan, JU, where the world of cinema embraced me.

This was the time when I discovered Gabriel García Márquez, and the art of magic realism fascinated me. *One Hundred Years of Solitude* had a deep impact on me, and I found the novel very relatable to the narratives of the subcontinent. I still remember the visuals the book generated; I remember how the blood of the murdered son travels across the streets and houses, finally stopping at the mother's feet. I wept. I rejoiced when Innocent Eréndira lights up the tent with her grandmother to escape slavery. The poems of Lorca—'As I have not worried to be born, I do not worry to die'—touched me. And Neruda made me weep . . . in fact, still does whenever I think of having lost You. The lines that come to mind are 'Tonight I can write the saddest lines, I loved her, and sometimes she loved me too'. When I was shooting in Manchester in 2015 for my only unfinished film, *Veda*, I was trying out magic realism as a style. I hope I can explore it someday, perhaps in some other context.

Naseer da and Tapan da had stalls right next to the Arts Faculty main gate and supplied us with endless chai and bread pakora, egg roll and chow mein as we sat in the lobby, dreaming about changing the world with our art. I didn't know till recently that Naseer da's real name was not Naseer. He had been renamed by my seniors as he looked like Naseeruddin Shah. Come to think of it now, he actually did. But unlike Naseer the actor, Naseer da was always smiling!

The walls in front of the Arts Faculty lobby were raised at some point, apparently so that passengers of the buses passing by did not see our girls smoking. Sometime after we left, the lobby was broken down, ostensibly because it didn't project an appropriate image of the university. It's as if they destroyed the memories of those evenings, and I miss seeing that space when I visit the university. Opposite the Arts Faculty building, there was a *jheel* (lake) with a cute wooden bridge, which later made way for an ugly steel bridge that reflected a total absence of aesthetics. The size of the *jheel* has also become smaller, but I guess these are all results of the passage of time. I suddenly feel an urge to go back and see how everything looks now, but it's also daunting to not find anyone around whom one knows and to see that so much has changed.

There were various groups in our class, and I think I was a part of two very different groups. One group was Aznive, Mohua, Paromita and I. We would often go to the National Library together. This grand British-era building had a large reading hall with high ceilings and dark, polished wooden furniture, countless shelves of books and this amazing magical aura . . . I can still recollect the seductive smell of those books. We spent hours at the library, going through many priceless books. My only problem was that in those pre-laptop days, I had to take notes in my own handwriting, and sometimes I couldn't decipher them myself! The National Library was built on sprawling grounds and there was a lovely garden outside, with large banyan trees and stories of ghosts of English women floating around.

An incident that occurred at the National Library really upset me. One day, I was asked to leave because I was wearing capri pants. I thought this was ridiculous in a hot and sultry place like Calcutta. Apparently, this was considered improper attire—we often experienced such moral policing in Calcutta in those days, and I hope things have changed for the better now. Coming from a place where the traditional male attire—the *kho*—was worn above the knee, this seemed ridiculous. But my anger was equally ridiculous, for I stopped going to the National Library for a few months. I mean, whose loss was it . . . I'm sure it didn't matter at all to anyone at the library whether I came or not!

After I had taken admission to Asutosh College, Calcutta University, I went to college wearing torn jeans and a t-shirt on my first day. The SFI union called me and asked, '*Tui drugs koris ki? Amon jama kapor pore aschish?*' (Do you do drugs or what, since you're wearing such clothes?). Nearly thirty-five years later, I read about the chief minister of Uttarakhand commenting about the impropriety of wearing ripped jeans and realized that not much has changed. Another day, the head of the English department of Asutosh College told me that my parents seem to have not taught me well since I was wearing a pink t-shirt. This is how the city of culture treated me, and I must say that I had never ever heard such unkind comments in Thimphu. Thankfully, I didn't have to stay at Asutosh College for more than two months. It was a happy, happy day when my name appeared in the JU Comparative Literature list—this was the third and the final list. Stepping into JU felt like liberation. I had finally found a space in Calcutta where I felt I belonged.

The Calcutta Zoo is right opposite the National Library, and there was a Bijoli Grill restaurant inside that served alcohol. At that time, many Calcutta restaurants would refuse to serve women alcohol unless accompanied by a man. So, when the four of us went to have a drink one afternoon, I felt good playing the role of the man whose presence was all-important. Till the waiter came and took the orders from my three female friends but wanted to check my ID for age. My male ego went for a toss.

The four of us shared our notes and went to the photography club together. That was another amazing learning experience— going early in the morning with the group to nearby rural areas, sometimes to cemeteries, to click photographs. We would be careful about each shot as camera rolls were expensive and we couldn't afford more than two for each trip. It was truly magical later to work in the dark room, to develop the negatives and then see the emerging prints.

This sounds like a cliché . . . but Jadavpur, I love you.

The other group of friends from my class consisted of Sangeeta, Nandini, Tanushree, Soma, Sabari, Mitali, Sharmista, Sulagna, Rini and the most studious, Debali. We used to have a lot of house parties and go for movies together. I watched my first 'adult' film, *The Blue Lagoon*, with this group. All the girls were teasing me after the film as I was feeling too awkward to look at them.

My JU professors Shibaji da and Subha di have been two very important people in my life. I loved attending their lectures, and they were always kind and encouraging. They helped me slowly overcome my low self-esteem. Among many other things, Shibaji da was the first person to discuss sexuality openly in a class without being judgmental. I think I was fortunate that the first discourse on sexuality happened with a non-judgmental teacher. While we discovered Orpheus, Narcissus and many other tales from Greek mythology, we were likewise made aware of the Ardha Narishwar or the Shakti and Sri concept from ancient Indian texts. We also spoke about Shikhandi and Lord Ayappa. Shibaji da was a fragile-looking man, with curly hair, a very sharp nose and an amazingly sarcastic sense of humour. His lectures were great fun as he brought in music, cinema, painting and culture into our discussions of literature.

Subha di was more classical and again someone I looked up to a lot. She was very approachable and even a little protective. When she found out from one of my seniors that I was doing weed, she called me to her office and said, 'I know exactly what all of you are up to. I know your parents are in Bhutan, and I'll inform them if you don't stop immediately.' Of course, I was very nervous and promised to quit immediately. She added, 'Don't think that I won't know if you nod your head here and go back and continue. I'll get to know everything.' I stopped for a week and then started smoking up again. I gave up after another year. But that is another story.

There was another group of friends that I had—the lobby gang. Some people considered us the no-gooders. There was O, who was one of my closest friends from the English department— he was a year junior. There were D and U, both two years my junior, from the Comparative Literature department. Then there was Arun John, a student of St. Xavier's, who spent most of his time with us in the JU lobby, and people started to think that he was a JU-ite. There also was V, Arghya, Roops, Moon Upala and H, another non-JU lobby-ganger. In my last year at JU, H lost both his parents within the span of a week. He was like a little brother to me and started to spend a lot of time with me. After I shifted to Bombay, one day I received an email from H saying that he was shifting to Bombay and needed to get a job as he wanted to marry U. He shifted, started doing really well for himself and got married. H and U remain two very, very precious persons in my life. One day, nearly fifteen years later, they called to say they were purchasing a home in the hills and wanted to purchase one-third of the property in my name. That love and trust for me is the best gift of friendship.

I think I started smoking weed in the JU lobby. I started cigarettes much later, when I was trying to quit weed. I remember O and I used to go to this place behind the Tollygunge tram depot; there was a masjid there, next to which we could buy weed. They had qawwali performances there on Friday nights, and it was kind of trippy. Very often, an old widow in a worn-out white sari would come and sit next to us and wait for her turn while the joint went around. There were also many nights on the terrace of my Calcutta home when O and I would lie down, looking at the stars and talking about poetry, cinema and painting. I know this too sounds clichéd, but those moments were beautiful. We shared an intense love–hate relationship, and though we did not know about each other's sexuality, we were very close friends. I think my need for his company was greater than his for mine, and so I would often end up feeling jealous, used and hurt. I sometimes felt that he never reciprocated my affection but sought it when it was convenient for him. All the same, I'll always cherish what I shared with him.

Our family was going through a lot of financial stress at the time I was in JU. Ma had not been able to come to terms with the changes in Bhutan, after twenty-five long years, especially when Baba was finally transferred to another school, now as an assistant teacher. She became very ill, returned to Calcutta and had to be hospitalized. She was in hospital for over three months, and we could have actually lost her. She never really recovered from the shock of losing what she had started considering her home. There were a few years of bitterness about Bhutan, which I too carried for many years, but she forgave sooner. I have learnt from Baba and Ma that it is much more important to cherish the love that we received than to dwell on those terrible last years. Both of them choose to retain only the fond memories of Bhutan now, of their friends, our home and our lives there. After Ma came back, Baba tried to keep working as an assistant teacher, visiting us in Calcutta whenever he could. This was a traumatic time for everyone, especially as Ma was so unwell, and he soon resigned. After twenty-five years of service with the education department of Bhutan, this was a rather sad end, and there wasn't even a pension to soften the blow.

Ma's hospital bills were huge and depleted the little savings my parents had—teachers in Bhutan weren't paid too well in those days. Being in his mid-fifties, it was too late for Baba to get a job in Calcutta, but he tried. He would roam around all day in the Calcutta heat, hunting for that elusive job, and come back defeated. I have never seen Baba so helpless. We sold off a small piece of land we owned, and Baba tried his hand at business and failed miserably, or rather, got cheated and lost some money. He tried to earn something by renting out our car, but that didn't really work, so he finally sold the car to his elder brother. He even tried running a bus service, but he just wasn't cut out for this kind of work. Eventually, he took up some work with an NGO, where he was paid an absurdly low salary. Those were dark, depressing days.

All of us started doing small jobs so that we could continue to chase our dreams. I used to do door-to-door market surveys for IMRB from 7 a.m. to 9 a.m. At times, when people just slammed the door on my face, it was very humiliating. But I also knew that I was intruding into their lives with a market survey form at a really inappropriate time. Of course, there were kind people too, and what kept me going was the knowledge that I could buy a book and continue with my Russian classes thanks to the extra money.

In the evenings, I used to teach English to two kids three times a week. Ayan Das was in Class 5 and his sister in Class 8. Ayan was an affectionate kid who got super attached to me, and I used to look forward to my time with the duo. He was in tears when I quit before my trip to Berlin; he kissed me on my cheeks and gifted me his photograph.

Ayan reached out to me many years later when I was in Bombay and a film-maker. He is settled abroad now. His sister unfortunately died in an accident. Writing about them and others from that time brings their faces before me.

When people message me saying, 'Sir, I have no family support, but I want to be an actor (or film-maker), just give me one chance', it kind of irritates me. I know some of it is true, but more often than not, these people feel that it's the job of their parents to not only educate them but also keep a bank balance for them, maybe even provide a house and a car, so that they can follow their dreams. They do not make any effort to use their time to earn or learn. Especially now, when there is so much that one can learn online without spending much money. But then, one is too busy with TikTok, Instagram, Snapchat and WhatsApp! People forget that apart from a few incredibly talented individuals, most of us need to learn our craft. If you want to be a doctor, you spend over five years plus a lot of money and effort to get a basic MBBS, but here you want to be a part of an industry that can bring you a lot of fame and money, and you want to achieve it without any proper effort. It took me ten years and a lot of hard work to transition from being an editor to a film-maker. And I never told anyone, 'I don't have the resources, but I have a dream, so please give me a chance.'

While in JU, I was learning German and Tamil in our department and Russian at Gorky Sadan. After I failed the FTII entrance exam, I joined Chitrabani for film studies. Didi was already learning film editing at FTII, and I had hoped to join too.

I have always been so terrible with exams that for the longest time, even after I became a film-maker, I would get these nightmares where I have an exam the next day and I am not prepared for it. Or I see myself as an unemployed film-maker who cannot get a job as he doesn't have a post-graduate degree. And believe me, these nightmares were terrifying.

Chitrabani had three kind souls who knew a lot about cinema and were willing to share that knowledge. There was the ever-smiling Father Roberge, a Canadian-French priest who loved cinema and opened the first space for film studies in Calcutta. He spoke softly as he imparted his knowledge of film criticism and theory. In *My Brother Nikhil*, I have named Nikhil's school principal Father Gaston Roberge as a small homage to my teacher. When I was screening the film at Montreal's Image + Nation film festival, someone from the audience screamed that Father Roberge was his friend! The world, at times, can seem to be a very small place. Chitrabani also had Biren da who always believed in me more than I myself did. He was like an elder brother, guiding us through the world of cinema. And there was the lovely Sunetra Ghatak who was in charge of the library. She would suggest books to read; sometimes with her would be this little boy who has now grown to be the super-talented actor/director Parambrata Chatterjee.

One day in 1990, Father Roberge called me to his office and asked me if I would be interested in attending the film-making workshop being held at Max Mueller Bhavan under the aegis of SFB/TTC Berlin. The workshop had already started the day before. I replied that I had seen the notice but didn't qualify for it as they wanted participants with at least two years' experience. He said, 'Did I ask you for the workshop details? I asked if you wanted to attend or not.' Biren da was the one who had suggested my name, and Father Roberge too had seen something in me that had led him to agree. At that point, I had low self-esteem, believing that everything good that happened was because of someone being kind and never because I deserved it. The next day, I was there and Dr Christian Grote—whom I will always remember as a mentor—was conducting the workshop. He must have been in his sixties—a tall man, so knowledgeable, a person who had travelled the world. One of the other guides/teachers was the brilliant Navina Sundaram, and of course there was Hanno Baethe who became a very, very close friend. Now, many decades later, my production company Anticlock Films is working on the English subtitling of the archival body of my teacher Navina Sundaram's work.

Hanno was a German documentary film-maker and teacher. His English was terrible, but somehow he managed to convey whatever he needed to. He was a wonderful teacher who taught me to think from my heart. Those days I would be running between P.G. Hospital, where Ma was in a critical condition, and the day-long workshop. It was during this time that I shot, along with three others from my group, my first documentary film—*Glimpses of College Street*. We shot right from the first tram of the day to the bookshops opening up and the street slowly waking up. We shot at the iconic Coffee House. I was finally doing what I had always dreamt of. I experienced for the first time how ideas transform into a script and then into corresponding images that we shoot and then string together. The role of sound, music and voice-overs, and, most importantly, the essence of a team—to realize that films are all about teamwork.

Years later, in 2017, I was back again in Calcutta, shooting my film *Kuchh Bheege Alfaaz*. I went back to shooting the trams, which have always held some magic for me—the sound of the bell, the way they move sinuously. I love them. I also went back to the College Street Coffee House. I think as a film-maker, you keep seeking old memories, of places and incidents, even as you are creating new ones. I went back to Dhakuria Lake, the place that held memories of my first crush and which also held memories of my last heartbreak. Ironically, one of the scenes I shot there was Archie's (the female protagonist) mother confessing to her about her love affairs. Of course, the landscape of the city had changed, and I can never recreate some of the memories. The JU lobby no longer exists, and the monstrous flyover in front of Gorky Sadan destroyed the look and the feel of the place.

I was making my first romantic film in the city where I came to understand about love and loss, where I was experiencing loss yet again and where I met PS two years later. None of my personal love stories have had any closure, and maybe that's why I wanted my characters to find closure, to smile and hold hands and walk away together into the horizon.

Talking of romance, I remember my first crush as an adult in JU—let's call her S1. She was a year junior to me and was the first girl for whom my throat would go dry out of nervousness whenever I had to talk to her. She was a very bright girl with a soft voice and thoughtful, tender eyes. Her curls gave her face a warm, ethereal beauty. My classmates knew that I had a crush on her and would tease me, especially since she often sought me out for advice, me being a senior and fairly good at my studies. By the time we became friendly, I realized that she was interested in someone from the engineering faculty. And being the good guy that I was, I started encouraging both of them. Then I fell in love with S2, a tall girl with a melancholic expression and a certain coldness about her. With her, I decided I needed to be brave and not wait too long. She was in the same class as S1 and the two would hang around together a lot.

At some point—I'm not sure if this is what happened—I think I told S1 about what I felt for S2 and she laughed her beautiful laugh, not in a mean way but like she was excited for me. S1 fixed a meeting for S2 and me, but S2 set a condition—that I should come to the lobby with roses at 7 a.m. the next morning and propose to her. At that point, I was this shy, left-leaning youngster who thought all this stuff with roses was stupid. I was also possibly scared that if I actually went with roses and found out that this was all a big joke, it would be awfully embarrassing. Yet I was also curious and hopeful. So the next morning saw me dressing up a bit more carefully than usual, and I set out for the rendezvous with a fluttering heart. I was pretty sure that she wouldn't be there, but as I walked towards the lobby from the 8B bus stand, I saw her sitting there. I did not know what to do as I had not bought roses and there were no shops open that early. The only shop open was the cigarette shop across the street, opposite the Arts Faculty gate. The fellow had no chocolates, and since the only thing available apart from cigarettes and bidis were NP chewing gums, I bought twelve of them for her. As I approached the lobby, she broke into a smile, but when she saw that there were no flowers, her face fell. I gave her the NPs, which she flung back at me before walking away. That was the end of my second crush.

I had one more rather major crush while in JU. But I want that one to remain locked in my heart. I never got to tell her, but I think she knew about it. True love is difficult to hide and, in any case, I am an absolute disaster when it comes to hiding my feelings.

A couple of months after the workshop, I remember an excited Biren da coming to me and saying, 'There's some good news, though it's not hundred per cent confirmed yet, but I think you will get it. Father Roberge wants to meet you.' Father Roberge asked me if I would like to be a part of a film editing course in Berlin at the SFB/TTC. I said I knew about the course and had not applied as one needed to be above twenty-five years of age and have at least two years' work experience. I was twenty and had no work experience at all. Father Roberge told me that there was one name being recommended by Calcutta Doordarshan, and Dr. Grote had said that I too should apply. He had said there was no guarantee, but I should try.

I think it took a month to know the final outcome. It was an anxious month. I knew that this would be an important step towards my becoming a film-maker. I had one small advantage—I had some knowledge of German as it was a language I was learning at JU.

The mud beneath swallows me,
Slowly,
Brown wet mud,
Spinning slowly as it draws me in.

You sit by the edge watching,
Your eyelids do not blink,
Calmly you watch me sink.

# 9

# Berlin

Two months later, in December 1990, I was on my way to Berlin. This was absolutely unthinkable, especially after Baba resigned from his job in Bhutan and we struggled to make ends meet in Calcutta.

I remember my trip was full of surprises. I had probably been on a flight only once before when my Jethu (my father's elder brother) had flown us from Dimapur in Nagaland to Calcutta. He was a forest range officer, and I still can taste the *luchi*, *begun bhaja* and omelette breakfast we used to have every morning in Rangapahar, Nagaland. I also remember the elephant rides with our cousin Gautam da and the late-night jeep rides through the forest as we headed back to Rangapahar after watching a film, followed by a Chinese dinner at Dimapur. Often, wild elephants would block the road, and there was also fear of militancy. But I digress.

The most difficult thing to deal with after I was offered the editing course in Berlin was that it meant I was to leave for Berlin one week before my post-graduation exams.

My British Airways flight itinerary was Calcutta–Delhi–Athens–London–Frankfurt and Berlin. I was nervous, as I didn't even know how to put on the safety belt properly. On the Calcutta–Delhi lap, there was an elderly gentleman sitting next to me who had tears running down his cheeks during the entire flight, and he would occasionally ask me about my parents. Just before we reached Delhi, he opened his briefcase and took out a beautiful sari and insisted that I take it as a gift for someone in Germany. He had bought it for his daughter; something must have gone wrong, and he couldn't give it to her on his visit. He also kept telling me that my parents were lucky to have a son like me. He gave me his card so that I could get in touch with him once back from Berlin, but somehow I lost the card. I will never forget that face. It was so full of grief.

Those were the stressful days of the Gulf War, and my British Airways flight from Delhi was getting delayed. At the airport, a young girl, also waiting for the same flight, became very friendly with me. When she heard the sari story, she got paranoid and made me take it out and check every fold for hidden drugs! Of course, there was nothing, and I felt so ashamed that I had so easily doubted the elderly gentleman.

When we were flying over the Middle East, I was worried crazy that the Iraqis would spot the British Airways plane and bring us down. I held on to the life jacket, convinced that it was a parachute. When we stopped in Oman to refuel, the airport was full of armoured trucks and tanks, the atmosphere tense. The next stop was Athens. It was early morning when we reached, and it felt like a dream to land in Europe. The runway lights seemed like stars lining up to welcome me, and all those white houses were so picturesquely perfect. From Athens, we flew to London, and since the flight was eight hours late, I missed my connecting flight, as did many others. The young girl came up to me and we got busy chatting about our arrangements for the night. We were to be put up in hotels, and the airline staff handed out forms for us to fill. When I ticked male, the girl looked totally shocked and kept saying that I must be joking. It took me a while to understand the reason for her confusion, and as I removed my hood and scarf, she froze, made some excuses and quickly disappeared!

I finally reached Berlin the following day, around midday. The course had already started the previous day.

For the editing workshop at SFB/TTC, we were sixteen students from eight different countries. It was no rocket science that the two participants from Pakistan—Fatima (who was from a radio station) and Parvez—became my best friends. What was surprising is that I did not get that close to my colleagues from Bangladesh. Maybe this was because they were much older and adopted a big-brotherly attitude which always made me weary. Fatima was fun; she wanted to try out everything that this trip could offer. A sip of wine, a puff from a cigarette, all kinds of cuisine—she was enjoying every minute. Parvez was more cautious and even judgmental in the beginning, but slowly loosened up. Then there was this Chinese guy from Indonesia who was very stressed about losing his girlfriend and would keep getting nightmares. I pretended to be an expert palm reader and dream analyst and offered him many pleasing interpretations of his dreams. Soon he was calling me every other night to discuss his dreams, and I started worrying that he was taking me too seriously, but I didn't have the heart to tell him that I had been making everything up. The storyteller in me was having too much fun.

All expenses for this trip were paid for by my scholarship, but I knew that I needed to save some money for when I would be back in Calcutta. I wanted to make a documentary film on my return and I also wanted to help my family a bit financially.

We were put up at the Kaiserdamm Hotel IBIS, where breakfast was included with the stay. Though we had to be at the studio by 8 a.m.—not an easy task on cold winter days in Berlin—I used to stuff myself at breakfast as I wanted to save money from my meal allowance. It was always a cold breakfast, and I did miss my omelettes and fried eggs.

I found the classes fascinating. In one of the early exercises, each of the sixteen participants was handed sixteen posters and a pair of scissors. We had to cut bits from the posters and create a storyboard. The next step would be moving images around, changing the narrative. We were given different kinds of footage each week—documentary, fiction, news, music video—and asked to edit. In the evenings, we watched films and interacted with each other and our mentor about forms of editing and the language of cinema. Words like 'form edit', 'action edit', 'concept edit', 'composite edit', 'sound edit' and 'continuity' slowly filled up my vocabulary. We were editing on Hi-Band, Low Band, Beta (analogue edits) and also started learning Avid, a non-linear editing system that would go on to change the way films are edited. At the end of each week, each of us would present our work to the rest of the group and answer any questions. I loved these sessions as they gave me an idea about how others perceived and experienced what I had thought out and executed.

Having editing as the base of my film education helped me learn the importance of economy, the importance of planning each shot and cut in your head, of understanding why you needed to go for a close up or a long shot. To know why one needed the camera to move, what that movement conveyed, how to create a rhythm in the edit.

Yes, there are rules, and rules are meant to be broken. Every editing rule can be broken, provided you know why you are doing what you are doing. As they say, you need to learn the language in order to reinvent it. Editing fascinated me—how much a blink could convey, searching for a small movement of the eyeball, a slight tilt of the head, a sudden breeze ruffling the hair . . . I could sit for hours in the editing room and didn't really look forward to the weekend. Weekends saw me waiting for Monday to be back on my editor's seat.

My training in Berlin also taught me how to respect time. At the institute, all our guides were very particular about punctuality and sticking to schedules, and till today the excuses people give for being late really put me off. We also learned to respect the machines we worked on. It breaks my heart when I see people treat equipment carelessly just because it's not their own. It's like a writer not respecting pen and ink. I learnt to pack things up properly at the end of my shift and to be organized and label things correctly. When I started working in Bombay in 1992 as an editor at Plus Channel, I would spend hours labelling tapes and arranging them, even though it wasn't really a part of my job.

The discipline came handy when I was shooting my first feature film, *My Brother Nikhil,* in 2004. My learning as an editor empowered me as a director. I made notes on the script about how I planned to shoot each scene. It was an indie film, and I was editing in my head. I didn't shoot any master sequence; I shot what I imagined as a close-up as a close-up and didn't shoot various possibilities. We were shooting on film, and this helped me shoot the film at a 1:4 ratio, thus keeping the expenditure on expensive raw stock under control and complete the shoot in twenty-seven days. Some people would say that I was limiting the editor's vision, but apart from the fact that I edited the film myself, I was fulfilling the director's vision of the edited film while shooting. Is that limiting? I don't really know . . . but I could stay within budget and complete my film. That is what I definitely know.

There are many ways in which a sequence can be shot and edited, but whenever I revisit my films, there is very little that I would want to do differently. Because they are a record of my growth as a film-maker, a record of history when we changed from celluloid to digital, from single screen to multiplexes and then to the digital format of film watching. My films evolve, trying to negotiate the space between what I want to tell the world and what the world wants to hear and between how I want to tell the stories and how the world allows me to speak. All these aspects are hidden in the visuals and sounds, and that is the magic of cinema. And, of course, there's my own vanity, knowing that there remains a bit of my soul captured in those images and sounds for all eternity.

During this time in Berlin, my guide Hanno and I became quite close. Though we were not yet what we call friends in India, he was very caring, and it was the beginning of a cherished friendship. Some months later, when he came to Calcutta for another workshop, I took on the role of workshop assistant. Later, Hanno, Swati (a friend from Chitrabani) and I went on a trip to Bhutan. I wanted Hanno to see the place I still call my homeland and miss every day.

In 1991, Berlin was going through a mammoth transformation. The wall had just come down and it was a historical time after the recent merger of East and West Germany. I soon knew how to spot the East Germans, and we were told not to venture into the Eastern parts of the city as there were incidents of foreigners being attacked. The East was having a hard time merging: people with leftist ideology and women who formerly had been a major part of the socialist workforce were suddenly jobless, and every foreigner was perceived as someone who was snatching their food away!

What I found strange is the way the West was dismantling everything in the East. From statues to buildings, all East German property was being broken and bought over by investors from the West. We're probably witnessing a similar zeal in India at present, in renaming places and roads and thereby disowning a bit of our past. It was mesmerizing for me to walk about Berlin, a city with so much history, and find bullet marks from the Second World War on the walls. Buildings that were destroyed by the Allies' bomb raids have been preserved for posterity, to remember those horrific days of German history. I remember going to the Holocaust Memorial near Brandenburg Gate, and when I saw the faces of countless Jewish children who were killed, I couldn't stop my tears. How did an entire society get brainwashed into enacting such a horrific crime? Today when I see what is happening with minorities in different parts of the world, I realize that humanity has not learned any lesson from all the earlier wars and genocide. We continue to nurture hatred and humiliate, torture and murder the other. Maybe the core of humanity is evil, something that religion was supposed to control but over centuries has only managed to magnify instead.

On returning to Calcutta after Berlin, I was gripped by a certain restlessness. I had to, for the first time, think about what death might mean, as someone close to me had attempted suicide while I was away. I was shaken by the thought that I might not have ever seen that person again. Maybe in some way that taught me to be stronger as I knew what it would feel like for those left behind, which is why not even during the worst phase of my personal or professional life have I thought of it as an option. I also felt not trusted and loved enough as I wondered about why I was not confided in. Slowly, over the years and for a very long time, I stopped sharing my angst with anyone. Maybe that is not totally true. I think I gave myself various identities, and there were different individuals in whom I would confide different aspects of my life. No one knew the whole me, and now as I try to write my story, I realize there are too many stories, so many that it feels like they do not belong to the same person. Just like there are so many lives that touched mine, and I'm not able to mention all of them, there are many people who became a part of my life for brief periods, and they were all important.

I was now finding it difficult to focus on completing my post-graduation. My batchmates had already graduated, and I started feeling that the degree was going to be of no use to me. I had acquired the knowledge that the space had to offer me, and I needed to take my next step. I continued with my studies only out of a sense of guilt, and I was not being honest.

At this time, when I was still a regular at JU, I remember doing something that I will forever regret. Two of my juniors who were a couple were both interested in cinema and had become my fans because of what I 'seemed to promise'. I used to find the boy very irritating while finding the girl attractive. Not that I really wanted to get into a relationship with her as I was still very much enamoured of my third crush . . . no, I'd rather call it love, as she meant much more. I realized that this junior was attracted to me, and I started to play with her emotions while also subtly putting down her boyfriend. The unsuspecting boyfriend did not foresee the evil designs of 'Anirban da'. They finally broke up. I remember she came to my house the evening they broke up, and as we sat chatting in my room, there was an obvious sexual tension. I was sure, though, that I did not want to have a serious relationship with her. Maybe I was just too much of a coward to deal with the responsibility of a relationship, or perhaps I was reading too much into what I thought she wanted and giving myself too much importance. But I didn't make any effort to comfort her or get physically intimate or encourage her in any way. I know that evening she left my place a bit more broken. Over the next couple of months, I slowly distanced myself from her. I think I was cruel and manipulative, and I hope if she reads this, she can forgive me.

Financial pressures were building up at home. Hanno recommended me to a German anthropologist, Bea Hauser, and I spent the next few months working with her. Ironically, it was while working as a research assistant to Bea that I had my first exposure to rural Bengal. It was a fascinating six months, but it also reaffirmed my belief that my soul belongs to the Himalayas.

# 10

# The Patuas

I was helping Bea translate the interviews she had recorded of the Patuas, the scroll painters of Bengal, from Bangla to English. The Patuas had a wonderful way of marrying moving images with sound through the scrolls they painted. They would open up the scroll, which was sometimes as long as twelve feet, one frame at a time, and these frames would depict some mythological story, mostly from the *Ramayana* and *Mahabharata*, but also some local ones. The Patua would sing about the incident depicted in the first frame and then open the second frame and sing about the incident shown there, and so on. The story would be completed at the last frame of the scroll. This reminded me of the exercise we had done in Berlin where we assembled different photos to narrate a story by linking one image to the next.

It was fascinating how many of the Patuas had dual identities. They were mostly Muslims who adopted Hindu names as performing artists. For example, Niranjan Patua also had a Muslim name, which I no longer remember. However, some like Kalam Patua had a single name. I loved how the women wore the bindi and *shakha–pola* (a pair of white and red bangles traditionally worn by married women in Bengal) even while they practised Islam. I've always thought that these are cultural identities that have been appropriated as religious identity. In Bengal and Bangladesh, the whole practice of wearing a burkha or a skullcap and growing a beard as a part of Muslim identity is rather new. In rural Bengal of the eighties or even the nineties, the Bengali identity was greater than the religious identity.

It was while sitting in the courtyard of Niranjan's mud hut in the evenings and listening to him sing in his high-pitched voice that I started smoking. I did it to be one with the men folk. I still have one of his paintings and also the small clay toys his wife and kids had gifted me.

Reaching these remote villages was in itself an adventure. We would take the train to the nearest small town and then board one of those terribly overcrowded buses. Then we would sit on the cycle *thelas* as they navigated the bumpy dirt tracks.

During one trip to a village, I did something I'm still ashamed of. The village had no toilet, and I was still a very shy young lad. There was a field for men to shit and one where women did the job, a pond for washing your ass and another for bathing. It was unthinkable for me to shit in an open space with no privacy. I controlled my bowels for three days—I ate less and smoked, hoping (forgive me, I know this is gross) that the stuff would not need to come out. By the fourth day, I was desperate, and that's when I did something unpardonable. I went into the bathing pond, waded into waist-deep water and did what I had to quickly and disappeared from the crime scene. Had someone caught me, I'm sure I would have been beaten up.

Bea and I were put up in adjacent buildings. After dinner, we would wish each other good night and retire to our rooms. I would then go to the roof of my building and she to hers. She would jump from her roof to mine and we would sit together to share a post-dinner cigarette!

Those six months of travelling made me realize, strangely, that even though I was a Bengali, I did not feel at home at all in these villages. It was as if I was visiting a foreign land, and I would be fascinated at times. For the rest of the time, I had to keep learning and negotiating what that space required of me as a 'man' to be able to work. I felt empathy, but not oneness. I was more at home in the streets of Berlin and Paris. My childhood in Bhutan had in a strange way made me more a global citizen, or perhaps a homeless man who found spaces of security and comfort in different parts of the world for diverse reasons.

Some spaces made me feel at home because of my language, some because of the acceptance of my sexuality; elsewhere, it was because of the colour of my skin, and some places because how morning bed tea felt or because of a view of the mountains from my window . . . or the comfort of your arms.

Long after it had stopped raining
And the earth woke up to the fragrance of monsoon,
I lay motionless,
Remembering many mornings ago,
When it had rained just like this,
And my two tiny feet ran out,
Laughter echoed in the mountains,
And there I saw you forty years ago,
Drenched in the rain,
By the willow tree.

But you did not know me then,
Nor I you,
But I recognized you so many years ago,
That rainy morning,
Your eyes had smiled at me,
And I knew I would wait to find you.

# 11

# The Fallen Hero and Other Stories

In the middle of 1991, Dr Grote and Hanno came back to Calcutta, and I worked as a workshop assistant this time. It was planned that after the workshop, Hanno would stay back in India, moving into our Calcutta home for a month as we wanted to shoot a documentary film and also planned to travel to Thimphu together. Our family friend, the Bhutanese film-maker Ugyen Wangdi, had organized a three-day film-making workshop for Hanno, and so the issue of Hanno's visa was sorted. As an Indian, I didn't need a visa to travel to Bhutan.

Travelling to Thimphu was emotionally overwhelming. I remember standing in front of Moothithang High School. Images of Baba presiding over the assembly every morning, Ma in the library, images of our last day filled me with so much sadness that I burst into tears. I went to look for my friend Binay—their family had a dry-cleaning shop in the upper market—but they were no longer there. I tried to find out about my friends Nima, Wangel, Subhash, Kado and Sonam Doma, but I couldn't find anyone. I hope to find them all some day, and I have recently reconnected with Sonam Doma and Kado on Facebook. It was a strange feeling to be back where I was uprooted from and to be still looking for my roots, hoping to find them there.

I remember going back to Yangchenphug Central School (YCS), where I studied in classes 9 and 10. As I climbed up the hill, memories came flooding back to me—of my classmate Rahul driving along in his Jonga while I walked up the road, teasing me for refusing to get into his vehicle because we had fought the previous day. Rahul was my best friend in YCS, and we shared a love for comics and table tennis.

In Calcutta, Hanno started shooting the documentary about his impressions of the city. Somehow, it always made me feel uneasy to see him shooting people sleeping on the footpath or a woman from a slum putting on her sari. It made me feel that, in a way, the Western sense of privacy and space was so fake and convenient. Later in 1995, when I was visiting Germany, the minute I would shoot someone sitting in a restaurant or a park, I would be told, 'Anirban, you can't just shoot people, you are intruding on their privacy.' So how come the same did not apply for the Indian pavement dwellers? Just because they do not protest or understand the notion of privacy, do you have the right to invade their space? I remember some of my other German friends like Dr Grote, Philip and Merle found this very problematic too. Though I was hoping to learn more about film-making while working on these films with Hanno, I did feel uncomfortable about this aspect. When I saw the final film *Null Diat* (Zero Diet), I was not happy. I loved the visuals and sound design, but the juxtaposition of haves and have-nots is such a cliché. It is also problematic when seen from the gaze of the West, which always absolves itself for what it has done to the subcontinent.

Hanno and I travelled by train from Calcutta to Pune. We were to visit FTII, where my sister was studying, and also have a screening of Hanno's film *Yearning For Sodom* for the students. That was my first trip to FTII, where, along with my future brother-in-law Ashwini Malik, I met a whole lot of people who would become a very important part of my life, as friends and also as collaborators. There was Amitabh Varma and Suresh Pai, who were editing students, and Vivek Philip, Pritam Chakraborty and Sumit Dasgupta from the sound department (we lost the soft-spoken, ever-smiling Sumit some years back). I also became friends with Arun Varma, Jatinder Sharma and Sachin Krishn from the cinematography department. I later shot three of my films with Sachin. Another person I became friends with was Charudutt Acharya, Ashwini's junior from the direction department. Come to think of it, I had become friends with my brother-in-law's batchmates and juniors, not so much anyone from my sister's batch apart from Arun Nambiar, who has worked as sound designer for all my films. This was probably because my sister was about to complete her FTII course at the time my visits began. FTII and its famous wisdom tree, the screenings, the very air of that place . . . there was so much cinema all around that I was totally envious of my sister. This was a place where I had always wanted to be but could not.

I remember going back in 1993 for Ashwini's diploma film shoot. At that time, I had a huge crush (apparently most of the other campus boys did too) on an editing student, Jabeen Merchant. So I allowed Ashwini to persuade me to give my first and only shot for a film because Jabeen was a part of the same shot! Jabeen had to zip me up inside a soft-cover suitcase. I had intentionally kept a little bit of my hair out so that she could push it in. The shot, sad to say, got edited out of the final cut!

After Pune, Hanno and I went to Goa. Travelling with a foreigner to Goa was not a great idea in 1991. I had no idea till I reached that people would simply assume that I was Hanno's toy boy. I looked very young, and Hanno was this tall, much older German man. I knew there were people calling me names in the local language which I did not actually understand, but the gestures and expression said it all. I told Hanno to let me handle all the cash payments when we went to restaurants so that it looked like I was the one paying. Not that it made much of a difference. My skin colour was the reason I was being discriminated against in my own country.

In those three months that Hanno and I spent together, I think both of us learned a lot from each other. When he left, we promised each other that I would soon visit Berlin for three months.

In 1992, I started working on a documentary film, *The Fallen Hero*, my first as an independent director. I had saved some money from my scholarship and was restless to do something on my own. There were three of my seniors from JU who were instrumental in making the film happen—Chitra di, Malay da and Arup da. I think Malay da was somehow related to Bijon da and introduced us to him. I hate the fact that my memory is slowly growing weak and that so many names, faces and details have just slipped away over the years.

Bijon Chowdhury was known for the strong Marxist narratives in his paintings. He was one of the founders of The Society of Contemporary Artists (1960, Calcutta) and in 1964, he had founded The Calcutta Painters. I saw his series 'The Fallen Hero' and was totally fascinated.

I remember taking the train to Bolpur to visit him in his home near Shantiniketan. He must have been around sixty-two years old then. Dignified, a little frail and soft-spoken, Bijon da lived in a modest studio-cum-home with his daughter. We chatted over cups of tea about his life, thoughts and paintings. His voice was lyrical and he explained everything to us with great kindness. I hungrily devoured every word that he spoke.

A few weeks later, we went back to shoot my first independent directorial venture. After the first meeting itself, I was clear that I did not really want to make a documentary on the painter Bijon

Choudhury; I didn't think that I was knowledgeable enough about Marxist art or painting as a medium. I wanted to adopt a more personalized approach to two series of paintings by him—'The Fallen Hero' and 'Return of the Heroes'.

While the first set of paintings depicted the 'heroes'—workers, farmers, the common man—going to war, the second set was about their return. They were carrying musical instruments, and there were women on horseback in this set. I felt what was missing in the paintings was the presence of women as a force of change, and when they appeared, they appeared as companions. I decided to have two female voices to fill that absence. These voices read out poems written by contemporary Bengali and international poets . . . all of which were about the struggles of the common man for equal rights. Chitra di read the Bengali poems and Tinnie the ones in English. My friends John and Indy helped out with the film's music.

At that time, we did not really know how to navigate the film festival scene. We screened the film for Bijon da, and it was a big relief that he liked what we had done as I was afraid of how he would react to my approach. We screened the film for JU students, and the feeling of having made my first independent film was exhilarating. Baba tried to help by approaching Doordarshan for screening the film, but years went by and we never heard back from them. A few years later, the only Hi-band copy of the film was destroyed when our Calcutta home was flooded. I was devastated, but luckily my friends from Berlin had a VHS and I could get a copy.

In 2021, Bijon da's grandson connected with me on Instagram and wanted to see the film, which was probably the only film made on Bijon da. That's when I decided to upload the film on the Anticlock Films YouTube channel. It can be watched there.

I also worked briefly as an editor for UGC Films. I used to enjoy the edits, but my colleagues irked me. Everyone behaved as if I was this youngster who had got a scholarship to Germany by a fluke and most definitely didn't deserve it. I would constantly be targeted in many subtle and not-so-subtle ways. What I absolutely hated was the 'dada' attitude. Just because I was younger than the others, I was supposed to quietly accept everything they 'advised'. This also pushed me towards wanting to explore new shores. When I eventually shifted to Bombay, I remember I started to cherish the city's work culture. No one cared how old I was, what my religion was or my caste was. The only thing that mattered was my work.

# 12

# Bombay Calling

Leaving Calcutta wasn't easy. The house we lived in had so many memories—the addas, the dreams that I had seen as a student. I felt I was betraying my Calcutta group of friends. Though I kept saying that I wouldn't last a year, I knew that I would probably never come back. Chitra di and Arup da gently goaded me, encouraging me to take the step. Perhaps they believed in my dreams more than I myself did. I remember one smoke-filled evening when I was feeling uncertain about my decision while sitting with Chitra di and Arup da. I felt that after moving to Bombay, I would somehow have to sacrifice the artist in me—something that has partly proved true. Over the years, I have started thinking not only as an artist who wants to simply express himself, but I also try to think about for whom, how and why.

My sister Irene was working as an editor with Plus Channel, and she introduced me to Amit Khanna, who became my first boss. I started by earning Rs 3000 a month. This was my first proper job as an editor, and I loved the work. Even in 1992, it wasn't easy to survive in Bombay with that much money. I was thrilled, though, for not only would I be a step closer to my dream of becoming a film-maker, I would also be close to my sister once again.

Other than Amit Khanna, I was working with Mahesh Bhatt, who headed the Bollywood stories section, and the legendary editor Renu Saluja. We were mostly a young and enthusiastic bunch and I made some amazing friends. Amit was unpredictable—he could be the nicest, kindest boss who would land up with food at two in the night because he knew we were working round the clock, but he could be unreasonable when it came to letting people grow or letting them go. The excitement about my first job was soon forgotten as the news of terrible events that were happening in the country engulfed us. The Babri Masjid demolition and the riots that followed shook us—first in December 1992 and then in January 1993. And with the multiple bomb blasts on 12 March 1993, which even targeted the iconic Bombay Stock Exchange building, our city changed forever.

I remember vividly the fear that we experienced that day in January 1993, and I hope I don't ever live through that again. In the morning, Didi and I had gone to Dadar station to receive Ma, Baba and Bhai, who were arriving from Calcutta. We had just shifted to a one-room apartment with a small balcony in PMGP, the Andheri East haven for struggling film industry newcomers. We were earlier staying temporarily in Ashwini's Khar West flat.

When we left to go to the station early in the morning, we had seen one building that was smouldering, but we thought that it must have somehow caught fire during the night. After we returned from the station, Didi and I went out to buy vegetables, when I suddenly sensed people whispering and looking at us oddly. Didi was wearing a green salwar kameez, and I felt a sudden sense of panic and kept trying to tell her subtly that we should leave. We went back home in a bit, not fully understanding what was about to happen. A little later, when I was in the balcony giving Bhai a haircut, the mob arrived. I remember the swords being brandished.

I remember us fleeing inside. We were on the fourth floor, and as the Muslim households in the building were targeted, we heard things being broken and people screaming. I was worried about Ma and Didi and overcome with fear. We panicked and piled suitcases against the door, even though we knew that it was of no use since the door was really flimsy. Ma was desperately looking around for something that could prove that we were Hindus. We did not have any deities around as we're not particularly religious, but at that moment I was wishing that Ma had carried one of her gods along. Finally, Ma remembered that she had some sindoor in her bag, and this was quickly applied on my sister's forehead and hers. The horrific cries seemed to be getting closer, when suddenly there was silence. The police had arrived and the attackers fled. We came to know later that the brother of a friend of Didi's, who had just arrived from the US, had been attacked when he tried to intervene. This friend, an editor–film-maker who also lived in PMGP, was later trying to stop a cab so that she could take her injured brother to a hospital and had to eventually scream 'we are Hindus' for a car to stop. There were no mobile phones then, and since we didn't have a television or a landline, we had no idea about what exactly was happening. Didi and I later went to a phone booth to call Amit Khanna and request him to send a vehicle to get us out of there. Amit did try, but the Plus Channel vehicle didn't manage to reach us. We also called Ashwini, who was in FTII, to tell him that we would have to move to his flat. That evening, we left PMGP and moved into Ashwini's flat. I will never forget that day. I was ashamed of and sorry for my country.

Our city was burning and people had gone mad with hatred. The footage that came to us had to be censored, but I don't think any of us can forget what we watched. Not everyone could manage to come to the office, but among those who came were some terribly brave souls who went and reported from the scenes of the worst carnage. It was very difficult to edit those stories, but we also knew how important it was to share those stories with the world. It broke us to see that human beings are capable of so much cruelty.

Eighteen years later, the Supreme Court of India acquitted all those who were accused of having led the demolition of the Babri Masjid.

Before the March 1993 bomb blasts, it was common for Urmi Juvekar, Anupama Mandloi, Guru and me to go for a late night walk on Juhu beach—even at 3 a.m. or 4 a.m.—without any fear. It felt good to take a break during a night edit. After the blasts, Bombay became a city that needed high security because it was constantly under threat of being attacked. The attacks didn't stop though, unfortunately, and even though the city bounces back every time, it hurts so much more each time. I wonder what people mean when they refer to 'the spirit of Bombay' each time Bombay gets back to doing what it does after a carnage—chasing dreams and surviving. What else are we supposed to do? What options do we have apart from continuing with our lives?

At Plus, the majority of my edits were with Urmi and Anupama. With Urmi, I would mostly edit stories for a Bollywood-based video magazine called *Bollywood Plus*. We would take turns to decide which song would get the top billing—her favourite or mine. Plus Channel also brought out a video magazine called *People Plus* which featured one of my favourite edits with Urmi: a story about the school for special children, Dilkhush.

One of my most memorable edits with Anupama was a story on Vikram Seth, also for *People Plus*. I remember how excited both of us were about the interview, which happened at a Khar bookstore called Danai, my favourite bookstore in Bombay. During college days, my favoured bookstore was a wall bookstore in the Oberoi Grand arcade where Tapan Chatterjee, or Tapan da as we called him, had an amazing collection of foreign publications. He almost always knew the books one was looking for and even managed to procure the elusive ones we sought sometimes. It was here that I had discovered Kundera, Neruda, Márquez and here that I had found books on or by Tarkovsky, Buñuel and Godard. These foreign editions were expensive for us students, but Tapan da trusted us and let us pay in instalments. The joy of being able to buy those books is very hard to explain, but book lovers will know the feeling. I have still not adapted to the idea of the Kindle. Books have a fragrance, the pages a texture, which lend a sense of intimacy that e-books cannot match.

I think reading was another habit I unknowingly developed while trying to imitate Didi. Every other night during childhood, Didi read novels by torchlight under the blanket after the lights were out. She was a voracious reader and hated to stop reading just because the lights were turned off. I think I wasn't much of a reader till Class 10. It was during the months of waiting for the ICSE results that I started reading a lot. Until then, it had only been Enid Blytons, Hardy Boys, Nancy Drews and comics. Tarzan, Phantom, Amar Chitra Katha, Asterix and Tintin—how we used to devour them all, how all the unread ones had to be read as quickly as possible! And how can I forget Archie! I was eternally in love with him and jealous of both Betty and Veronica! I also loved Casper the friendly ghost, although I was never too sure about Richie Rich. He always reminded me of my brat of a schoolmate in Bhutan who was the son of a brigadier. After Class 10, I found myself finishing novels of Charles Dickens, Jane Austen, Thomas Hardy and even reading Shakespeare. And I was loving it!

I was quite popular as an editor, enjoyed editing, and I could happily spend hours in the edit suite. But I had not lost sight of my goal. I wanted to direct. Whenever I would see a team heading for a shoot, in my heart I would long to be with them. I did go for a few shoots with Urmi and Anupama, but I think after editing for about eight months, my restlessness started to grow. Apart from editing stories for the three Plus video magazines, *Business Plus*, *People Plus* and *Bollywood Plus*, I was also editing for Vikram Bhatt's show *Mere Saath Chal*, which was hosted by Pooja Bhatt. I went up to Amit one day and asked him to give me the opportunity to direct a segment. He refused, saying that I was an excellent editor and I should stick to my job.

Around that time, I had been offered to direct a music video, something that Ashwini, Didi and I co-directed. I took three days off work for the shoot, which featured the recently crowned Miss India, Madhu Sapre. I came to know two precious people through this shoot. Our director of photography (DOP) was the gentle and kind soul Rajen Kothari, the man who had shot films like *Damul*, *Dacait* and *Ghayal*. Didi and I later edited a series that he directed, *Arjun Pandit*. Even back in 1993, Rajan strongly felt that I would make a good film-maker. The other person was Buri, the production designer Sharmishta Roy. I learned a lot about production design by observing her. Sometime in 1995, Buri called me and asked me if I wanted to do art direction for seven episodes of a TV series. She had to leave for New York for a film shoot, and I was thrilled that she thought I would be capable of filling in for her. I had always loved doing up our home, and this prospect fascinated me. It would also mean that I would learn another aspect of film-making. I took it up, and I learnt two things right away. The first was that photographs shouldn't be placed too high on the wall for they would always be missed when the shot was framed. The second was why flowerpots shouldn't be used whenever a space seemed empty. I hated how often the direction team would want a flowerpot moved into the frame . . . I believe every space must have its own properties and those should own the space.

After the music video was ready, I was showing it to some of my Plus colleagues when Amit was passing by. He stopped, smiled and congratulated me, but I was called to his office a little later. He told me that I couldn't take leave to direct music videos. I knew he was within his rights to demand this and I told him that he should then let me direct a segment! He again asked me to stick to editing. I told him that in that case, I would have to give him a month's notice and leave as I needed to move towards my goal. I am sure he never meant it, because Amit is essentially an extremely sweet and warm person, but what he said at that point was not very kind.

I packed my bag and left immediately.

I was scared that Amit Khanna was such a powerful man that he would send the police after me. Yes, I was that naive! I went to my sister, who was in Pune, for refuge. I was angry, but I was also feeling guilty as I had behaved unprofessionally by quitting without serving my notice. I went back to meet Amit a month later to apologize, and he accepted my apology with a smiling face. As I walked out of the office, he sent a colleague after me to tell me that I could come back if I wanted to. It was generous of him, but I too had my pride to consider. I would have gone back if he had asked me directly, but because it was through a colleague, I didn't. Plus Channel became the first and last real 'job' I ever had. Thanks to Amit, I rediscovered my free spirit and embarked on a difficult and yet extremely rewarding journey as a freelancer.

The first few months were difficult. Didi was also going through a difficult phase personally and professionally. We had shifted to a one-room apartment with a shared bathroom off Linking Road, Bandra. Though the location was lovely, the shared bathroom was an absolute nightmare. Hygiene and cleanliness were not our landlady's forte. She was an elderly east Indian lady who was quite an alcoholic. Therefore, there was this strange, stale smell about the flat at all times. I clearly remember those days of surviving on *vada pav* and boiled eggs.

But I soon started getting interesting editing assignments again. I began editing Vikram Bhatt's first fiction series, *Aasman*

*Se Aagay* (1994). My friend Anupama too had quit Plus Channel and she joined as an assistant to Vikram. Viveck Vaswani was the producer of the show, a person with whom it's very difficult to be angry for too long over anything. He knew the art of talking, and the ever-cheerful face made your anger evaporate every time there was a crisis.

I also started editing for *Dekh Bhai Dekh* and *Chandrakanta* (1995). Those were some of the big-budget series of those days and amazing learning experiences for me. The series that I enjoyed working on most as an editor was *Aasman Se Aagay*, an adaptation of Ayn Rand's *The Fountainhead*. I used to edit in an editing studio in Juhu that belonged to Neeraj Bhakri. Looking back at the number of hours I spent editing every day, it was almost as if I was addicted to the machine. The minute the rushes would come, I would be restless till I set about syncing the sound, logging the footage and then editing. So much has changed from those days of analogue editing to the present non-linear world. I was getting to work on so much fiction material for the first time, and it was exciting to be able to apply all that I had learnt in Berlin. It was also enjoyable because Vikram listened to other points of view and always allowed me enough breathing space as an editor. Sometimes, when I did not agree with what he was suggesting, I would kind of sulk, and then he would allow me to do what I wanted! Of course, I think he also did that because he was convinced that what I was suggesting was not bad. Because of the freedom that Vikram gave me, I always had a sense of ownership. I was not just doing a job. At the same time, I never did forget that as an editor, I had to understand and deliver the director's vision.

I learnt how important it is for a film-maker to give that sense of ownership to their team. This is one reason why I never allow the credits to read 'A film by Onir' or 'An Onir film'. It goes as 'Directed by Onir'. Film-making is a collective activity, the film a result of so many dreams and energies coming together. Yes, my vision is central to the process, but ownership cannot be singular.

Didi and I had shifted to a tiny flat in Chuim Village in 1994. That flat had so much positive energy and has seen so many people as guests. I remember Didi, Ashwini and I sitting with our friends from FTII on a *chatai* on the floor—Charudutt Acharya, Arun Nambiar, Arun Varma, Suresh Pai, Pritam Chakrabarty, Vivek Philip and Amitabh Varma—over Old Monk, tandoori chicken and fish fry (from Charu's mom's kitchen on a lucky day) and dreaming of cinema, planning to do things together. There were so many dreams in that tiny room those days, with young lovers of cinema from all over the country trying to find our roots in the industry. Charu had written this fun song *'Bukhar chad gaya, tere chumme se'*, and I wanted to use it in a film some day. It was at that time that Pritam had sung his now famous song to me, *'Alvida alvida ab kehna aur kya'* and had promised me the song.

By 1996, I had graduated from the typewriter to my first PC, and for the first time I was enjoying writing. Till that time, writing was a daunting task as I hated my handwriting, and spellings and grammar were an absolute nightmare. I now started putting down the first script ideas that I had. I was developing something called *Realm of Shadows*, a docudrama series based on paranormal activities. I think Charu was working with me on the concept. I used to often be alone at night as Didi would be working night shifts. We had a sofa-cum-bed in the main room with a window just behind the sofa. The nights I was alone, I would frequently get spooked while writing, imagining what if someone came and stood just outside the window? I would quickly get up and shut the windows and get back to writing. And then the thought would come: what if someone just appeared inside the room, and with the windows closed, no one would hear me scream! So I would quickly open the windows again. The tension would finally get so overpowering that I would end up switching off my computer.

Then there were planchette sessions with friends, probably a result of my research on the paranormal at that time. I remember one particular session with Pritam and Sumit one night. The 'soul' who 'appeared' happened to be that of a murdered sex worker who predicted that things would go wrong with Pritam's upcoming trip, that the train would be delayed at start and reach Calcutta twenty-four hours late. Pritam still recalls vividly how they were waiting at Dadar from 6 a.m. and as the big clock turned to 4 p.m., the train finally arrived. Pritam's new pair of Nike shoes were stolen in the train, and the train got diverted because of another accident and arrived in Calcutta a day late.

This was a short period when planchette became kind of an obsession. It was a way of telling stories—all kinds of strange souls would be created with fascinating back stories. I don't remember why, but somewhere along the way we stopped having those sessions.

Power cuts weren't that uncommon in Bombay in those days, and if I was alone, I would be scared to go to the bathroom that was attached to the inner room as I would have to pass a mirror fixed to the cupboard, and the thought of that would freeze me. I had read somewhere that if you stood in front of a mirror with a candle for long enough, you could see the ghost present in the room. I dreaded that while going to the bathroom with a candle, I would see something that I didn't want to in the mirror. I am actually embarrassed to say this, but the truth is that even while writing about it now, more than two decades later, I feel my body grow tense with an inexplicable fear. Now you know that I will probably never make a horror film!

Coming back to the post-Plus Channel days, the process of editing *Dekh Bhai Dekh* was initially a lot of fun, although slowly but surely it turned into a nightmare. Unlike Vikram Bhatt, my director here liked the edit to be exactly the way he wanted it. Though I was learning a lot from his vision of how to edit comedies,

I felt more like an operator than an editor. Maybe that is why I never felt any ownership of what I was doing, and the hours felt excruciatingly long.. This is also where I learnt what not to do with my team. The editing that had started with so much excitement ended up with us just waiting for it to get over. The director would make an editor redo every single cut innumerable times, and all the time he spent in the editing room would be devoted to praising himself. An episode that should ideally have taken a week to edit took fourteen to sixteen hours of work every day for over a month. When I could take it no longer, I quit. Unfortunately, I had to quit *Aasman se Aagey* around the same time. Both Anupama and I had decided to leave as there were differences between the director and producer, and there were talks of changing the director. We wanted to quit because we were working on the show primarily because of Vikram.

It was around this time that I first did some work for a film. I cut some song promos for film-maker Sai Paranjpye's film *Papeeha*. I was thrilled after I got the call from her—the director of the film we had all loved so much, *Chashme Buddoor*. This was in late 1993; I remember Sai had booked a hi-band studio somewhere close to where I lived, and we were supposed to be working from 9 p.m. to 5 a.m. as night shifts were cheaper. The first night, I was nervously waiting for Sai, and in she walked on the dot at 9 p.m. I remember her vividly from that night—short grey hair, capri pants and a long floral-print shirt. The first thing she told me was, 'Anirban, I would like you to call me Sai, and not madam or *ji*.' I immediately fell in love with her. That is one lesson I learnt from her. I prefer people calling me by my name rather than sir or *ji*. And when people argue saying 'but I respect you, sir/*ji*', I explain that respect has nothing to do with the word 'sir'. They can call me 'sir' and still be disrespectful enough.

Editing with Sai was memorable because of the person she was—full of warmth, smiles and stories. Sometimes she would bring miniature bottles of alcohol and some snacks. We would take a small break after midnight and then continue. A year later, Didi and I co-edited a TV series for children that Sai was directing, *Partyana*.

I must talk about an incident that seems kind of hilarious when I look back at it now. I could have probably easily dealt with the situation myself back then but instead created some drama around it! I was editing for a film-maker who, I soon realized, was trying to get a little too cosy with me for my comfort. He would only arrange for night shifts, when there were not too many people around. It began with innocuous comments like 'I love your socks, my wife has similar ones'. I was standing near the edit console one day while he was sitting and telling me about the changes he would like, when he suddenly slipped his hand under my t-shirt and followed it up with a ridiculous comment, 'What a beautiful colour for a t-shirt.' I was wearing black! At that time, there was a close friend who enjoyed watching edits and on whom I had a huge crush. I asked her to come and sit with me whenever she was free! This went on for maybe a few weeks, and we used to joke that she was my bodyguard!

Another day, while I was sitting and making changes on the final edit, he kept complaining that he had a body ache. He called the watchman to press his shoulders, and after a couple of minutes, started screaming at him, 'C****ya, *theek se massage karna bhi nahi aata, main dikhata hoon massage kaise kartein hain.*' He swivelled my chair so that my back was towards him and started massaging my shoulder and back. I was so mortified and put off that I quit soon after this incident.

In 1994, I started work on another big serial—*Abhay Charan*, produced by ISKCON and directed by Tarun Dhanrajgir. That was a unique experience for me, for I was an atheist and not a big fan of ISKCON notwithstanding the yummy food, but I learnt to edit the serial with love and genuine interest. This might have been because Tarun was a wonderful director to work with. Both Tarun and Vara—who was married to him and acting in the series as well as handling a lot of the creatives—were lovely human beings. They treated me with love and pampered me. This was when I also started to work with people with whom I would end up having long working associations. Amitabh Varma, who was Didi's junior from FTII, worked as my editing assistant and later went on to write the lyrics of the music albums that Nameeta Premkumar and I produced. Amitabh has also worked on all my films as lyricist. I keep telling young film aspirants that film-making is all about creating your circle of cinema lovers who believe in you and will be there for you in your journey as a film-maker. Only make sure that your camp has open doors and windows so that new talent can constantly flow in as well. Pritam did the background score for *Abhay Charan,* with Vivek Philip (who later did the song '*Le chalein*' for *My Brother Nikhil*) as the programmer.

I remember the first serial that Pritam gave music for. He was still studying at FTII, and I would book the Hi-band editing suite for a night shift so that none of the other unit members would be present. Pritam had just bought a very basic keyboard and was learning how to use it. He was staying in my Chuim Village flat, and while I was editing, he would spend the day trying to figure out how the keyboard functioned. At night, he would come to the editing room and record the background score. By the time we started work on the final music, Pritam had mastered the keyboard, and the music he finally composed was really good.

Afterwards, Pritam worked on the background music for a lot of TV serials that I edited. He used to come down from FTII for a few days, mostly over the weekend, and stay over at my place and work on the background music. I had always been interested in music and thought it would be fun to make some music together. Nameeta loved the idea too, and we got together to produce *ARIA*. That journey had a lot of drama too . . . but I will come to this later.

To come back to *Abhay Charan*, I had to go to Hyderabad for one edit schedule. I was staying at the ISKCON guest house and was rather miserable about the fact that I would only be served vegetarian food. Imagine being in Hyderabad and not being able to have Hyderabadi biryani! Impossible. The ashram was in Banjara Hills, and I soon discovered that if one walked down the road, there was a shady little joint that served beer and biryani.

Mornings were also painful as they wouldn't serve tea at the ashram. I told them that I wouldn't be able to work without a constant inflow of tea into the editing room. Finally, Maharaj Bhakti Charu Swami relented and allowed green tea to be served to me. He would walk into the editing room every morning and greet me with a 'Sri Krishna Prabhu, Anirban', and I would reply, 'Good morning, Maharaj.' I guess I was being childish, but that was me, and I think Bhakti Charu Swami saw that and always had a kind and benevolent smile for me. Towards the end of my Hyderabad editing schedule, when he walked in one morning, it so happened that he greeted me with a 'Good morning, Anirban', and I simultaneously said, 'Sri Krishna, Maharaj.'

I used to love to scandalize the young devotees there. They all loved me, and I could freely discuss with them what my notions of sexuality and non-vegetarianism were in the context of religion and culture. I realized that when there is mutual respect, people listen and are willing to understand even if what they practise is different.

During this period, I felt a distance growing between Didi and me. At least I thought so, and this went on for many years. I felt I knew a lot more about her life, her woes and happiness than she knew about mine. I stopped sharing details about my life with her, and she didn't know that Kamros, my internet alter ego, existed. She didn't really ask me much about my life apart from the usual leg-pulling. Different people knew about different aspects of my life, and there were very few who knew about what was happening in totality. My friend Nameeta Premkumar was one of those few, and the other was Mukesh Sawlani.

I first met Nameeta in 1995 while working as an editor for Rashmi Uday Singh's TV show *Health Today*, for which she was assistant director. I later directed some short segments for the show as well, but the best part of working with Rashmi was that she would often take Nams, as I call Nameeta, and me to different eateries to do the food tasting and reviewing with her. She was what we call a true SoBo snob. I remember her taking me to this happening place, The Ghetto, in Breach Candy. As the manager and staff were fussing over her, she introduced me to them saying, 'Meet my editor, Anirban. He has come all the way from the suburbs to see this place.' I wanted to disappear.

Nams soon became like a soulmate. She helped me set up my flat, bringing an extra TV set from her home for me, gifted me my first mobile, supervised the clothes I bought. We were inseparable. Nameeta's mom and dad were also fond of me, but her boyfriend used to be a little unhappy about the fact that we would share hotel rooms while travelling outdoors for shoots. There were many times that Nams, Candy and Sophie stayed back at my Chuim flat, and we would party till dawn. We used to go dancing in nightclubs at least twice a week, and since we shared our birthdays, we would organize a joint party at Madh Island to celebrate. We would book a bungalow and I would do a lot of the cooking. Eric Pillai, an audio engineer at the sound studio Spectral Harmony, would be in charge of light and sound—he was the official DJ. There were three of them at Spectral Harmony—Vikram, Anish and Eric. I really loved them. They looked up to me as an older (not really wiser) friend, relationship advisor and more. There was also the chief sound engineer Biswadeep Chatterjee and Shantanu Mukherjee, who always treated me like a younger brother. I honestly miss those days; there was so much positive energy and love in that space.

Once, I made up a sad story about myself to Eric which I told him not to share with anyone. This was after he had asked me why I was so serious and always looked unhappy. I told him that I had been married, divorced and had a baby girl whom my wife did not allow me to meet. I took care of their expenses but missed my child. Eric believed the story, but he didn't keep quiet about it. Soon, everyone in Spectral Harmony knew the sad story and always looked at me with a sympathetic smile, until the story reached Sadhana Rana, the studio manager. Sadhana, who was very fond of me, was very hurt that I had confided in Eric and not her. That is when I had to confess that I had just been pulling a fast one on Eric! Eric was so furious that he did not speak with me for many days afterwards.

The moon
Had retired.
The wind silent,
The glow of dawn touched the weary eyelids,
Awaiting the presence that never came.
The lamp had extinguished long ago,
Unnoticed,
Yet the flowers kept raining,
Drenching me with memories of what never will be . . .

# 13

# Berlin Revisited

In 1995, I decided to take a three-month break to visit Berlin and stay with my friend and teacher, Hanno. Ever since he had married Zaki, he had been asking me to come over and spend time with them so that I could get to know her. It was a big deal for me to not work for three months and travel just to be with friends. I was excited that I would be in Berlin during Christmas and New Year.

Being in Germany as a visitor was a different experience. It hadn't been easy for me to save money for the airfare and basic expenses and just take off for three months. But I had wanted to do it badly. I had also wanted to upgrade my editing skills with a little more knowledge about using Avid, a non-linear editing software that was gaining popularity in a big way. The first few weeks were amazing. Hanno's wife, Zaki Omar was from Indonesia, and we Asians bonded immediately. I know Hanno had been anxious about how we would get along, but Zaki was probably happy to connect with a fellow Asian, to chat with someone who looked differently at life than the Western way.

At that time, Hanno was also teaching in Hannover. So we would travel from the Schellingstraße Berlin apartment to Hannover and stay there for three days, spending the other four days in Berlin. We would keep drinking coffee so that Hanno would not fall asleep while driving on the expressway. There used to be many accidents on the expressway in winter because of the icy roads.

One week, we went to the Black Forest, the forest of Hansel and Gretel and of many other stories heard during childhood. Hanno had a small cabin there, and like in rural Bengal, shitting was to be done in the forest, except that here we were supposed to dig a hole and cover it up afterwards. And we had to shower outdoors in the ice-cold waters of a German winter. This apparently was good for health, but I would die each time I stepped under the shower.

After the first few weeks, the excitement of being back in Germany slowly started to diminish. I started feeling restless—I wanted to learn something new or shoot a documentary. But Hanno would keep insisting that it was holiday time and that I should relax. It wasn't possible for me to shoot something alone, and Hanno was busy. He would also be constantly cautioning me about not intruding into people's privacy, and even at home, I slowly started becoming more and more conscious of what was 'my space'. I would dread cooking anything in the kitchen, afraid of scratching the expensive kitchen tabletop or maybe the expensive Spanish tiles in the kitchen.

I do not blame Hanno for my discomfort; it is just that in India we approach a guest in a different manner. It's difficult to explain, but when I have any of my friends over, I make space for them to feel comfortable and be free with me. I did not have that sense of freedom with Hanno.

Towards the end of the third month, I went off to Hamburg to spend some time with Bea. Bea had planned out this wonderful road trip from Hamburg to London. We took the overnight bus to Brussels so that we could spend the entire day walking around and exploring the city and then again took the night bus to the Port of Calais. I remember the exhilaration at the thought of crossing the English Channel. The bus was stopped at the border and the British border police started to check visas. I was asked to step out, and the grilling began. I was asked all kinds of ridiculous questions about why I was going to the UK. It was embarrassing as the entire bus had to wait for me. The 'why London' questions would just not stop. Why was I not visiting other European countries since I had a Schengen visa? I was exhausted and past caring when I finally said, 'I want to go to the UK to have a look at how my colonial masters live.' I was immediately allowed in.

I instantly felt at home in London. In Germany, people would look at me with suspicion, as Indian tourists were not a common sight in those days. They would try to figure out if I actually wanted to settle there. Even the Bangladeshi guy selling flowers outside the restaurant would look at me questioningly, as if asking, 'How come you are sitting and dining here?' In London, no one seemed to care. People from the entire world were in the streets of London, and one could just blend in. Language was another advantage, and I realized that there were people with accents far worse than mine. The constant drizzle did not dampen my spirit as there was so much to take in. The Asian and African displays at the British Museum made me angry—to see stolen artefacts from temples and pyramids made one acutely aware of how unfair the West is about certain things. After the Second World War, the West got together to rebuild Germany, but the British left India bleeding from a wound that we are still trying to heal. No one ever returned our stolen artefacts.

Back in Hamburg, I realized that I was getting into Bea's space. As she lived in a small flat, my presence was disturbing her work. Both of us were trying, but it wasn't easy. In Hamburg, I started shooting at the historical Rote Flora, which had recently been burnt down by the right-wingers. Rote Flora was a space for leftist artists, and I felt connected because of my JU background. On the second day of shooting, there was a huge protest. Thousands were out marching, when suddenly the riot police attacked. I was terrified because if I got arrested for being a part of the protest, my visa would probably get revoked and my travel plans would go kaput. Though my legs were not as long as the Germans and I could not run as fast, I did manage to get away. Unfortunately, many of the protestors were arrested, and I could not proceed with the documentary under the circumstances.

One fun memory of Hamburg I have is of visiting Reeperbahn with Bea. We would go from one sex shop to another, inspecting all kinds of sex toys, gadgets and accessories. I had never seen anything like that and would burst out laughing. There was also a group of Indian mariners huddled together, looking sheepish and gathering the courage to approach a prostitute sitting in one of the many glass windows. What struck me was that while there was so much talk about respect and freedom for sex workers, most of the women looked like they were from Asia, Latin America, Africa and East Europe. That says a lot. Besides, everything was designed for toxic patriarchy—all the sex workers were women and many of them probably victims of trafficking, doing what they were doing not really as a choice but to survive or after having been forced into prostitution. I wonder how it is that men don't choose the same profession because of poverty. Don't women desire sex as widely as a service, or is it a male privilege? I don't recall seeing any windows where men stood naked and women or queer men could shop for them.

I returned to Berlin sooner than I had planned. Honestly speaking, I now wanted to be back in Bombay. Zaki and Hanno must have figured that out and were a little disappointed, but there was no way they could travel with me to Paris as I had initially expected and hoped. So they gifted me four days in Paris on my way out of Berlin. A day before I left, the evening was cold and Berlin covered in snow, and I met some very special people. Hanno had brought home four visitors—Merle, Philip, Tina and

Joerg. They had all been his students once, and as Philip and Merle were supposed to come to India in a few weeks, they wanted to meet me. That was the beginning of an incredible story and a very precious friendship. Meeting them was the best thing that happened to me in Berlin. The truth is that a distance had slowly grown between Hanno and me. I felt that the three months he hosted me in Berlin were somehow payback for the three months I hosted him in India. He failed to understand what would have actually interested me. If only he had introduced me to this group of his former students sooner, they would have happily given me access to their Avid editing systems, and maybe I would even have managed to shoot something with their help.

# 14

# Paris and New Friendships

I used to have a postcard of Paris as a child, of the fountain in front of the Louvre. Since then, Paris had been a destination at the top of my wish list. Over the years, the romance around the city had grown. Now I was finally here—in the city of Godard, Truffaut, Bresson, Monet, Renoir, Cézanne, Baudelaire and the French Revolution, in the country that first raised the all-important cry of 'Equality, Liberty and Fraternity'. Today, if a teacher gets beheaded in France for talking about a cartoon, you want to stand by the nation that has made freedom of expression its anthem. I was breathing that air, marvelling at all the majestic buildings, the grand arcades and museums. But then a lot of the romanticism was eclipsed—at the thought of the years of slavery, exploitation and violence over the African, Asian and Latin American nations because of whom France acquired the wealth it now possesses. The romanticism died when I thought about the freedoms that were taken away. And now, it dies at the sight of the thousands of young students and migrants in the streets of Paris, protesting against the human rights violations that migrants face.

Every morning, I would eat a very heavy breakfast at the hotel, then take the metro to one end of the city and start walking back towards my hotel with the help of a map, exploring places of interest en route. I would eat fruit while walking by the Seine and have a French omelette with bread and wine at around 6 p.m. The second day, I was walking by a gay pub near Bastille around 9 p.m., when I noticed a man getting out of a car. He was wearing a long black overcoat, a black suit and a hat, and he was rather attractive. I think I looked at him for a bit too long, and he noticed me watching him. I was mortified and quickly started walking away. After some time, I realized that he was following me. I was excited but nervous too as my experience in Berlin told me that I needed to be careful of racism. I did not take the next metro back home though, but kept walking around the nearby blocks, occasionally looking back to see if it he was still following me. I was kind of thrilled that he did not stop even after an hour. By 10 p.m., it was getting deserted, and although it wasn't as freezing as Berlin in January, it was still terribly cold. Suddenly, I was gripped by panic, too frightened to take the tube as it would be nearly empty, and if I walked, there would be parts that would be totally deserted.

So I stood at the bus stop, wondering what next. He stood close by and watched me. As I finally gathered the courage to look at him, a smile spread across that kind face. He walked up to me and started speaking in French. I stopped him and told him I understood nothing. He invited me for a beer. That was my first time in a gay bar in Paris. It was funny how we struggled with language as we tried to communicate with each other. And then, at some point, he just kissed me. I was overwhelmed, happy, nervous, excited . . . it was the first time I had kissed a man in a public place. No one looked, no one seemed to bother, and I felt strangely liberated. Needless to say, the next two days in Paris were beautiful. I do not remember his name.

A few weeks after my return to India, Philip and Merle arrived in Bombay. I remember going to meet them at this matchbox of a hotel in Colaba on 19 January 1996. I hated how the hotelier looked at me, as if I had come to sell drugs to the foreigners. I found it sweet that my German friends had put up a huge map of India on the wall of their hotel room to make that miserable space look better. Since our flat in Chuim Village was also matchbox-sized, I asked them if they wanted to move in as a guest at my brother's hostel at TIFR. And, of course, they were welcome to spend their days in our Chuim flat. The next day I met them at Churchgate station and brought them back with me on a local train to our Chuim Village flat, where we spent the entire day over beer and the food that I had cooked. That became a routine, and slowly they learnt to navigate on their own. This was the beginning of a special friendship.

There was a reason why they were in Bombay. When she was twenty-five, Merle's mother had told her that the person she grew up knowing to be her father was not her real father. The story is right out of a Bollywood film. In the 1970s, her German mother, then already married to a German man and with a little daughter from that marriage, had fallen passionately in love with an Indian marine engineer visiting Hamburg. After they had been meeting regularly for several years, she found herself pregnant. The marine engineer had wanted to marry her and bring her to Bombay with him, but she had been afraid to leave everything and come to India. Meanwhile, her German husband was willing to continue their marriage as long as she destroyed photographs and all traces of the Indian man, which she then did. When Merle was born, her parents decided that they would not tell her about her real father. She grew up distinctly different from her blonde sister as she had dark hair and her skin tone was not exactly white. And here she was, twenty-six years later, in search of a father she knew nothing about. All she knew was that he was originally from Bombay, that he was a Gujarati, his name was AM and he had worked in the merchant navy.

From the next day, we started going through the telephone directory and calling everyone with the name we were looking for. We would also spend time walking around different parts of Bombay and cooking together, and there would be evenings with beer/rum and tandoori chicken. I don't know how the three of us bonded so quickly, but we never seemed to run out of things to talk about, and that is something that has not changed in these twenty-four years. When we meet, we talk endlessly. And when we part, it always feels like time just flew by and there was still so much to talk about.

I think it was on the third day that we called a number where we learnt that a person with the same name used to live there but had died a couple of years back. Merle's face turned white, and we all literally froze. Then Merle checked if the deceased used to work with the merchant navy, and it turned out that the dead person was someone else. We were all a little shaken after that. What if this 'ghost' of a father was actually dead?

After two more days, we finally managed to locate the man. He had migrated to London, was married and had three children. Merle managed to get his UK phone number. I will never forget the image of Merle inside the STD booth at the Khar Danda and 17th Road crossing, talking for the first time to a man who was supposed to be her father, while Philip and I paced up and down the road in stress. When she finally came out, she enveloped us in a tight hug.

Her real father was now a very successful merchant navy man. A few months later, Merle and Philip went to London and finally met him. I find it sad and shameful that he didn't have the courage to officially accept the daughter who found him after twenty-six years or introduce her to his family. Merle found and lost a father, but in the process, we found each other. We formed a relationship that's hard to define—a sibling, friend, working partner—but now I have a place in Berlin that I can always call home. Over the years, we've made it a point to meet every year, either in Berlin or in India. When I was filming *My Brother Nikhil,* Merle advised me on the script and edit. Philip and Merle came down to Goa when we were shooting and covered the making of the film. They were here with me in Bombay when *Bas Ek Pal* premiered. When I was working on the stories for *I Am*, I ran away to Berlin for a couple of weeks. I wrote the first drafts of the *Omar* and *Abhimanyu* segments, and then Merle read them, made suggestions and we arrived at the next draft. When I am with them, I feel so much at peace—going for morning walks with Merle and the dog, having my favourite coffee and croissant at the corner coffee shop, writing all day . . . Philip brewing coffee for us, and then all three of us going for evening walks, cooking an early dinner and then having a beer or two at The Roses Bar, or sometimes just sitting at home and watching a film.

My soul celebrates life,
When I bask in your presence,
And in your absence it celebrates longing,
Like a mirage.
You make me dream,
Of the rain,
Of the rainbow,
Of the Milky Way.

# 15

# Making Music

By 1996, Nams and I had started planning to get together to produce a music album with Pritam. I remember Pritam calling me up at night from Pune and singing tunes for the album. Then we would do conference calls with Nams. Nams and I worked on instinct, going for melodies that stayed with us when we woke up the next morning. At the same time, we also started thinking about how we could make this album unique. We decided to create what I think was India's first mixed performing group. As we were deciding on the melodies, we also started with Pritam's FTII batchmates—Amitabh Varma on the lyrics and Vivek Philip on arranging the music.

Nams and I auditioned over 300 aspirants and finally zeroed in on four singers to record our album with. The singers were Sona, Subrata, Raghuram and Aparna. Both Nams and I were always thinking about how we could make it more fun and unique and get people talking. We decided to call the band *ARIA* and rename our singers—Subrata became the I in '*ARIA*', Ishaan; Raghu became Reeshav and Sona became Asia. We brainstormed intensely with Pritam and Amitabh and decided that the music would be an Indo-Western mix. Sona was trained in Western music, while Aparna was more in the Indian space. Pritam started designing the songs and the actual recording started around early 1997.

Didi and Ashwini got married in March 1997. In a way, this was a new chapter for me because as long as Didi was around, she was always the boss. Now I was officially living on my own.

The year 1997 was also the beginning of another long association for me. I edited the music promos for the film *Darmiyaan* directed by Kalpana Lajmi, the music of which was done by the legendary Bhupen Hazarika. While editing the promos, Bhupen da felt that I had a good sense of music and wanted us to work together in the future. I started working as an editor on a series produced by Bhupen da called *Glimpses of the Misty East*, a travelogue narrating stories about the seven states of the North-East. That was again a very precious learning experience, as I was editing hours and hours of documentary footage and trying to find a rhythm in them. Didi was working on the editing script, but we had to work with material that was shot with no real sense of direction, and the whole exercise was rather challenging. Years later, I faced a similar challenge while editing an Indo-Australian documentary, *Raising the Bar*. This was a film about children and young people with Down's Syndrome, produced by emotion21 and the Indian Film Festival Melbourne. There were a couple hundred hours of footage and no script, and while I know that a lot can be done at the editing table, I think it's absolutely indispensable to have some structure or approach in mind while shooting a documentary. This can change at the editing table, and one should also be flexible while shooting—to allow things to happen, to allow oneself to be surprised. But a documentary (unless we're talking about one where one has planned not to pre-plan) needs planning. Otherwise, God save the editor!

My time at Spectral Harmony has left me with some amazing memories. It seemed as if the entire studio was booked with work in which I was involved. I fondly remember the collaboration with Biswadeep Chatterjee, Shantanu da, the super-talented Eric Pillai and studio assistants Vikram and Anish (who is no longer with us). Then there was Rahul Sood and Sadhana Rana from the studio management who ensured that I was always given first preference for everything. We were like a family that ate, drank and slept music. Nams used to order biryani from Candies so often that it almost became our staple diet. I learnt a lot about music and sound design from Biswadeep, Pritam, Vivek and Eric as I sat inside the studio during the voice and music recordings and during the song mixing.

It was fascinating how so many channels played different music and vocal tracks and then how they would be mixed non-digitally as was done in those days. That learning was invaluable. To be able to interact with a music director, lyricist, musicians and singers about every nuance was amazing. To know the why and how was very important for me, and it helped when I was making my feature film debut. This training helped me while briefing KK, Sunidhi and Shaan when we were recording 'Le chalein' for *My Brother Nikhil*. I would tell them the synopsis of the film, about the character to whom they were lending their voice, the reason behind the lyrics. I think that knowledge is important for a singer. If instead of singing for a faceless person, they have a face, a situation and a space to fill with their emotions, they proceed to do that. I remember how Sunidhi broke down when she heard about the situation for which she was to sing. I believe that it's because she was so moved that the song became memorable. She always recalls it as one of her favourite songs. I remember KK hugging me after I explained the context of the song and saying, 'Thank you, bro, for giving me this beautiful song.'

After *My Brother Nikhil*, I developed such a bond with these two singers that a film would almost feel incomplete if they hadn't sung any song for it. Very often, when I didn't have the appropriate budget, both of them would forgo their fee, saying, 'But you offer us beautiful songs.'

Coming back to *ARIA*, we faced a challenge with one of our singers, Sona, once we had completed the recording and had started hunting for a music company to back the album. She didn't feel comfortable about a contract with a music label, and for us it was important that they made a minimum commitment to stay together as a band for a certain amount of time. Both Nams and I realized that it was a mistake to form a band artificially, and it turned out that the two of us, Pritam, Amitabh and the entire Spectral Harmony team were more enthusiastic about the album than the artists themselves! Sona's departure was a nightmare, and we had to replace her with another singer, Arasha. This wasn't easy as the tracks had already been recorded and songs had been created to suit Sona's pitch. It was sad that the strongest singer of the band quit, but we still went ahead and redubbed and remixed the album, even though we now sensed that the band could not last long. As creative producers and also managers of the band, we realized that each singer thought that they were much better than the rest and therefore deserved much more than the others. They didn't dream as a band.

In August 1998, we went to Moscow to shoot the music videos for *ARIA*. I had to be in Berlin just before the shoot for a workshop organized by my friends Merle and Philip, called 'Hungry Minds Think Alike'. This idea for the workshop had developed during an ICQ chat that Philip had set up, where people from various countries logged in to chat under the caption 'I Shit You Shit'. This was a fun project that started during one of our endless conversations. When Philip and Merle were in Bombay, they would struggle to coordinate the movement of the rice-curry mix from the plate to the mouth using their hands or trying to drink water from a bottle without touching their lips to it. I would tell them how I used to find those Berlin toilets without bidets or mugs so difficult to use. I would never feel clean enough and would end up taking too many showers even in the cold Berlin winter. My friends always thought that using one's hand to wash one's derrière was dirty. While I found their effort to eat with their hand hilarious, I struggled to figure out which spoon or fork to use for which dish . . . and which was the correct glass! To burp during meals is pretty natural in India because of the kind of food we eat and also as an expression of satisfaction, but it would be considered rude in Europe. I would get quite put off by people blowing their nose during dinner in Berlin, something they're probably comfortable with due to the weather. Basically, the chat room was about diverse perceptions and cultures and to celebrate them all. The workshop 'Hungry Minds Think Alike' was an extension of the chat.

Urmi and I were to attend the event, but my visa just didn't arrive in time, and when Philip and Merle came to the airport to receive us, they discovered that it was only Urmi who had finally taken the flight. I managed to get there after two days but was to leave for Moscow in two days' time for the *ARIA* music video shoot. My friends were really hurt, and I think Merle and I spent most of the last night crying over bottles of beer.

We landed in Moscow at the time of the infamous Russian ruble crisis. The ruble's value just kept plunging and there was total chaos, but it was too late for us to cancel the shoot. A lot of money had already been spent, and we were in Moscow. The only thing we could do was to cut down the number of shooting days. We had planned to shoot the two videos over eight days, but with the new situation, we knew we would have to complete it in four days and head back.

That first trip to Moscow was really no fun, and our woes started right from the airport. The airport authorities refused to release our stock. We were shooting on 35mm and Rajen Kothari was the DOP. Nams and I were taken into a security room where there was a Russian policewoman sitting with her legs on the table, filing her fingernails. She didn't even acknowledge us for a while and then pretended that she couldn't understand English. After two hours of negotiations, she finally agreed to release the stock if we 'gifted' her a bottle of vodka. I know this sounds like it is out of a C-grade film, but I'm not making it up.

*ARIA* was also the beginning of a lifelong friendship and a long working relationship with my friend Mukesh's sister, Anita. In those days, designer Anita Dongre worked out of a small workshop in Santa Cruz East in a narrow lane where a car couldn't get in. I remember meeting her there—the warm, generous smile and a confident, towering personality. Anita designed the artist costumes for the music video. In 2004, Mukesh and Anita helped us get a sponsorship deal with WEEKEND for *My Brother Nikhil*, and Anita took care of any additional requirements for clothes. Anita has always treated my films with special love. She makes it a point to read the entire script and has so many things to say about the film that, as a film-maker, you feel blessed. We have spent hours discussing each character and how that person should dress. She made me understand that most of us have our favourite colours and how we can use that to reveal character traits. Now, when I write about my characters, I like to imagine the colours they would wear, if they would iron their clothes or wear them unironed . . . How an actor owns a character also comes from the clothes they wear in the film. For the character of Nigel in *My Brother Nikhil*, Anita suggested that Purab come to the workshop and paint a few of the T-shirts that Nikhil and he wear in the film. I later extended the idea and scribbled poetry on the walls of Nigel's bungalow in Goa.

While shooting *Bas Ek Pal*, we worked a lot on the colour schemes for the characters. Blue for Juhi Chawla's character Leena as it reflected a certain calmness, black for the sinister and deeply introverted Nikhil (Sanjay Suri). Sameer (Jimmy Sheirgill) wore white, as his character was pure, and finally it was red for Anamika (Urmila Matondkar) as she was passionate and fiery. Of course, this didn't mean that they would only wear these colours, but that these shades would dominate their wardrobes.

I enjoy the process of dressing up my characters. By the time we did *Sorry Bhai!* (2007), thanks to what I had learnt from Anita, I was working on the styling of the male characters. I remember calling up Sanjay, Sharman and Boman from shops in Melbourne, trying to figure out sizes for their shirts, T-shirts and shorts. It was fun and worked out fine.

I also remember another incident around the *Sorry Bhai!* costumes. I was told that Shabana Azmi is very fussy about the clothes selected for her character and had apparently reduced one well-known film-maker to tears because she thought the clothes chosen were not appropriate. I remember anxiously discussing options for Shabana with Anita. I was actually very nervous the day we were supposed to go to her house for trials. It was kind of the first day of work with her. I had always wanted to work with her and Naseeruddin Shah, and one dream was getting fulfilled. The other dream remains unfulfilled—I had approached Naseer for the role of Neel from *Shab* (the film was called *Kaash* then). He had told me that the role didn't appeal to him, and I was quite heartbroken. Coming back to the costume trial at Shabana's Juhu flat, at the end of trying out all the nineteen options (yes, I still remember the number), she sashayed across the room with a wide smile and said, 'Onir you are lucky, I loved all the costumes.'

In 2009, when we resorted to crowdfunding for *I Am*, both Mukesh and Anita supported the film with funds. Anita's husband Pravin Dongre, a Dubai-based cousin Sumit Valrani and their friend Pradeep Jethani also contributed for our film. I can say that one of the four stories was made from their contributions. Anita also styled Juhi, Manisha Koirala and Radhika Apte for the film. Anita has always styled the look for my films because she passionately loved the stories and wanted to support the storytelling.

Anita has not only helped me with the styling for my films but is also always available when I need something or some advice, even though with the growth of her brand, it has become logistically impossible for her to continue styling for my films post *Sorry Bhai!*. For years, I have just called up Anita to help me dress, be it for the National Awards or for my trips to various film festivals. The only thing that I miss these days, ever since Anita turned vegan, is the mutton curry that used to be cooked in her house which she would often send us.

~

I don't have too many memories of Moscow apart from how hectic the shoot was. There was a strip club called 'Hungry Ducks' that all of us had headed to one night post shoot. It was very sad to see what was happening to the economy of a country that I always perceived as powerful, and of course women are always the worst hit. Women were constantly coming up to us and offering themselves for 15–20 dollars. The ruble was not being accepted by anyone as it was getting more and more devalued every day. Most of us left after a while, except for Pritam and Ishaan who stayed back on the dance floor. The next day, one of them had a bad infection on his lips, and none of us missed the opportunity to tease that person endlessly!

Another incident that I recall happened on the metro ride back from the flea market. Pritam's hands were loaded with CDs of East European and Turkish music, stuff that wasn't so easily available in India back then. As both his hands were occupied, he couldn't hold on to the overhead bars and kept losing balance and falling on other passengers, till one guy shoved him back. He looked at us accusingly for not standing up for him, but none of us had the guts to take on the tall Russian man! It was actually quite amazing how Pritam did not drop a single CD and also managed to retain his balance, and luckily our station came soon afterwards.

Somewhere around this time I had another misadventure that I won't ever forget. Ma was admitted in a Bombay hospital for her knee replacement surgery. I was on my way to meet her and running late. I saw a fast train to Churchgate leaving the platform and I ran and got into a compartment, only to realize that it was a ladies' compartment. I apologized profusely and promised to get off at the next station. When the next station came, I promptly got off, only to be caught by the railway policemen. I still looked very young and was anyway someone who was scared of the police. I was put in the lock-up, and I kept pleading to be allowed to leave. The lock-up was filthy, with a stinking open toilet, and the other couple of guys in there looked like crooks who had been there before. I was terrified. After much begging, they brought me out and asked for Rs 2,000. I didn't have that much with me and asked them to come with me to the ATM. They refused, took my wallet and emptied it of all the money I had, finally letting me go with a warning, 'We have your address. If you ever tell anyone, we will come for you.'

I was also dealing with a very problematic relationship in 1998. I don't know what to call that relationship—I was in love with this 'straight' guy, but his interactions with me weren't that platonic. The signals were extremely confusing, but Nams and our gang thought that he was surely in love with me but confused or in denial about his desires. Didi was now married and living with Ashwini, and the man in my life moved into my Chuim Village flat. I think living with someone always brings out his or her truth, and very soon I realized that I was playing the role of a doormat partner. I would be cooking or doing some other chores while he would be busy chatting on the phone or watching TV. I think it was partly my fault because I hadn't set the rules about sharing the work at the outset. This was probably because I thought that it would come to him naturally, and I was also enjoying taking care of him. I cringe to think of what I had reduced myself to on the pretext of love. That was the first time I was living with someone with whom I imagined a relationship, and I wanted it to slowly become a complete bond. I was happy waking up with him and holding him close, his hands in mine. I would usually wake up before him, make tea and then gently wake him up by running my fingers through his hair, caressing his face and then tickling him if he didn't wake up by then. As he woke up and overpowered me, I would pretend to resist but would actually be in seventh heaven. All this was okay for some time, but my sense of what's right started to make me notice things. We would go out shopping for me, and while I was trying to figure out what I wanted to purchase, he would suddenly point to something that he really liked, and I would very often end up not buying anything for myself but buying what he had wanted for himself.

In the middle of 1999, I moved from Chuim Village to the Juhu flat of Candy's friend. The family was visiting the US for three months and I could stay in their flat during that period. He too shifted to Juhu with me. Slowly, we did fewer and fewer things together. What started really irritating me was that after I had made dinner, he wouldn't join me at the dining table for the meal, but load his plate and sit on the sofa, watching TV while having dinner. I think we stayed together for about three months before I asked him to find a place and move out.

After *ARIA*, Nams and I went on to collaborate with Pritam, Amitabh and Vivek for two more albums. One was called *MTV Loveline—Pyaar Ke Dhun* (1999). It was a concept album, and the concept was Pritam's. The idea was to take old Hindi film songs and restructure them. I thought it was very smart of Pritam to have thought of something like that. He would take the *mukhra* and *antara* of a song and turn them into the musical interlude, and the melody of the song became the *mukhra* and *antara*. That year was also when we started work on our third collaboration with Pritam and the team.

Both Bhupen da and Kalpana loved good food, and as I love to cook for friends, I would often have them over. Lunch at Kalpana's office also used to be a lavish affair, and she was a very generous host. All of us would sit on the floor inside the small office room and both Dada and Kalpana would constantly cajole me to eat more. It was while we were working on *Pyaar Ke Dhun* that I invited Pritam, Vivek, Amitabh and Nams to join Bhupen da and Kalpana at my place one evening. I now lived in Manish Nagar, and this night was all about food and music. Pritam and Vivek played the guitar and sang, and Bhupen da too sang a couple of songs. This was the evening when the idea of *Voices of Brahmaputra* was born. We were going to recreate some of Bhupen Hazarika's famous songs in Hindi and get various singers to sing them. It was a prestigious project for all of us.

For me, the making of the album was also about learning so much about music. To be guided by a maestro like Bhupen da as we reinterpreted his music was incredible. The album also led to us working with many legendary singers. We had Kavita Krishnamurthy, Hariharan, Alka Yagnik, Shaan, Rekha Bharadwaj, Dominique, Usha Uthup and Shweta Shetty as the voices for the album. Each song began with Bhupen Hazarika singing the original track in Assamese and would lead in to the new track with Hindi lyrics.

Later that year, Kalpana started work on her next feature film, *Daman*. She asked me to edit the film and also help design the songs along with Dada. I was excited that I would finally be editing my first feature film. Pritam and Vivek were designing the songs and background music, and I was closely involved with the entire music process. Closer to the shoot—I think somewhere in October 1999—Kalpana asked me if I would be open to the idea of directing the songs. She had no budget for a choreographer and thought that I had a flair for visualizing songs. She was a little hesitant as she couldn't offer me any money, but I didn't have to think for a moment before saying yes. How could I say no to directing something for a feature film? Here was an opportunity to move closer to my goal—the dream that I had been nurturing since I was in class 6 and actively pursuing in Bombay since 1993.

# 16

# Kamros

A few years earlier, I had bought my first desktop and discovered the world of Internet chatting. Didi would often work night shifts, and I had our tiny Chuim Village flat to myself then. And when she got married and set up home with Ashwini, I had the flat to myself, except when our parents were visiting. Chuim, like the name suggests, was a little East Indian village, inhabited mostly by Goan Catholics. There was a small tandoori chicken shop close by from where we would often order, and then there was Hotel Samudra, where we would sometimes go for a dosa breakfast. There was also a wine shop near Pali Hill, where we would go when we ran out of alcohol (mostly rum and coke and the occasional beer) at 2 a.m. during the many drinking sessions that happened in our tiny flat, which was often packed beyond capacity. We would go to the 'closed' wine shop and knock on the shutter, and someone would come out and supply us with the required alcohol. But I'll come to all that later. What I was coming to is that with the Internet, I now had the space to explore my sexuality without being under any kind of scrutiny.

That is when I created another identity for myself. I have always been honest and open about who I am, and the photo and description were honest, but I used a nickname for my chatroom profile and for M2M. 'Kamros' was the name I gave myself, and the surname I added was 'Dreamseller'. 'Kamros' was a combination of Kama, the Hindu god of love, and Eros, the Greek god of Love. Whenever I donned that name, I transformed. While Onir was a shy, soft-spoken workaholic, Kamros was wild, raunchy, imaginative and adventurous. My nights transformed, and I started going out to meet other guys from the site. There have been times when I had three dates on the same night. All of them didn't end with sex, but many did. And some became friends for life. On one such rendezvous, I met Mas, who is now one of my closest friends.

I think it was a night in 1997 when Kamros was chatting with Mas, and then they went on a drive. I remember being nervous like I would be before each such encounter. He was waiting in his Honda City, bespectacled, in a white shirt and grey trousers. Later that night, I got to know his name. I don't think we were attracted to each other when we first met and I don't actually know what he thought of me, but I knew from his eyes that he was a kind and gentle man. And soon he became an integral part of my life in Bombay, especially my discovery of the gay spheres of life in the city—he was my partner in crime, and our friendship went beyond those wild nights to include our families and even work.

With Mas, I ventured to Voodoo, the only gay nightclub in Bombay in those days. Saturday nights would find us there, drinking, dancing and looking for hookups. There would be a constant threat of police raids, and I remember us escaping through the back exit a few times. I remember us being there till dawn on some occasions, then walking to the Gateway and having a chai before heading home. Mas also lived in Khar Danda, so it was convenient. We used to spot and encourage each other in our attempts at finding that weekend's lust story!

His number is still saved as Mas on my phone and he still calls me Kam.

One night, I had hooked up with this hot and dusky guy. I was taking a cab back with him, and midway, he told me that he wanted to pick up another friend. When we reached Bandra, he made the cab stop near a desolate alley, where the two guys assaulted me and tried to rob me. I was terrified, but an auto driver saw what was happening and approached us in such a way that I could free myself and jump in as he drove away. I lost some money, but thanks to the kind auto driver, I was saved from serious damage.

It was common in those days for gay men to be assaulted and blackmailed. But I think the need to explore oneself was so overwhelming that those setbacks never stopped us. As Onir at work the next day, I told people that I was mugged while taking a late night walk. Only a few close friends knew the true story.

I think that we gay men often lived in two different worlds, and those nights as Kamros, I inhabited a world totally unlike my daytime one. Usually, my Onir time was till 11 p.m., and then my Kamros avatar took over till 7 a.m. Weekends were also Kamros days. Chatting on M2M could get frustrating at times as it was connected through the landline and the connection would sometimes snap when one was in the middle of a passionate chat! At times, the line wouldn't reconnect, and sometimes a reconnect happened after several attempts. Often, the guy one was chatting up would have left the Gaybombay chatroom by then.

One of my most memorable rendezvous was at 3 a.m. one night. I had been chatting with this guy for hours. I knew it could be dangerous, but the urge to live life on the edge was strong then. He was waiting in his car, and since he looked like Aamir Khan from *QSQT*, I immediately decided to remember him as AK. Anyway, I never did get to know his real name. As soon as I got into the car, we saw a police car approaching. To chat in a parked car wouldn't be a good idea, so he started driving. He drove and we chatted. I was feeling pretty sure that he didn't like me enough to spend the night with me. After an hour of driving, AK asked me, 'Are you going to invite me for coffee or are you gonna make me drive you around all night?'

I laughed nervously and invited him home. There always was an element of tension if I invited a stranger home—what if he attacked me, or blackmailed me, or worse . . . I made coffee and we continued chatting till he asked to see my palm as he wanted to read it. I wasn't a fool to not know what that meant and happily gave him my palm. In another five minutes, we were making passionate love. We were connected for six months, during which time we met very often. He had the number of my mobile phone, but he had told me not to call on his landline as his family was very conservative and nosey. After six months, he suddenly disappeared. He wasn't online and he never called either. A couple of weeks passed and I was getting restless. So, I decided to call the landline number he had given me one day, the one that I wasn't supposed to call. No one by the name he had given me lived there.

He had told me that he lived somewhere in Pali Hill, and so every night I would take a post-dinner walk up Pali Hill, coming back to Chuim Village via Carter Road. During one such walk, I got mugged once again. Two guys on a bike, both dressed in black T-shirts and black jeans, passed by. They were staring at me, so I stared back. They went ahead and turned around and crossed me again, still staring. I thought that perhaps they had seen me at Voodoo, and so I stared back to see if I could recognize either of them. The third time they came by, they stopped. One of them held me by the collar and asked me to hand over my pouch. They were speaking to me as if I was a tourist—I had never realized that the pouch around my waist made me look like one. I knew I was in trouble and that if they got off the bike they could bash me up and rob me. There was a cigarette shop open on the other side of the road. I hit the guy holding me by the collar on his chin so that he loosened his grip, and I started to run to the other side of the road. One of them kicked me on my calf, and I was lucky not to fall as I could have got run over. I made it to the other side of the road to the cigarette shop, my eyes brimming with tears because of the pain. I was trembling with fear, for I couldn't see them and was scared that they could suddenly appear and stab me.

Four months later, AK was back in the chat room. He said he had to suddenly leave for Canada, that he was back now and had missed me a lot. I knew he was lying, but I called him over. We made love, and then I told him that I thought he was a fraud and I didn't want to see his face ever again and that he should leave. Two years later, I bumped into him once more at a nightclub. He had walked in with a girl, and when he saw me, he froze and left immediately. Not that I would have accosted him.

Those years were full of drama; I don't know how I had so much energy. Work was pretty hectic, yet I had energy for the chat rooms almost every night. I guess my earlier stint at Plus Channel had conditioned me to long working hours with no sleep on occasions when the story simply had to be prepared. For example, when the Bombay riots happened, we were editing stories round the clock. At one point, I hadn't been home for three days. We were dealing with devastating footage of rioting, and it was important for all of us to get those stories ready. I remember that I was standing and editing one night so that I would not fall asleep. Those were the days of Hi-band and Lo-band U-matic tape editing, and during every cut, the tape would pre-roll for 5/7/10 seconds. And when the tape went for a pre-roll, I dozed off and fell straight on the machine.

To come back to the Kamros adventures, there was a night when the bell rang, and I opened the door to a boy who seemed to be below eighteen years of age. He was very cute, and I invited him in, made some tea and lectured him for two hours about how unsafe his behaviour was. I told him that he should never land up at someone's doorstep the way he had—he could have got assaulted. He left at 5 a.m., and we never met again. Till about five years later. He was a Bollywood journalist by then, and I met him with Raveena Tandon at a party. I didn't recognize the handsome young man, but when we got a little alone time, he reminded me of that encounter. He told me that he had come for some action that night, and all I had done was lecture him! We laughed about that incident and since that time have become good friends.

Mas and I mostly hung around and partied with a fixed group of friends. There was Sandy, who later became Mas's partner for life. There was P, who at that point was seeing Sandy, and there was B. There also was Chocoboy, whom I had a huge crush on. He was studying hotel management and used to cook really well, but he was from a conservative Muslim family and totally paranoid about being found out. I once convinced him to come to Nameeta's house for a party and cook. The food was too spicy and the whole event a disaster. Maybe he was too nervous.

One night, it was raining very heavily, and Sandy, his boyfriend P, Mas, Chocoboy and this beautiful stud had all come to my Chuim flat. At that point, Sandy and P were staying in my house as P had run away from his family. He was a Muslim boy and his family had vowed to kill both him and Sandy.

Khar Danda was flooding, but Mas left for home as he stayed very close by. Chocoboy and Stud decided to spend the night with me. I had two extremely tiny rooms. The inner room had a tiny single bed that Sandy and P took. The outer room had a sofa-cum-bed. I lay down in the middle, with Stud on one side and Chocoboy on the other. Stud had been trying to flirt with me all evening, but I was being loyal to my crush, Chocoboy. We went off to sleep. I woke up in the night and realized that Stud was going down on Chocoboy. I was ready to start crying as I felt betrayed, when suddenly there was a lot of commotion. Sandy was in the room, and he slapped Stud hard, screaming '*ehsaan faramosh*' (ungrateful). My friend Sandy was outraged that this guy who had taken shelter in my house was making a pass at my love interest. Stud was promptly thrown out of the flat into the rainy night. I let Chocoboy stay till dawn. He had tea and then left. I did not see him again for months, and then he migrated to the US. We remained friends, and he now lives with his partner in Canada.

During this period I reconnected with a friend from Calcutta, S. After years of marriage and a child, he had realized he was gay. He had a rough divorce and was now open and wanted to reconnect. He lived in Ahmedabad and would come for weekends to be with me and explore the 'Voodoo world' with us. He was a very handsome man and soon had many admirers. Some years ago, I got to know that he had died of AIDS.

Mas and I had become very good friends by then. He did not mind meeting my other friends, and my closest friend Nams had met him too.

This brings me to one of the most embarrassing episodes in the Kamros chapter.

# 17

# Mas

The infamous 'Gay White Night' party at Madh Island took place on 21 June 1999. I remember going there with Mas and a few other friends. The night was getting wild. There supposedly were dark rooms into which I never ventured, partly because my idea of adventure was not that bold and partly because I was kind of shy about getting physical with anyone in a public space. At some point, when I think I was very drunk and snogging someone, Mas came up to me and said that we should leave. I don't remember the sequence of events, but he kind of slapped me as I wasn't behaving 'properly'. I promptly interpreted this as jealousy, and we left soon enough. We got to know the next day how lucky we had been, as the police raided the venue soon after we left. Many were arrested and humiliated—yes, being gay those days was fraught with danger, and our act of being together and having a good time always came with high risk.

At that time, many of my friends thought that I should date someone. Especially Nams. She thought that Mas and I would be perfect together and that I was being an idiot and not recognizing the love he had for me. Somehow, Mas was one person about whom I hadn't really thought romantically from day one but always as someone whom I could trust blindly and reach out to anytime. I now started thinking that there could be something wrong in the way I perceived romance. Maybe I needed to look at the kind and gentle soul with a different gaze. Over the next few months, this thought kept running in my mind, till one day I thought I needed to actively explore this possibility. I thought of how he always came to the airport to drop and pick me up whenever I went out of the city. And whenever he returned from his trips abroad, he would take me for a drive at night, his car dashboard lined with chocolates for me. He had always made me feel special, and now I finally thought I knew why.

So, one morning I sent an email to Mas, writing about us. I can write about it so easily because Mas is what he is. I think he replied that evening that I was a very important part of his life, but that he had always thought of me as a best friend, almost a brother. To be honest, I was not heartbroken, nor did I feel rejected, but I was so filled with embarrassment that I immediately wrote to him saying I didn't want to ever meet him again. He promptly dismissed my email, saying that I could take my time, but I was too precious to him for this to be acceptable. As always, he was being more mature and thoughtful than me. I think I refused to talk to him or meet him for six months, and then one day I realized that I was being stupid. It's not often in life that one comes across such amazing people, and I would have been an idiot to lose him. We met, laughed about the episode and were soon back to our night cruising together. Mas remains one of my closest friends and has a separate equation with my family, especially with my mother, whom he calls 'Ma'. Ma feels it's her right to call him whenever she wants to regardless of the fact that he is no longer living next door. She asks him to send his car and driver for her trips to the doctor. Baba enjoys making *payesh* (kheer) for him, and is very disappointed that Mas has now turned vegan and he can't offer him *payesh* any more.

P and Sandy broke up as P couldn't handle the family pressure. I think he got married and moved to Dubai. Sandy and Mas started seeing each other, and I think they have been together for over twenty years now. Sandy knew of the episode, but he has lived with me, loved and trusted me. For the longest time, he used to treat me almost like I was a part of his in-laws' family, in whom he could confide. I would advise him about work, relationships etc.

When it comes to Mas and our escapades, I can't but mention another incident. One night, Mas, B and I had hooked up with three guys at Voodoo. We decided to go to B's house. He said his mother would be fast asleep, and I didn't want to go to my flat alone with a casual date as I had discovered on waking up one morning previously that my hook-up had disappeared with my mobile and some cash. Anyway, we were in B's room, each in a dark corner with our respective dates, when suddenly there was loud banging on the door. B's mother was awake and suspicious. We panicked. The three guys were quickly locked inside the bathroom, and Mas and I hastily dressed. B opened the door to his mother. She knew Mas and me and relaxed a bit, but still went around the room screaming and checking if anyone was hiding, her sixth sense telling her that something was fishy. She even checked under the bed and then finally started to move towards the bathroom. B panicked. All of us panicked. He stopped her even as she kept screaming and led her out of the room. We quickly locked the door and opened the bathroom door where the terrified guys were locked up. Thankfully, it was the ground floor and they could leave through the window. Mas and I left through the front door. It was a narrow escape and we swore, never again!

There came a time when I started wondering who I actually was—the relentless, restless creature of the night Kamros or the gentle, shy, sensitive workaholic Onir. The boundaries between day and night would merge at times and so would the boundaries between Kamros and Onir. I realized both were me. And what is true is whether it was a one-night stand, a relationship or my work, I have always approached things with as much honesty as I can. At least I have always tried to. That doesn't mean that I haven't made mistakes or not hurt anyone. Yes, I have faltered, hurt and been hurt and learnt. I am human.

Futile,
These words.
Yours,
Mine . . .
They keep us apart

~

When I started making *My Brother Nikhil* in 2004, I decided to rename myself Onir. I like the sound of Onir and that it preserves the essence of Anirban—a flame that doesn't burn out. I also knew that at that point I was the first Onir. The Dr Onir character of *Pavitra Rishta* owes its roots to me. I also thought that this would be justice for Ma that I finally had no surname, though she hasn't been happy about my mutilating the name she had given me. Many years later, my niece Trisha sought my help when she turned fourteen—she wanted to change her surname. I thought she would want to add 'Dhar' to the 'Malik' she had inherited from her dad, and so I readily agreed. But what she was thinking of revealed a different perspective. She wanted just Dhar—not because she loved her father any less, but because of two points that she had reasoned out. One, she had lived without her mother's identity for fourteen years, so now it was time to set the balance right by living without her father's identity. Two, my sister Irene had taken up her husband's surname. She had become Irene Dhar Malik after marriage, but her husband hadn't added her surname and become

Ashwini Malik Dhar. I was made aware of this hugely flawed gender equation in our society by my fourteen-year-old niece. Patriarchy has normalized that it will be the woman who will leave her house and will give up her surname and sometimes religion to become a part of the man's family. It's the woman who has to always fit in and adjust. I must add that my younger niece (my brother's daughter) has both her parents' surnames, and perhaps the times are changing.

The sunset over the desert,
Immersing my soul in an orgy of colour and light.
The magical universe
Whispers into my ears its beauty,
The promises of the mysterious night.
When I shall be immersed in the multitude of colours
That resides in the depth of your eyes,
That shimmers with love and sadness,
Mine forever . . .
Or just a mirage.

# LIVING THE DREAM

# 18

# *Daman*

This is a story I tell anyone who tells me that they're an outsider to the industry, without family support, without enough finances—that you have to want it so bad that you stay alert and open to opportunities and then just go all out. It's important to not just know your goal, but explore and analyse the routes available and take whichever suits you the best. Don't keep comparing your life and opportunities with someone else's; forget that shit and focus on your own goals.

I started thinking about this opportunity and what I could do with it. I knew that to make my own film, I would have to have the support of actors. I thought that I would have to somehow impress Raveena Tandon, Sanjay Suri and Sayajee Shinde with my work. I would have to win them over as friends. Apart from wanting to learn as much as possible, this too was my goal. You may think that is being shrewd, but like I said, I wanted to make the most of the opportunity that was available to me, *but* it would never be in a dishonest manner.

In December 1999, I flew to Guwahati to be on my first feature film shoot. That is where I met actor Sanjay Suri, who later became my best friend. We were shooting in a remote village near Guwahati where there were no hotels, and we were staying in guest houses with very basic facilities. I got into the habit of being the first person on the set, checking the art and costumes and making small changes if necessary. It wasn't really my job, but I was interested, and I didn't care if those responsible for the job weren't as interested. I felt that many of the crew members were treating the shoot like just another job. For me, this proved to be a learning ground for many things.

Kalpana had a very sharp eye; she knew that I was going out of my way to make things better and she always appreciated and acknowledged my efforts. I met the dancers to figure out the song choreography, and this was a little embarrassing as all of them immediately wanted to touch my feet and treat me like a 'Masterji' that I wasn't. But I wouldn't behave like a novice nor seem nervous, even though I was very nervous the day I finally shot with Raveena Tandon.

I explained the shot to her and went, 'Music . . . roll camera . . . action!' Raveena stopped me and asked me to give her the count '1 2 3 4', which is how a professional choreographer would do it. I had no idea how to do that, so I tried to the best of my ability which was not good enough. I could see that she was getting irritated. This continued for two more days, and I started feeling that maybe she didn't like me directing her. After all, she was here for the National Award-winning director. I could not sleep that night, and I made up my mind that I would talk to Kalpana the next day and ask her to let me go. It wasn't an easy decision as I had so many dreams around the first film I was working on. I felt dejected and like a total failure.

I told Kalpana that I didn't think Raveena was comfortable being directed by me and that I wanted to go back to Bombay (though the transition from 'Bombay' to 'Mumbai' happened in 1995, it took many of us many more years to internalize the change). Kalpana looked worried, as she knew how passionate I was about my work, and she had started depending on me a lot. I don't know if she actually spoke to Raveena or if Raveena did it on her own initiative, but after that day's shoot, she said, 'Listen, why don't you join me for dinner, it will be nice.' I was a little confused but also flattered. At dinner, Raveena told me that how nice it was to have me on the set and that she felt she could connect with me and chat in a way that she couldn't with the others. She was talking to me like I was her friend. I remember telling her that if she treated me as a friend, I would also treat her as one, and I hoped that was fine with her. From that day onwards she became 'Ravs' for me and I became 'Bon', and true to her word, she has been a precious friend for over two decades.

*Daman* was perhaps one of the most important steps towards my becoming a film-maker after my training in Berlin. It was fascinating to be there on set—the energy was electrifying, and I learnt how important it is for a director to win over an actor's confidence. Soon, Sanjay Suri joined the team—it was I who had initially suggested his name to Kalpana—to play the role of the brother-in-law. With Sanjay, my friendship developed slowly and in no way as dramatically as that with Raveena! He was a little reserved, but we were soon talking about cinema and the stories we wanted to tell. When Raima Sen joined the cast, we hit it off right from the first day, and whenever I think of Raima, I think of her as that young, crazy, warm, beautiful girl. She reminded me of her grandmother Suchitra Sen—she had those same dreamy eyes, that beautiful smile. Though I was a decade older than her, she always treated me as if I was her age. Her energy is infectious, and I have many stories about her crazy ways. In Bombay, when Raima and I would be sitting in an auto, people would often stare at her —maybe because of the neckline of her outfit or a long slit. She would suddenly fling herself all over me and exclaim, '*Hai, in pe nazaar mat dalo, ye mera hai!*' (Don't look at him like that, he's mine!).

Raima means to me memories of downing shot after shot while she and her sister Riya were happily guzzling down water shots as they goaded me on to drink more and more. Obviously, I would get totally destroyed. One night, I remember her father walking into the living room where I was lying sloshed on the sofa. I loudly asked what this strange man was doing in the living room so late at night! I remember another instance when Raima, Riya and I were dancing at Hawaiian Shack . . . and I was trying to swing Riya in my arms . . . I lost my balance and somehow all three of us landed on the floor.

The thing about Raima that used to mortify me the most and make her gleeful was that every time she wanted to get rid of the man in her life, she would flirt with me excessively in front of him. I would tell her that someday one of them would definitely beat me up! When I meet Raima now, I see the same nineteen-year-old girl—beautiful, feisty, naughty.

During the shoot, Kalpana at times needed to attend some urgent meetings or coordinate security issues. It was not an easy location, with the ULFA crisis still on, and since this was a very low-budget National Film Development Corporation (NFDC) film, we couldn't afford to waste time. I was fortunate that she trusted me more than her direction team, and I ended up directing a few scenes with Sanjay and Raima. This was my first real experience of directing actors, and while directing the scenes, I wasn't nervous. There was a strange sense of energy, confidence and happiness, because I was experiencing film-making. When I was interviewed for *My Brother Nikhil* and asked how it felt on the first day of shoot, I said that I definitely didn't feel nervous. It was all about doing it right within the time I had.

Sanjay was the first person to actually listen to the story ideas I had with patience and respect, and he told me that I should start writing down my ideas. That was how, in the year 2000, I started writing my first feature film script, then titled *Kaash*, which I

With ma, 1969

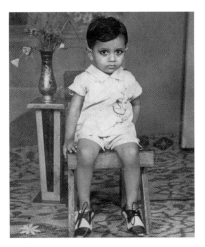

Me at age four

Didi, Bhai and me

Our home in Thimphu

Berlin 1991

Calcutta 1992

My first registered script, 2001, later renamed *Shab*

Candy, Mukesh, Sandeep and me, 1997

With Nameeta, 1997

Family photo at Didi's wedding, 1997

With Trisha

*My Brother Nikhil* shoot, with Purab, Goa, 2004

*My Brother Nikhil*,
BTS, with Juhi and
Sanjay, Goa, 2004

*My Brother
Nikhil*, 2005

FOUR FRONT FILMS
presents
my brother...Nikhil
DIRECTED BY ONIR

With President
A.P.J. Abdul Kalam,
2005

With Sanjay, New York, 2005

Philip, Urmi and Merle, 2006

With Raveena Tandon, 2000

With Nandita Das, *I Am*, 2010

With Sanjay and Urmila, *Bas Ek Pal*, 2006

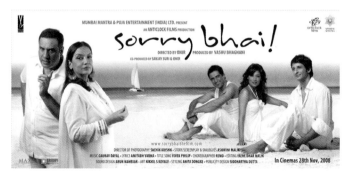

*Sorry Bhai*, 2008

*I Am*, Juhi and Manisha, 2011

Receiving the National Award for best Hindi Feature film, 2012

With Ambika, BTS, *Shab*, 2015

*Kuchh Bheege Alfaaz*, 2018

With Aryan, Aditya and Ashish, 2015

My 50th, 2019

The premiere of *Raising the Bar* at Indian Film Festival Melbourne, 2016

finally shot fifteen years later as *Shab*. I wrote the script and gave it to Sanjay to read. Then started the process of trying to get a producer on board. The journey that began then culminated with the making of *My Brother Nikhil* in 2004.

Coming back to *Daman*, Sanjay, Ravs and I bonded famously during the shoot. Some nights, Ravs would take us out for a drive, during which she would suddenly switch off the headlights for a few seconds and we would be driving in pitch darkness. Those few seconds would seem endless, out of this world.

Unfortunately, during this first feature film shoot, I also experienced the not-so-nice side of our industry. The insecurity that plagues the industry shocked me. While Kalpana was extremely generous in terms of money and credits, acknowledging work and talent, I would soon realize that all these were mine as long as I was content with remaining an 'associate', as long as I did not aspire to be an independent film-maker. The growing friendships were not being taken well. I was told to be careful and not get emotionally attached as a friend (I don't know how there can be any friendship without that) and that Ravs would forget about me the moment she went back to Bombay. Honestly, I was no longer thinking so far ahead but just enjoying the work and my new friendships, which I found stimulating. Ravs packed up a few days before the final wrap of the film. She told me that I should call her once back in Bombay, no matter what time it was, as she wanted to meet before she went off for a three-month world tour.

After the wrap, Kalpana and Dada took Raima and me to Shillong for a few days. That was my first trip to Shillong and I fell totally in love with the place. Of course, even back then, what used to break my heart is a common feature in most Indian cities—a total lack of town planning and architectural planning and no careful nurturing of nature. I remember when I travelled to India from Bhutan for winter vacations as a kid, I would often start imagining how I would have changed things if I could have.

I would talk to myself about how I would preserve old heritage buildings and have more trees and a proper architectural design. I sincerely believed then that I could someday make it all happen. I would even end up talking loudly to myself at times and then suddenly notice that people around me were laughing. Nowadays, it's very rare that I end up talking to myself aloud, I suppose as one grows older, one slowly starts discarding certain dreams. Now I realize how impossibly foolish and unattainable those dreams of mine were. I have to be content with my window garden in Bombay. My building has a strange rule that plants are not allowed on the window ledge, in spite of there being a grille. Apparently, the water dripping from the flowerpots can damage the building and the trays can become a breeding ground for mosquitoes. Both reasons are ridiculous. No one seems to be bothered about water leaking from ACs, whereas I have trays below each pot and make sure there is no stagnant water in the tray. I have to now be satisfied with as many plants as I can possibly accommodate indoors.

It was a late flight that got me back to Bombay, and it was 10 p.m. by the time I got back home, and so I didn't call Raveena. She called me at midnight and abused me for not having called her, and then asked me to come over for a small party at her house the next day. She wanted me and Sanjay (her new friends) to meet her other friends. It was at her house 'Shiv Kuthir' in Lokhandwala that I got to meet Rohini and Afifa. Both of them remain close friends till today.

Meanwhile, I also started work on the editing, my first feature film edit. The added excitement was to see how what one had imagined while shooting translated to the screen. I don't remember how I got more and more involved in various aspects of film-making with this film, but while editing, I was also working closely on the background score and sound design with Pritam and Vivek. I think the independent film-maker in me was already thinking about what would happen once the final print was ready, and I started to try to find out how we could possibly release the film. Till 1997, I used to edit a lot at producer Rakesh Malhotra's studio and we had become friends. He started advising me about distribution strategies and also introduced me to film distributors and exhibitors. So, pretty early in my film career, I learnt end-to-end film creation and marketing! In those days, there would be distributors from different regions who would offer an MG (minimum guarantee) for the film to be released. Some of them were crude enough to say, '*Bas ek hi rape hai film mein, woh bhi husband, toh rape kaisa hua?*' (There is only one rape in the film, that too by the husband; so how is that even rape?) In 2022, when the Supreme Court is considering whether marital rape should be considered rape, I wonder why there even is a debate. Nobody has any right to a woman's body, and marriage does not mean that a man owns his wife.

I got to learn a lot about the trade in purchasing the film from the NFDC and then handling its worldwide sales. The overseas and satellite rights were bought by Mr Chabbria, who later also helped in the overseas distribution of *My Brother Nikhil*. I'm mentioning all this because I think what empowered me as an independent film-maker was the fact that I did not stop myself from doing anything related to the film if it needed to be done, even if it was not directly related to directing.

My friendship with Sanjay slowly grew after we returned from Assam. That is when I thought of the idea of *Shab* (then called *Kaash*). I had already worked with Urmi, and we had a lot of comfort working together. We had long sessions discussing the story, and Urmi started writing the script. The film had the character of Neel (then called Nigel) even then, but no one ever asked me why I had such a major gay character or why the film had so many gay characters. For both Sanjay and Urmi, the sexuality of the character was not the only defining factor; they found the characters interesting and wanted to hear their stories. Maybe that was also the way I wanted to be seen—to be loved, respected and heard as a human being who is perhaps interesting. My sexuality is a part of my identity, a very important one, but not the all-defining factor. I am gay. And more. Sanjay made it seem like my dream was something that could possibly come true.

I would for the longest time not discuss my adventures with Sanjay, not because I was worried about what he would think, but more because he always felt more like a brother than a friend. And while I share some stuff about my romantic life with my sister, I could later tell Sanjay's wife Ambika much more. I think it's only after 2011 that Sanjay started teasing me about my love stories. I had asked him if he had ever wondered about my sexuality. He told me that it had never mattered and that he wanted me to talk about it only when I was ready.

I think it was somewhat similar with Urmi as she did not know that Kamros existed for the longest time. Urmi is now writing a lesbian romantic comedy for me, and what excites me about this film is that no one is taking 'baby steps'. We will all have a blast watching this extravagant love story.

The year 2000 was also precious as a very important person came into my life. My niece Trisha was born that year. Twenty years later, as I see her bloom into a beautiful young woman, fiercely independent yet very much connected to the family and gifted with the art of playing with words, I feel such happiness. I am also jealous at times of how beautifully she writes. I remember her falling asleep on my chest on so many occasions, and to feel her little heart beat against mine was bliss. She is a precious bouncing board for me now; her thoughts and ideas help me remain connected to the younger generation. I am glad that she treats me almost like a friend, and I feel no inhibitions in telling her all about my life.

In December 2013, when the Supreme Court of India overturned the Delhi High Court verdict on IPC 377, thereby criminalizing homosexuality, she went to school wearing black as a sign of protest and to show her solidarity with me. She used to proudly tell all her friends, 'My *mama* (maternal uncle) is gay.' I was the proudest *mama* that day.

This was also the year when I bought my first and only car—a second-hand Maruti 1000—from Kalpana. My brother, Abhishek, had learnt to drive in 1983 as an underage driver, but I had given up after a few attempts. I finally learnt to drive now but was an emotional mess while doing it. I would manage to drive late at night or early in the morning when the streets were not terribly busy, but I never really enjoyed the experience. I used my car so little that the ever-charitable Sanjay would often volunteer to leave his car outside my building and drive in my car to any event we were both attending. That way, my car would get some much-needed activity! Six months later, I had an accident while driving. This was at the Four Bungalows signal in Andheri, and while it wasn't very serious, I ended up hitting a bus, a car and an auto. All I can remember now is everyone screaming at me, including the guy who was sitting next to me. I froze and couldn't do anything at all. He asked me to get out of the car and let him drive us out of that mess. I have never gotten into the driver's seat again. I sold my car six months later, and since then have only used public transport. That's one regret I have—that I just don't seem to have the courage needed to be able to drive again. I always wanted to take my lover for a drive, but that seems like an impossibility. The idea of being driven around by a driver has never appealed to me.

I also edited my second feature film in 2000—*Rahul* was directed by Prakash Jha, a film-maker I love and admire. Unfortunately, I had the misfortune of being a part of his worst film. I witnessed how a director's vision could be totally destroyed by a producer who wanted to play power games. That experience made me careful of working with a producer who didn't understand my vision as that can be a film-maker's worst nightmare. I would edit during the day with Prakash, who loved to make changes on every cut. 'Add one frame, go back two frames . . . now it's perfect.' After a while, I would cheat him at times, pretending that I had made the change but replaying the exact same cut. Prakash wasn't so familiar with the non-linear editing system at that time, so I could get away with this. I hope he will not murder me now if he's reading this! Evenings would be a nightmare when the producer arrived and wanted to change everything Prakash had done. I didn't enjoy this as I had wanted to work with Prakash. And no disrespect to him, but I wasn't so keen on working with the producer.

By 2001, Urmi had finished the story outline of *Kaash*, and both Sanjay and Raveena were keen to be a part of my first film. My friend Rakesh Malhotra was planning to produce the film, and he signed up Sanjay as my lead actor. At this point, Kalpana was facing some challenges starting her next film as *Daman* hadn't done well commercially. I introduced her to Rakesh so that they could try and explore the possibility of doing a film together. I think Rakesh backed out of my film a month or so later. Many months later, I got to know that someone from the industry had told him that I wasn't very stable mentally and was capable of suicide. That person had also added that my choice of actors and writer was immature and not the best possible ones and that going ahead with the film might cause Rakesh a major financial crunch.

Meanwhile, I had started working on Kalpana's next film, *Kyon*. Sanjay started trying to pitch our script elsewhere.

During the first schedule of *Kyon*, I met DOP Arvind Kannabiran. I was directing one song, and Arvind and I bonded during the shoot. This is how I decided to reach out to him to shoot our film *My Brother Nikhil*. After the first schedule of *Kyon*, I began focusing on the edit. At some point, Kalpana came to the edit suite to watch the first cut. After watching the cut she said, 'Bon, I am very disappointed. I feel you aren't focusing on the edit as your mind is on too many other things. You need to focus. This is terrible. I need you to sit with my assistant and do an assemble edit first and then the first cut. This is rubbish.' I was a bit shocked at this extreme reaction, and while I was absolutely okay with changes and re-edits and in trying to achieve the director's vision, what was never acceptable to me was being treated with disrespect. I told her, 'Kalpana, please tell me what does not work for you, and I will make all the changes.' She insisted that everything was wrong and that I should not be egoistic and just sit with her assistant for an assemble edit. She said she could not waste her time in the editing room explaining things to me as nothing in my first cut was worth retaining. I told her that if she thought that I was incapable of doing an assemble edit on my own, then I must be the wrong editor for her and that I would like to quit. She started getting extremely aggressive, saying that I could not just quit when she was in the middle of a project. I told her I couldn't work where I was made to feel so incompetent. She said that if I quit, I had to make sure I found her someone as good as me. This made no sense to me at all as she was also telling me that I was doing a terrible job. I quit. I later realized that she had possibly found it difficult to accept the fact that I was on my way to becoming an independent film-maker.

I never could understand how a person who was so kind and warm to me could transform in this way. The warmth that we had shared was lost forever. I could never make myself revisit the relationship. It just ended.

Sanjay got married to Ambika in 2001. I think that was the first North Indian wedding I attended and probably the first traditional wedding I went to as an adult. I am wedding-phobic and usually find them terribly boring. But Sanjay's wedding was fun for me as, by then, his family was like family to me. So I was an insider without having to do any of the rituals that a family member might have to engage in. When Ambika came to Bombay, I was very anxious that we should get along. A close friend of ours had recently got married, and he would have to sneak out during his wife's afternoon siesta to come and meet us! Ambika and I bonded very quickly and very soon had our own equation as friends, and I wouldn't treat her only as my friend's wife. Actually, I would always feel much more comfortable telling Ambika all about my escapades than I would with Sanjay. I would feel shy with Sanjay who is younger than me but behaves like an elder brother.

Ambika would later become an integral part of many of our films. She was a bouncing board for my scripts, and being creative by nature, would be very proactive on the sets. During the making of *My Brother Nikhil,* when we weren't managing to procure what we needed for our art department due to a lack of budget, she went from shop to shop along with Shubha and even to some houses in Goa to convince them to let us use their furniture, curtains and other household stuff for free. She always had a solution for any problem. I remember her doing the same in 2009 when we were shooting for *I Am* in Kashmir. She went to Azaan's house—he was an AD on the shoot—and to the house of Sanjay's family friend to borrow stuff so that the film's set looked real.

Sanjay and I gave up trying to raise finances for *Kaash* in 2002. Most people we approached found it too 'non-commercial'—not only was the lead male actor a toy boy, the lead female actor was a bar dancer. And to top it all, the script had many gay characters, and I wasn't willing to change that and neither did Sanjay ever suggest that I do.

I now started writing my second script called *Time Time ki Baat Hai.* This was a romantic comedy set in the film industry, a story of friendship and conflict between two friends who come to Bombay as strugglers, one trying to become a director, the other an actor. Once again, we could not find producers to back the film, this time because the scale was too large. I was a newcomer and Sanjay was not a 'big' star. I was learning all about the ugly side of the industry now that I was getting closer to my goal. I totally ditched the idea of making this film in 2009 when *Luck by Chance* released. There were too many parallels, and I didn't feel like making this film any longer.

In 2002, Sanjay started work on Sujoy Ghosh's *Jhankaar Beats*. Sujoy had a very clear vision of what he wanted but no film-making experience. Sanjay asked me if I would like to help Sujoy by being at the shoot for a few days till Sujoy was more at ease. I wanted to meet Sujoy first, and we got along really well. I loved Sujoy's verve and how honest he was about what he knew and what he did not. Then I met Rangita Nandy and Pritish Nandy, the producers, so that I could be on the film. I told them that I would do it for free and did not want any credits. I don't know why, but I had a thing about either being an associate or the head of a department and didn't want to be an assistant.

It was a lot of fun sitting with Sujoy every day and working on the shot breakdown of the film and the floor maps. By then, I had shifted from Manish Nagar to Heena Apartments on Yari Road. Sujoy's assistants would come during the second half of the day and the discussions would continue. This was when I first met Shubha Ramachandran, who was working with Sujoy as AD. She later worked with me on *My Brother Nikhil* as first AD and started as script supervisor for *Sorry Bhai!* but took over as first AD after a few days of the shoot when she realized that the first AD was not being able to handle the responsibilities.

Shubha remains saved on my mobile as 'Smile'. She has the most beautiful smile I know and extremely kind eyes. That does not stop her from her being a hard taskmaster on the set. Many years later, she sweetly confessed that the first time she met me, I was coming down the stairs of Heena Apartments with Trisha in my arms, and she was disappointed that I was married as she found me attractive. She realized much later that I was single and gay! I find one major difference between the women ADs that I have worked with and the male ones. The male ADs mostly recreate the shot division the way they want the film to be, whereas the women mostly try to understand what I want and help me achieve that. This is why I think I mostly have a woman-heavy team! Here, I must add that there are exceptions like Amar Kaushik, whose standard line whenever I hesitated about shooting something because of logistical issues was, 'Sir, *bataiye naa ap ko kaisa chahiyeh*' ('Sir, just tell me how you want it').

I attended some music sessions Sujoy had with the duo Vishal–Shekhar, and they offered to do some songs for *Kaash*. They were kind enough to record three scratch songs for our film. I still remember two of the songs—one was '*Phir na kehna*' and the other was '*Door se paas bula leh*'. They held on to the songs for me for the longest time and finally gave them to Sanjay Gupta for *Musafir* (2004). I especially regret not being able to shoot '*Phir na kehna*' and the fact that we have not yet managed to work together.

I helped Sujoy for one entire shooting schedule and then discontinued as I got busy with various editing assignments. Viveck Vaswani, who had produced *Aasman Se Aagay*, was true to his word and signed me up for editing two films he was producing—*Funtoosh* and *Agnipankh*. Imtiaz Punjabi, the *Funtoosh* director, was fun to work with. He would call me up from the shoot to ask what was working and what wasn't and if I needed any additional shots. I liked the way he acknowledged the importance of the editor as a creative force who had a major contribution towards the film. Later, when I was making *I Am*, Imtiaz became one of the co-producers of the film. I always say this and I will keep repeating it: film-making is all about building relationships—building relationships with people who believe in your skills and conviction and will stand by you in your journey.

Rangita Nandy, having observed me on set, thought that we should do a film together. I had signed up with her company to start working on a film script. The film was to be a suspense thriller called *Ashq*. I was super excited about how I had shaped the script, and we had even started recording songs with Pritam.

I went location-hunting in Goa, started having meetings with choreographers, art directors and costume designers, and the direction team was making my floor maps. Yes, I was that close to shooting this film, which was to have Sanjay Suri and Jimmy Sheirgill. We only had to finalize the female lead, and then suddenly the film did not happen. I was heartbroken, and doubly heartbroken because my songs again went to another film, Vikram Bhatt's *Ankahee*. I was especially close to the song '*Ek pal ke liye hi sahi*', and I can still hear KK and Sunidhi singing the songs at the recording studio. As a director, I am very attached to every element of my film and especially attached to the songs. These songs were composed for a situation—the lyrics were written accordingly and even the music arrangement was something I was very particular about.

In 2003, I had brief stint working with film-maker Ram Gopal Varma. I was called in for a meeting to pitch for cutting the promos for *Bhoot*. At that time, getting a call to work with RGV itself meant celebrations. So, that night there was rum and coke with tandoori chicken!

I went to meet RGV the next day. I was nervous, excited and desperately wanted the project. He asked me how much I would charge for the promos. I told him to give me a shot, and once he liked my work, he could decide how much to pay me. Didi and I used to work together on some projects and I roped her in for this, and we started work on the promo edit at Spectral Harmony. Imagine a chicken like me working on the promo edit of *Bhoot*. I was eternally in a state of nervousness. When I went home in the evenings, I would feel very scared to enter my flat, remembering the dialogue from the film, '*Har ghar mein koi na koi toh mara hoga* (There must have been a death in every home)'. I must have spent countless nights long after the edit was over and the film released with the bedroom lights on through the night, chanting 'Ram Ram Ram, Durga Durga, Kali Kali . . .' Dadabhai was no longer alive, but the mantra he had taught me as a child helped me deal with the *bhoots*!

There was another opportunity for me to direct a film in 2003 through rather unfortunate circumstances. Anant Balani, who was directing *Chameli*, passed away after a heart attack. Rangita, the film's producer, asked me if I would like to do the rest of the film. I half-heartedly agreed and was kind of relieved when things didn't work out, possibly because Kareena was not keen on working with a new director, and that's when Sudhir Mishra stepped in. In hindsight, I am glad that it did not happen for I would have never been able to establish my identity with a debut film that did not belong to my soul.

I also started writing *Bas Ek Pal* in 2003, and Sanjay and I shopped around a bit, but again could not find any takers.

Around that time, I edited a talk show where a section dealt with the story of Dominic D'Souza, who was the first known HIV-positive case in India. In February 1989, he was arrested by the Goa police and kept in solitary confinement. He was twenty-nine years old when he became Goa's patient zero. He was kept in confinement for sixty-four days and released only after a prolonged campaign by human rights activists and lawyers. He died of AIDS in 1992 in a Bombay hospital. His face, his smile and his story shook me and touched me deeply. I would keep thinking about his helplessness, confusion, fear, loneliness and sometimes my eyes would just be wet.[*]

I told Sanjay that I was thinking about writing a script inspired by Dominic's life. Sanjay was moved as well and encouraged me to start writing. That is how the journey of *My Brother Nikhil* began.

---

[*] 'Dominic D'Souza', *Wikipedia*, https://en.wikipedia.org/wiki/Dominic_D%27Souza. Accessed on 14 March 2022.

# 19

# Milestone—*My Brother Nikhil*

Sometimes you feel so deeply about something that when you start working on it, thoughts simply flow. There were a couple of ideas in my mind, which I discussed with Sanjay before I started writing *My Brother Nikhil*. We were both tired of knocking on doors in the quest to finance our film. By then, we were also certain of one thing: that our sensibilities about cinema were similar, and perhaps more importantly, that our vision of life was similar and, decided to write the film in the style of a documentary for two reasons.

One, a lot of the film was to have characters addressing the audience directly, breaking the fourth wall. This would reduce the shooting time and stock exposed (we shot the film on 35 mm Kodak). This also worked creatively for me, as it gave a sense of reality. I wanted the audience to know that this was not just fiction but something someone had lived through—that this was a real story.

Two, I was thinking about how I wanted to tell this story. I thought about whom I would trust the most to tell my story if I died, and the answer was Didi. So *My Brother Nikhil* became a story about a brother narrated by his sister. The person I missed the most during the entire process of making *My Brother Nikhil* was also my sister as she was based in Pune at the time. As Trisha was still very young, Didi couldn't really be a part of the creative process of my first film in any manner.

I wrote the first draft of *My Brother Nikhil* in fifteen days. I would act like each of the characters and then, as they talked to one another, I would keep writing. I wrote the dialogue draft as the first draft. I have never formally learnt scriptwriting and have no idea about the three-act structure or other technicalities. I know my scripts often have many technical flaws because of that. I write from my soul. I write what I see and hear. While writing *My Brother Nikhil*, I would at times get so moved by what was happening in the script that I had to take a break to get hold of my emotions. I would think a lot about Dominic and try to imagine how he must have felt. At that point, I had not got in touch with anyone who knew the real person as I wanted him to remain an inspiration and create Nikhil without being burdened too much by facts.

The name 'Nikhil' happened because I had a huge crush on actor Nikhil Bhagat from the time I watched Prakash Jha's film *Hip Hip Hurray* (1984). Whenever I wrote a script, the male lead ended up being called 'Nikhil'! I loved the name 'Anamika' as it means 'one who is nameless' and also because of this very beautiful friend of my sister's from her Lady Brabourne College days.

Nigel's character was what I would have liked my boyfriend to be: gentle, beautiful, kind, an artist and activist, flirt, loner, rebel . . . I know that's asking for a lot! But I did create a Nigel who embodied all these elements. It's kind of funny how *Hip Hip Hurray* was significant for me in other ways as well. I had edited a TV series directed by the lovely Nupur Asthana called *Hip Hip Hurray* (2001), and I had really liked one of the actors—Purab Kohli. Later, while writing *My Brother Nikhil*, I would imagine Purab as Nigel, though I had not reached out to him yet. I just needed images while writing.

Similarly, I had imagined Juhi Chawla as Anu while writing. I had met her briefly during the *Jhankaar Beats* shoot, and I always thought of her as one actor who has this incorruptible smile, and her eyes smiled along with her lips. I wanted a sister who had kindness and love in her very appearance, and I felt that Juhi had that. I know she will scold me if she reads this, but I find it impossible to imagine her as someone vile, scheming and hateful. Also, when I had discussed the initial idea with Sanjay, he had mentioned that it might be a good idea to take the script to Juhi as she was very accessible and seemed open to interesting scripts.

For the father's character, I had imagined Victor Banerjee since I had been a huge fan of his from the time I watched *A Passage to India* and wanted to work with him. Lillette Dubey came along as the mother when we started casting.

I was a bit anxious when I gave the script to Sanjay and Ambika to read. I think we met the next day, and I found that both Sanjay and Ambika were totally overwhelmed by the script. Till then, I had only imagined Sanjay as Nikhil, but that day I found my Nikhil. The way he spoke about the script, I knew that only someone who could connect deeply with a character could do that. His eyes were constantly moist as he spoke about the character and he said, 'Let's make this film.' He was not worried at all about playing a gay character and thought that the role was a challenge he would cherish as an actor. I don't remember ever sitting with Sanjay and discussing the 'gayness' of the character. For me, that was in his gaze on Nigel. I have never believed in or agreed with the way gay characters were perceived and portrayed in most mainstream Hindi films. For me, Nikhil was gay and more. And with Nigel, I wanted an element of the 'feminine'.

I kept working on the script based on various feedback. I interacted a lot with my friend Merle on the script, and she helped me be more objective. It was Sanjay's idea that I should establish the happy family space a little more before people discover that not only is Nikhil HIV-positive but also gay. We were aware that this was not going to be an easy space to negotiate with the audience. Even after all that caution, I had people telling me that some of the audience walked out of the theatre when they realized that Nikhil was gay. And it was mostly men!

While I started figuring out our crew, Sanjay started to look around for financing. One of the potential financiers even suggested that it should be Bipasha Basu who gives him AIDS in the film! They just refused to understand that Nikhil was gay. Another producer suggested that we should cast Yana Gupta as Anu. Sanjay spoke to Juhi Chawla and fixed a meeting. I was supposed to go along with him and give her a narration, which is something I am still terrible at! Juhi had kept aside about three hours for the narration. Sanjay and I met her in the garden for the narration, and I was done in fifteen minutes! Juhi looked confused and concerned, and Sanjay told her that I was terrible at narrating and that she should read the script and then decide. We left with heavy hearts.

Juhi called me three days later. Actually, it was K.S. Sanjay, who was manager to both Sanjay and Juhi at that time, who called and passed the phone to me. Juhi told me that if she had gone by the narration, she would have never done the film, but she had read and loved the script. One step closer to my dream, I spent a sleepless night, happy and nervous. KS soon became a close friend who always comes in to advise and cheer us when we start a new film. KS also became a co-producer for *I Am*.

I had couriered the script to Victor Banerjee in Mussourie. He read it and instantly agreed to do the film. Purab too was so moved by the script that he didn't feel insecure about playing Nikhil's lover, Nigel. One of the moments from the shoot that I always recall fondly is Ambika sitting by the monitor, weeping while watching some intense scene, and commenting, 'Their chemistry is so good.' I feel so blessed to have found friends who always accepted sexuality without any clamour—no lectures were needed, no sensitization workshops required.

At one point, when there seemed to be no hope of getting any financing, Sanjay was contemplating the idea that we should just shoot on Hi-8. Eventually, he was not convinced about that and wanted us to make a 35mm film that could be released in the theatres. We still didn't know how that would happen. Sanjay then decided to talk to his film-maker friend, the late Raj Kaushal and producer Vicky Tejwani. The four of us got together to form Four Front Films and produce my first film, *My Brother Nikhil.*

I knew we would have to be very careful at the shoot as our overall budget was not much. Every can was precious. We would be shooting at a ratio of 1:4, and believe me, that's not easy. This is where my editing skills helped. When I was doing the shot breakdown, I decided not to take any master shots. I would decide from which point to which point I would be using a CU (close-up), MCU (medium close-up), LS (long shot), OTS (over-the-shoulder), back shot, trolley . . . And we shot exactly according to what I had imagined the film needed to look like at the edit stage. Of course, there was the disadvantage that I didn't have too many options to play around with at the editing table, but I preferred having the rushes of a complete film in hand than play with incomplete footage. I think that clarity helped, because during the shoot my DOP and I would hardly need to discuss shots, apart from when some improvisation happened while the actors rehearsed or due to a location crisis. This helped save on shooting time.

Getting together the key crew was not that difficult as ten years of working in Bombay had established connections with various people. Arvind Kannabiran was the DOP, Arun Nambiar became the sound designer and I edited the film myself. Amitabh Varma, who had already assisted me in editing for a while, wrote the Hindi dialogues. Because my knowledge of Hindi wasn't great,

Sanjay spent a lot of time with us doing script readings to help make the dialogues as natural as possible. I think both Amitabh and Sanjay were rather kind because I can be foolishly stubborn at times. Sounds fascinate me, and sometimes I would keep insisting on using a Hindi or Urdu word just because I loved the sound of it even though it didn't actually fit the bill, much to Sanjay's frustration. Amitabh would play the pacifier.

Pritam was initially supposed to do the music for the film. Jeet and he were a team at the time, and they had a beautiful song, '*Kaash*', for me. Just before the film shoot, the two of them had some differences, and since the song belonged to both of them, I could not use it. I think my jinx with Pritam began there. But the rather happy consequence was that I got one of the best songs of all my films composed by Vivek Philip, with lyrics by Amitabh. We did three versions of '*Le chalein*' as I wanted different voices for each character. So Shaan rendered the version for Sanjay, Sunidhi for Juhi and KK for Purab. '*Le chalein*' became like the theme song or musical motif for the film. It became a song that celebrated the brother–sister relationship, their memories together. Later, when Nikhil has AIDS, Nigel sings the song for the brother–sister duo, and in the process becomes a part of the deep connection. I tried to portray this not only through the owning of the song, but also through costumes. I wanted Nigel and Anu to wear Nikhil's T-shirts when he was ill. It's an act of intimacy, warmth and love, and we see the slow transformation of Nigel for Anu, from being her brother's lover to almost a brother.

Anita Dongre did the styling of the film, and my friends Philip and Merle came from Germany for one whole schedule to be with me and support me during this most precious journey. Philip and Merle also shot the making of the film. Apart from Shubha, who was the first AD, there was Tina Nagpaul and Sharmistha in the AD team. There was one male assistant whom I had to unfortunately ask to leave. We were quite a woman-heavy team, including a woman camera assistant, Menosau Kevichusa. Reddy was the other camera assistant and Ambika primarily handled the art. I remember Arvind telling me mid-shoot that one day Reddy had observed, 'There is nothing wrong with this, this is also okay.' He was referring to the relationship between Nikhil and Nigel. I could see acceptance happen on the set.

The first day of shoot was when I decided that I would keep the monitor off while taking a shot as I preferred to stand next to the camera and watch the actors. I feel one could see much better that way than on the monitors we had in those days! And next to the camera, the energy was different. Arvind and I had agreed that we would only check a shot after both of us had okayed it. This would save us time during the shoot. I also requested the actors not to ask for a replay unless actually needed as that also leads to a waste of time. Above all, I didn't want anyone else to make comments and suggestions and disturb the flow of the shoot with unasked-for advice. The film, with its mistakes and flaws, had to be my vision, and judgment and inputs were only welcome from the relevant departments. Shubha was the only one allowed to give feedback all through as she was also keeping track of continuity.

The first few days we were shooting at Nigel's house, where I had scribbled my favourite poems and quotes on the walls of Nigel's room. I had carried my books, including my García Márquez collection, as I didn't want random books from a props rental shop to populate Nigel's bookshelf. I wanted the books he read to reflect the person he was. We had one painter, one carpenter and one helper on the set. Nigel's kitchen was designed the way I wanted it to be, open and minimalist. Ambika, Tina and I carefully chose every art object. Our line producer from Goa, Dilip Borkar, was one of the kindest line producers I have worked with. He treated the film with so much love and went out of his way to ensure we got the right locations at very low costs. It's not easy when you are directing your first film to also worry about production logistics at the end of each shooting day. It was a very difficult task for Sanjay too. To be in this intense space as an actor and the next minute to look into some production nitty-gritty is a daunting task. But I suppose the need to make this film in the best possible way kept both of us sane.

During the first few days of shoot, Juhi was feeling anxious that I was not shooting enough close-ups and that a lot of the shots were not sufficiently lit. We weren't shooting sequentially, and Arvind and I had planned a certain look for each of the main locations. Sanjay too was getting a little anxious, but he also knew that I must have a good reason. Soon enough, Juhi too got the hang of how we were working. During the first schedule, we shot everything that was supposed to happen before Nikhil became HIV-positive. The sea was blue and the overall tone of the film warm. Once Nikhil is found to be HIV-positive, from the time he's put in jail, we decided to make the look starker. We took a two-month gap between the schedules so that Sanjay could lose about 10 kg. He also stopped working out so that his body would look like it was slowly surrendering to the disease. Sanjay also insisted on shaving off his hair instead of wearing a wig, even though it meant that he wouldn't be able to do any other shoot for at least three to four months. The second schedule was shot during the monsoon. As the family goes through turmoil, the raging, choppy seas reflect their turbulence.

Directors can sometimes be selfish to the point of becoming inconsiderate, and I remember two very distinct instances when I was rather unreasonable. I wanted Sanjay to swim in the River Mandovi which was behind Solar Culacos Bungalow, Nikhil's home in our film. Though the river looked safe, we were told that it had strong undercurrents since this was the lagoon area close to the sea, and we had one hour in the morning when it was considered safe for swimming. The first day we were supposed to shoot, Sanjay had tested the water and it was not easy since each time we needed to retake a shot, he had to swim against the current. Moreover, we did not have funds for safety nets, lifeguards and boats. We couldn't complete the shoot the first day as Lilette did not reach the set on time. By the time she reached, the current was too strong. I knew that we would have to somehow manage to shoot the scene the next day as we didn't have the location after that. The next day too, Lilette was not there, but being a writer-director has its advantages. I quickly reworked the scene without her character and shot it. By the time she arrived, the scene was already shot. There was one more sequence with the river where she was needed. I managed to shoot that with her in a cut-away minus over-the-shoulder shots of the river.

The second instance of my being inconsiderate was when Sanjay had to go out into the sea and swim across the waves. The monsoon had arrived in Goa, and the sea was not the safest, but Arvind and I kept pushing Sanjay to go deeper and deeper into the sea so that the shot would look better. It was dangerous, and me telling Sanjay that this wasn't dangerous was kind of a joke as I don't have the guts to swim even in waist-deep water in the sea! Ultimately, the shots do look beautiful in the film. The sea and river added a layer to the narrative all through the film. Right at the end, we see Nikhil in the wheelchair, looking at the same sea and river and reminiscing about the time when he used to ride the waves. Nigel says that after Nikhil's illness, they would love to watch the dawn, as it meant that another beautiful day was gifted to Nikhil.

On the first day of the shoot, I was wondering how I should explain to Juhi about the way I wanted her to act in the film. She made it easier for me by telling me, 'I'm a director's actor, you'll have to tell me exactly what you want out of the shot. Tell me what Anu was thinking of before the sequence and what will be happening after the sequence.' I would talk to her a lot about what I wanted Anu's state of mind to be. I feel that the eyes reflect what's on the mind even in silent shots and in pauses. I would tell her the pace of action and at which point I wanted her to cry. Come to think of it, in many ways I was a little restrictive, but then I had imagined Anu when I had written the script; I wanted her to totally break down only once in the film. So I would tell Juhi not to cry till that sequence. Yes, there were sequences when she would be a little teary-eyed or her eyes overflowed. But I wanted the ultimate breakdown to happen only when she tells Nigel in the end, 'I cannot be strong any more.' Juhi, Sanjay and Purab would listen to me with a lot of attention, trying to understand what I wanted of them, and then each of them would add subtle layers to the scene or the character.

There were times when each of us would end up crying while rehearsing the lines. One day the make-up man told me that I should do the reading before he did the actors' make-up as otherwise the make-up would get ruined.

As a film-maker, I have some shot-taking peculiarities that I have now discovered when I watch my films. My actors would find it a bit odd that during an intense scene, I would sometimes have two characters sitting side-by-side, looking at a waterbody or something else, and talking. I wouldn't want them to look each other in the eye and talk. The camera would be behind them and at times shoot over-the-shoulder profiles. There is a scene between Nigel and Nikhil at the sanatorium where Nigel expresses how hurt he is. Sanjay and Purab were initially not convinced about standing side by side and not looking at each other while talking about something so intense, tender and intimate. I told them to imagine that the window that looked outside the sanatorium symbolized space and freedom and to speak with that yearning as they looked towards it. That is another of my favourite scenes in the film.

Sanjay and I would have huge creative arguments at times, and everyone would think, 'Oh shit, now the shoot is going to get affected.' But the fact is that we were capable of having a heated debate about something one minute and then going back to being pleasant the next. We respected each other as professionals, accepting that we might have different approaches to certain things, professionally and/or personally, and we could either try to convince one another or learn to live with the differing viewpoints. Here, I must add that Sanjay never used the power of producer/actor to pressure me about anything. Actually, he made it clear to all our partners that the ultimate creative call was mine as a director. When we started producing under the Anticlock Films banner, Sanjay would be the lead voice when it came to production, marketing and distribution since he has the calmness that one requires. I'm all over the place when it comes to finances and production. I think we could make films like *My Brother Nikhil*, *I Am* or *Chauranga* within a certain budget only because Sanjay would sit for hours with the production team after each day's shoot, going through the expenses and planning for the days ahead. And despite all the constraints, whenever I needed a little bit of extra stock, he stood by me as a producer. I can without hesitation say that, in a way, Sanjay has spoilt me. He has been the best possible producer to work with. I find it difficult to realign myself to other producers when I have to do so. I have seen Sanjay do the same with other directors too, and when we were producing *Chauranga*, Sanjay would never impose on Bikas Mishra as an actor who was also producing the film.

The second schedule of *My Brother Nikhil* was during the monsoon and it wasn't an easy schedule at all. It would start raining at any time, and we knew that we had to somehow manage and finish the shoot despite that. Apart from the look, another reason for shooting during the monsoon was that it being non-tourist season, everything was much cheaper. We had taken a risk, and with every outdoor location that we shot in, we kept an alternate indoor location nearby on hold. In case it rained, as it often did, we would all quickly run to the other location and continue shooting.

I had written quite a few night scenes at the beach. My lack of shooting experience was the reason. I liked the idea of night scenes by the sea and hadn't realized that unless we shot day for night, we wouldn't be able to see any of the sea, given our budgetary limitations with lighting. We eventually shot those sequences day for night, and when you don't have the luxury of time, it isn't easy to schedule the shoot for the golden or blue hour (an hour before sunset and half an hour after sunset). At this time, the quality of light works well for a night feel as it's soft and flattering. When I look back now, I feel that I should have rewritten the scenes as day since it wouldn't have greatly affected the narrative and definitely made life easier for Arvind.

One of my biggest weaknesses is that when I'm upset, I sulk instead of screaming. And on Hindi film sets, screaming is what makes people move. One day, when I was irritated about the pace of things and was unsuccessfully trying to raise my decibel level, Govind, one of the spot boys, walked up to me and said, 'Should I do it for you, sir?'

So the responsibility for shouting and making things happen on set fell on Sanjay and Arvind. I sometimes wonder how Sanjay could so easily switch between the role of producer and Nikhil. After the first schedule, his vocal chords were affected by all the shouting as he is otherwise a soft-spoken person. The selfish film-maker was of course happy as this rasping voice worked fine for the second half of the film. When Nikhil's health starts failing, his voice too sounds unwell. It was only after the dubbing for that part was over that I got seriously concerned about Sanjay's vocal chords. I needed his normal voice back to dub the first part of the film.

Arvind's booming voice was what most crew members were terrified of, and it got them working at once. I owe a lot to him, for he risked becoming unpopular so that we could complete the film on time. And the truth also is that the voice was never raised without reason. Overall, we were a peaceful unit, which is fairly uncommon. As a film-maker, I get extremely anxious if I feel any tension on the set, and it affects my work. It's rare that I raise my voice, and abusing is almost unheard of. I hate the misogynistic abuses that have been normalized on film sets, and I'm happy that this is now changing. I know of film-makers who hit assistants, and I find that kind of behaviour totally unacceptable. I tell those who have been abused that if they have made a mistake, they can be reprimanded, sacked even, but they should never let anyone hit them. Either hit back or walk out after abusing the person, but don't accept it. While shooting for *Kuchh Bheege Alfaaz* in Calcutta in 2017, I lost my temper twice and screamed. I didn't feel good about it.

Mostly, when I am upset about something not getting done, I start doing the chore myself. Then, when whoever is supposed to actually do it runs up to me and tries to do it, I don't let them take over. I would rather they feel guilty that the job wasn't done earlier. This strategy works better for me than screaming, but there are times when this strategy doesn't have the desired effect or is too impractical to implement. That's when I feel at a loss, unless someone else takes over the responsibility. Over the years, Sanjay's right-hand man, Govind Rathor, has taken pride in executing the task of getting people to hurry up!

The best thing about the shooting of *My Brother Nikhil* was how the entire crew slowly became like a family that was working towards a common goal. Juhi was put up at the Taj Village for security reasons, and the rest of us were at a hotel in Candolim. I remember that after a few days of shoot, Juhi said that she did not want to be at the hotel on her off days but rather come and help us on the set or just hang around. She also suggested that we send her the *dabba* food from the set as she didn't want to order food at the hotel.

One location that I wanted to shoot in and didn't manage to get was a church for Nikhil's memorial service. All the churches in Goa refused permission to shoot about a gay and HIV-positive person. I rewrote the sequence as a memorial service in his school. I would have ideally also shot Juhi's wedding sequence in a church but decided against it for two reasons. If the permissions for the memorial had worked out, we could have clubbed the shoot for the two scenes, but to have a separate location only for the wedding was not financially feasible. The other reason was perhaps the bigger one—we did not have the funds to get enough junior artists to make the wedding look authentic. And so I chose to do a more intimate house party.

A lot of friends came together to be a part of our film. Sanjay's friends stepped in to do supporting roles—Shweta Kawatre did the role of the lawyer, Gautam Kapoor was Juhi's husband, Sayan Munshi became Sanjay's rival at the pool and Pia Ray was Sanjay's friend. Not to forget that Ambika doubled and acted in many scenes as Nikhil's friend. There also was the lovely Dippannita Sharma who played Nikhil's fiancée. Arvind was so smitten by her that he would always want to wait for the golden hour to shoot her. Sujoy Ghosh came to the shoot for a few days to extend support and ended up playing Sanjay's coach.

I have this memory of the last day in Goa, a few days after the wrap, as I drove to the airport. It suddenly hit me that I had just taken a stupendous step. All my life, I had been dreaming about this, and I had finally completed the shoot for my first feature film. Not on the first day of the shoot, not after the first shot, not at wrap, but when I was sitting alone in the taxi, I let the tears of happiness drench me.

The post-production was mostly smooth apart from the tension of organizing funds. The nearer we came to the first print, the greater was the anxiety about the release. I was editing the film on Hi-band, after reverse telecine, at Spectral Harmony. Those were exciting days—to see what one has written and then shot slowly take the shape of a story, a film. I could see what was working and what seemed problematic, and I looked for solutions for the problem areas. As we had shot according to how I had visualized the edit, I didn't have too many options to experiment with. There was very little that was finally edited out of the film. At that time, there was Jolly ji, the 'negative cutter' at Adlabs, the person who had spliced the negatives of hundreds of films. He must have been in his mid-fifties—grey, lanky and always smiling—and you could sense how much he loved his job. After the edit, we would take out the edge numbers, check each cut very carefully and give Jolly ji the numbers to start cutting the reels. Any change would mean losing a frame. It was always stressful and exciting to watch a reel on the big screen, minus sound, to check the cuts. It was also not an easy process as one had to make decisions without sound and music. This was because each print cost additional money, and an indie film couldn't afford to keep taking out test positives.

We didn't have the budget to take *My Brother Nikhil* to Adlabs for our prints, but that's the place where I met one of the most passionate lovers of good cinema—Krishna Shetty, who used to be in charge of Adlabs before it became Reliance Color Labs. This kind and gentle man told me one day when I was there for some other film screening, 'We haven't done your first film, but I loved your film and you as a director. From your next film on, I want you to come to Adlabs. I won't let you work anywhere else.' As long as Krishna ji was there, we always took our films to Adlabs. He went out of his way to provide discounts and credits and at times even waived bills because he understood cinema. I miss him and Jolly ji. Jolly ji was one of the early casualties of the new age digital editing and film processing. Suddenly, almost overnight, he was without a job. He didn't survive long. With Krishna ji leaving Adlabs, the personal touch was gone, and suddenly one felt like just another client. I missed that gentle look, concern, smile and support. Most importantly, the driving energy for Krishna ji was a passion for cinema. Very often, when we were having our first test screening, he would come and quietly sit at the back and watch. You felt safe knowing that your rushes were in the custody of this man.

It was so exciting to watch the prints getting dispatched just before the release. Those aluminium cans contained our hard work. Each jumbo reel was usually 16–20 minutes, so a two-hour film like *My Brother Nikhil* had seven jumbo reels. I have travelled to so many countries with those seven cans, struggling with the weight across continents. It felt like something precious. I know this will sound old-fashioned, but I don't get that feeling with a hard drive.

Once we were ready with the film, we started hunting for distributors or a studio to partner with us. That is when the nightmare began. I think one of the first screenings we had was for Shyam ji and his brother. They were embarrassed and bored by the film and found the two hours way too long and the film too non-commercial for them to get attached for distribution. The screening I had at the then UTV boardroom with their marketing and distribution team was a humiliating experience. I understood the difference between a Krishna ji and a Jolly ji, who loved cinema, and these marketing people from the corporate world, who saw cinema merely as a product to sell. They were doing a job with no special love for cinema, so why would they break their heads in trying to position and market a 'gay' film without any 'big' star? In our sexist industry/society, women are not considered as big 'stars' as men, and women after a certain age are not considered 'stars' or 'commercial' enough. The UTV screening was in a boardroom with about twelve people. The room wasn't dark enough, and people were walking in and out of the room, talking on their phone. One of the guys gently asked me if I was showing them the rushes or a documentary. I was appalled at how cinema-illiterate these people were and arrogant on top of that. Even now, I realize that much hasn't changed. I'm discussing the script of a docuseries with the creative team from a leading OTT platform. All the examples they are giving me are from fiction shows! But I no longer get dejected now, nor am I surprised—I just feel more cinema literate.

The months of 'trials' were heartbreaking. The word 'trial' sounds terrible. It's almost as if the film-maker is on trial to be judged by a court. 'Special screening' or 'preview' sounds so much better. With the coming of studios and platforms, cinema has become more of a commodity than the creation of an artist. More often than not, depending on who has the power (it's a myth that platforms and studios are democratic), the platform or studio will have trial screenings and the film-maker will be told to make changes according to how the 'test group' has reacted or what the marketing and distribution teams have suggested. So you are trying to please a maximum number of invisible people. Imagine any film-maker whose films you've loved being told how to re-edit their films or rework the script from the beginning once a platform is attached, acting on the advice of a group of people who have never made a film. Imagine Tagore being told by a publicist what poems to pen and Van Gogh what to paint. The so-called digital revolution is actually murdering the artist film-maker and transforming them into content creators responsible for grabbing the most eyeballs. *Pyaasa* may have never gotten made today.

At some point, as a last resort, Sanjay reached out to Karan Johar and asked him to watch the film. Karan came to the Spectral Harmony studio, and I remember playing him the Hi-band edit. We stayed outside as we did not want to embarrass him if he didn't like the film. I think I must have smoked twenty cigarettes in my nervousness. After the screening was over, Sanjay went and chatted with Karan for ten minutes, and when they came out, Karan's eyes were swollen from crying. 'You made me cry so much, I have a headache now.' This was said with kindness and for the first time, I felt some hope. Once he left, Sanjay told me that Karan had spoken to Aditya Chopra as Dharma didn't have the infrastructure to release a film in 2005, and he thought that Yash Raj Films (YRF) might be able to help. Adi was supposed to be travelling in two days, so we quickly made a VHS of the edit and sent it to him. The next two days were filled with anxiety.

I will be forever grateful to Karan for making that call. Adi liked the film and offered to distribute it. When we met him, I was really nervous, wondering what I would do if he wanted to change everything. But he did not. He had two suggestions, but it was up to me to implement them. I liked one idea and made that change. Next, he asked me to cut five music promos and five dialogue promos for marketing. At this point, we interacted a lot with Tarun Tripati from YRF's marketing team, discussing how to position the film. Sanjay, Tarun and I would spend hours having discussions, and the great thing was that Tarun loved our film and there was so much positivity in his approach. I cut ten dialogue promos and ten music promos and showed them to Adi. He liked all the edits and told us to choose what we considered the five best ones.

Sanjay and Tarun came up with the campaign idea of having various celebrities say, 'I care for my brother Nikhil. Do you?' We had decided that while the campaign wouldn't focus on the gay or AIDS aspects directly, it wouldn't pretend to be about something else. When we were discussing the film's title, someone suggested that we should have named it 'My Lover Nikhil', but I had never wanted to tell the story from a lover's perspective—I wanted it to be the story of a brother who happens to be gay, told by his sister. Maybe I didn't want it to be a lover's story because at that time I hadn't really experienced what a lover could mean. Nigel was the lover I was seeking . . . am still seeking. In my life, lovers have walked in and out, but my sister has always been there. Yes, there have been instances of distance, but she has never left me. Just like Anu stood by Nikhil when he needed her the most, my sister Irene stood by me when I was falsely accused of molesting someone in 2011.

Sometimes it feels uncanny how my films have shown things that I have experienced later. I shot Omar's story as a part of *I Am* in 2009. The story is about how the gay character Jai, played by Rahul Bose, was humiliated by a cop because of his sexual identity. I experienced something similar when I visited the police station to file a case against the guy who falsely accused me. It was only because my associate Amar Kaushik was there by my side, giving me strength and support, that I did not crumble. The police understood that the allegations were fake and joked about the fact that someone so much physically stronger than me had made these allegations, but that didn't stop them from humiliating me verbally for being gay. I realized then that if I faced this in spite of belonging to the privileged class, gay men and women from less privileged backgrounds and the trans community must be dealing with unspeakable horrors. There must be so many untold stories of violence and humiliation. That is why I write this now, even though it is extremely painful to relive those days. Of how a publication made front-page headlines of an allegation that was not proven and drove me to the verge of ending my life. I did not, as death would have meant accepting defeat and perhaps even guilt. I could not let my family and friends down. I had to stand up for the truth.

Once *My Brother Nikhil* was ready, it suddenly struck us that the film had to be certified by the Central Board of Film Certification (CBFC). Those were the days when Section 377 was still a part of the Indian Penal Code, and the film was dealing with gay characters. I was nervous—what if we got an 'A' certificate? That would mean not being able to sell satellite rights of the film. What if the film did not get cleared? The day of the censor board screening was another smoke-filled afternoon. I had no idea who the five people watching our film were, the people who would judge if the film was to be allowed for public consumption. Sanjay and I were waiting anxiously at the door when we were told that one person had to go in and face the members. My knees were shaking and I was feeling queasy as I stood in the centre of the room looking at those five faces. They were cold and silent, and when one of them said, 'We liked your film, but there's a problem', I was ready to collapse. They then proceeded to explain that all of them loved everything and would give us a 'U' certificate, provided I added a disclaimer in the beginning that everything was fictitious and not based on any real story. They were worried that the government of Goa might not like that Goa was shown as the home of patient zero. This was one of the reasons why we didn't put a card saying that the film was inspired by Dominic's life story, but we acknowledged it in every press talk we had. One of the things I kept stressing is that the docu-feature structure of the film was to help reinforce that this was not a fictitious story but a real one. I wonder if *My Brother Nikhil* would still get a U certificate with the current guidelines. And with *I Am*, an FIR would probably be filed against me today!

For our marketing campaign, we shot with Rahul Dravid, Sania Mirza, Mahesh Bhupati, Karan Johar, Saif Ali Khan and Abhishek Bachchan. On 24 March 2005, we had the premiere of our film at Fun Republic in the Bombay suburb of Andheri. It was a magical night and truly overwhelming. The YRF marketing team had organized the media coverage in the best possible way that I could have imagined, and we had a great turnout in terms of people. All the screens at the venue were packed. I do regret that I couldn't be inside the theatre when the screenings started, as Juhi, Sanjay, Purab and I were outside giving interviews till nearly two-thirds of the film was over. Post that, I slipped in once but felt too nervous to stay. Sanjay slipped in once too and came back smiling. 'People are sobbing,' he told me. Then the show finished and as people started to come out, we watched them nervously from a distance as we didn't want people to feel obliged to like our film. But they were seeking us out to just hug and tell us how much they loved the film, loved Nikhil, Anu and Nigel. Some related to the film as a father–son story, some as a mother–son story, some with the sister, some with the lover and some were just reminded of love and loss.

I don't have any clear memory of what we did that night, but for me it was like the end of a phase of my life. Ever since I was in Class 6, I had unknowingly wanted to be a film-maker; consciously, since I was in Class 10. Having lived with the dream for so many years, working for this one day . . . I had finally transitioned from dreaming to becoming a part of that dream. I know I had already been working in the film industry for about ten years, but this was a huge moment. I had always told myself that I wanted to have the opportunity, at least once, of seeing my work as a film-maker, and if I didn't like what I saw, I would quit film-making and do something else, But I needed to do this at least once. The box office matters, but the fact that my films haven't fared well commercially hasn't broken me either. This is primarily because—and I don't know if I should call it a strength or a weakness—money was not the driving force for me, the need to tell the story was. That is the force that made a film like *I Am* possible. The need to keep making memories . . . for what is cinema but a reservoir of the memories of a society, time and culture?

The next few days were full of excitement and some heartbreak. The film got very good press overall, apart from one really stupid review where the critic said I had copied it from some documentary that I hadn't even heard of! Even though I was welcomed as a film-maker with a difference, the heartbreak was that not enough people went to the theatres to watch our film. The minute the reviews were out, people knew that the protagonist was gay. Men were largely reluctant to go into the theatre or show interest in the film because they were scared to be perceived as gay. Those who watched were mostly overwhelmed, and I was flooded with emails

and calls from unknown people about how much the film meant
to them.

Anupama Chopra, reviewing the film for *India Today,* wrote:

> *My Brother Nikhil* is that rare and remarkable thing: an
> understated, heart wrenchingly moving Bollywood melodrama.
> Debutant director Onir creates a lump in your throat with his
> first few scenes and then, with a finely crafted script and first-
> rate actors, holds you between teary smiles and all-out bawling.
>
> It is both exhilarating and exhausting cinema. Told mostly
> through in-camera conversations and flashbacks, *My Brother
> Nikhil* goes where few mainstream movies have gone before:
> AIDS and homosexuality; a loving relationship between two
> men; and a bewildered mother and father who flee at first but
> then eventually accept their dead son's lover as their own child.
>
> Onir treads lightly so that no point is hammered in and
> no emotion underlined. The actors, without exception, follow
> his cue so the tragedy never descends into bathos. The pacing
> occasionally lags but *My Brother Nikhil* is a triumph for its cast,
> crew and for us, the audience.*

Sukanya Verma, writing on rediff.com, said:

> *My Brother Nikhil* is an impressive debut by Onir. Though
> it begins meekly on a trite note, it develops into a serious
> film, which tries to educate without being overtly preachy –
> whether about an individual's constitutional right to freedom
> or the distinction between HIV+ and full-blown AIDS. It

---

* Anupama Chopra, 'Film Review of *My Brother Nikhil* starring Juhi
Chawla, Sanjay Suri', *India Today*, 11 April 2005, https://www.indiatoday.
in/magazine/your-week/story/20050411-film-review-of-my-brother-
nikhil-starring-juhi-chawla-sanjay-suri-788628-2005-04-11.

maturely handles the subject of homosexuality without a single suggestive scene.*

We did not recover the costs; YRF was gracious not to charge their commission on the sales and only recovered their marketing expenses. We recovered some monies from various overseas rights and sold the satellite rights to Sony TV, but that was not enough. In spite of being one of the first mainstream Hindi films from India to have a queer theme and deal with AIDS, despite having travelled to more than forty international film festivals, being shown in universities, NGOs and inclusive conferences, it didn't find a home for six years on any platform or TV channel. Sanjay and I were weary of hearing that the film was not entertaining enough or light enough or that it was too dark for the audience. There was a time when *My Brother Nikhil* had completed its contract with Sony and they didn't renew it. We released *I Am* and the film received two National Awards in 2012; yet all platforms and satellite channels refused to show it. Yes, it was heartbreaking that after years of failure, we had to finally option the film to an agent, and then it was once again leased out in 2017. Our film *Chauranga* (directed by Bikas Mishra), which won the India Gold at MAMI 2014 and best film at IFFLA 2014, was released independently in 2016 after having failed to get a distribution partner because of the subject of the film—Dalit lives did not seem to be interesting enough for the moneybags. We managed a Netflix deal for three years for *Chauranga*, after which it languishes, waiting for a home.

That is the most difficult thing to deal with—you navigate various challenges to make a good film and it wins accolades, but releasing it seems to become tougher over the years. This aspect of film-making has been so disheartening and stressful that we

---

* March 25, 2005, https://www.rediff.com/movies/2005/mar/25brother.htm.

have now become sceptical about producing what are termed as
'unsafe' films. The other day I was having a friendly debate with
a well-known film-maker on Twitter where he was going on and
on about how times are much better now, and I was telling him
I didn't feel that way. I found it a little strange that he should
refuse to acknowledge that it might be better for him, but that
does not mean it's the same for someone primarily known as a
queer film-maker. Stories set in 'B' towns have now become viable
and entertaining enough as 'A' cities have suddenly woken up to
the 'other' India, but the fact is that they have still not woken up to
show as much interest in queer lives, nor are they involved enough
to find queer stories 'entertaining'. Yes, my shortcoming is that I
could not make a comedy like *Dostana* out of *My Brother Nikhil*,
nor have I managed to do a *Shubh Mangal Zyada Saavdhan* out of
*I Am* or *Chauranga*.

Maybe my shortcoming as a film-maker is that I am drawn
to the grey side within us, to loving smiles and tears a little more
than loud laughter.

In April 2005, Sanjay, Purab and I were invited by Assam
Rifles Wives Welfare Association (ARWWA) for a screening of
*My Brother Nikhil* at the Armed Forces Conclave in Shillong in
the presence of President A.P.J. Abdul Kalam. Our hosts were
the warm and gracious Winnie Singh and Lieutenant General
Bhupendra Singh, and that was the beginning of a cherished
friendship. For three days, the film was shown to school students
and the forces, and we would interact with the audience after
the screening. Before the first screening, Lt. General Bhupendra
Singh told me, 'Don't forget this is the armed forces that you
are addressing. You can talk about HIV/AIDS, but not about
homosexuality.' My face fell, and then he smiled with a twinkle in
his eyes and added, 'But you are an outsider, go ahead and speak.'

Come to think of it, I feel we have regressed as a society.
Now, in 2022, my film *We Are* is facing a peculiar problem

at the pre-production stage. These days, you need to take an NOC from the Indian Army if you portray anyone from the armed forces in your film. I had watched an interview of Major Suresh on NDTV in 2020 where he spoke about why he quit the Indian Army. It was because he could not be open about his sexuality. Even after the Supreme Court ruling on IPC 377, the LGBTQIA community is not accepted in the armed forces.[*] I had decided that the first story in my film would be based on this—the story of an army man falling in love and then quitting the army as he could not be honest about his identity and express the basic human feeling of love. I sent an email seeking an NOC from the Ministry of Defence on 16 December 2021. I received an email stating that the NOC was refused on 19 January 2022. I was told on a WhatsApp call that the reason for refusal was that my protagonist was a gay army man.[†]

The irony is that I made *My Brother Nikhil* in 2005, *I Am* in 2011 and *Shab* in 2017, and all these films had LGBTQIA protagonists. I could make those films at a time when homosexuality was criminalized by law. And now . . .

It was while we were in Shillong that I received a call from New York—the Asia Society in New York wanted to screen our film. That was the beginning of festival invitations for *My Brother Nikhil* which went on for years, taking me to over fifty cities across the globe, to film festivals, film clubs, museums, embassies and universities. I can never forget that evening at Winnie and the

[*]   Major J. Suresh, 'I Was an Officer in the Indian Army, I'm Gay and Very Proud', *NDTV*, 8 July 2020, https://www.ndtv.com/opinion/i-was-an-officer-in-the-indian-army-im-gay-and-very-proud-2255980.
[†]   Priyanka Dasgupta, 'West Bengal: Defence Ministry Rejects Onir Film Script Inspired by Gay Major Who Quit', *Times of India*, 21 January 2022, https://timesofindia.indiatimes.com/city/kolkata/mod-rejects-onir-film-script-inspired-by-gay-major-who-quit/articleshow/89027628.cms.

Lt. General's bungalow, when I got the call from Mallika Dutta, inviting us across some truly terrible telephone network. I had always dreamt of travelling to various countries, but I didn't have a US visa yet. By the time we were ready to leave, we had received invites for two more screenings—for the New York Asian Film Festival (NYAFF) and Frameline at San Francisco.

I landed at JFK Airport early on the morning of 17 June 2005 on a Lufthansa flight. I had 200 USD with me, seven cans of our film and my suitcase. This was my first trip to the US and I was nervous and excited. As I stepped out of the airport, a friendly Mexican-American guy walked up to me with, 'Welcome brother, are you from India?' He was a taxi driver who offered to drive me to my hotel in Manhattan.

There I was, sitting blissfully in a sedan, happily chatting with the cabbie and taking in the amazing sights of NYC. Soon we were outside the hotel and the driver was unloading my luggage in the middle of the street. I gave him 100 USD as I had no change, hoping he would charge the fixed rate of 45 USD. Suddenly, the friendly cabbie started to argue with me aggressively. His wasn't a yellow cab and he wanted 200 USD. I was literally in tears as I begged him not to charge me so much, and he finally agreed to 150 USD. So I gave him another 100 USD. He returned 30 USD to me, saying that I needed to tip him 20 USD. Before I could react, he was inside the sedan, driving away. Simultaneously, like in films, Sanjay and Ambika, who had travelled on a different flight, arrived in a yellow cab. They paid their cabbie 45 USD! Till today, Sanjay and Ambika tease me about my inability to distinguish between a yellow cab and a luxury sedan. After that, when I paid the bellboy 2 USD for helping with the baggage, I felt miserable since I was left with 28 USD for the rest of the trip.

We were flying to the West Coast the next day, to San Francisco. Our first ever international screening was going to be at Castro, the iconic theatre that hosted the Frameline LGBTQ

Film Festival. I was excited to be at a queer film festival for the first time in my life. The area around Castro itself was special, and to see so many queer men and women move around expressing their identity freely was empowering. I knew that our audience would be primarily queer, and I was curious about how my community from a different culture/history would react to our film. The Castro screening was truly overwhelming; Sanjay and I could hear the crowd sobbing in the dark.

Let me quote novelist Sandip Roy:

> When the lights came up after a screening of *My Brother Nikhil* at the Castro theater in San Francisco, my eyes were raw and red from weeping.
>
> I was sitting at the famous Castro theatre in San Francisco's gay neighbourhood watching Onir's *My Brother Nikhil* at a film festival. For a San Francisco audience, the film must have seemed mild, especially in gay terms. Its lead couple never kissed. Their status as lovers had to come across just through body language, the way one got the other tea in the morning. But grown men who had lost lovers to AIDS, men who were living with the disease, tough men and women who had marched in protests against senators and presidents, wept like children as Nikhil's family grappled with their love for him and their fear of the disease he had contracted.*

In those days, I used to be terrible at handling the stage, but the warmth and the love showered by the audience towards our film slowly started giving me courage. Sanjay and Ambika would tease me about how I would scratch my head while answering. Sanjay

---

* Sandip Roy, 'Ripples of Change in Indian Film', *AlterNet*, 30 June 2005, https://www.alternet.org/2005/06/ripples_of_change_in_indian_film/.

was the charmer on stage, and in Castro that night, many a heart was broken when they found out that he was travelling with his wife, Ambika.

The next day, when we were walking around Church Street, there were people screaming at Sanjay from across the street, 'Nikhil, we love you.' Both Sanjay and I could not stop smiling; the journey had proved truly rewarding. We had one more screening at Parkway Theatre, Oakland, on 21 June, which was again charged with emotion.

We were heading back to New York on 22 June. I consider myself to be very organized, so when Ambika asked me at the hotel lobby if I had carefully checked and packed everything, I shrugged and said I was ready way before them. We reached the airport and got into the check-in lane. Sanjay asked me for my ticket; I opened the zip of my pouch and my face turned white. I had forgotten my flight ticket, my passport and about 1000 USD in the hotel safe. My brain stopped functioning as the flight was in two hours, and to reach the hotel would take at last an hour. Sanjay did some quick thinking and called the girl who had dropped us—she was halfway back to SF. She rushed to the hotel, by which time Sanjay had called the hotel, and they had opened the safe and put all my stuff in a packet, which they handed over to the girl. She reached the airport just in time, before the counter closed.

But the drama was not over. Mid-flight, the engine suddenly started to make a strange noise. The flight attendants seemed stressed and people started to panic. After a while, the pilot announced that one of the engines was not working and we would be making an emergency landing at Salt Lake City. There was silence as we all prayed for a safe landing. The noise kept increasing and the pilot announced that we would be landing in five minutes, but we should all be prepared for a rough landing as the second engine too had stopped working!

Later, as we waited for another plane to come from New York, we were served complimentary pizzas. No pizza has ever tasted better.

We stayed for a few days in the New Jersey flat of Ambika's cousin. Every day, Sanjay, Ambika and I would take the tube to NYC and walk for hours, exploring Manhattan, Union Square, museums and art galleries. The best way to discover a city is to walk. The good thing about New York is that, unlike Los Angeles, it is pedestrian friendly. Soon it was time for our New York premiere. At 6:00 p.m. on 27 June 2005, *My Brother Nikhil* was screened at the Asia Society and Museum, New York City.

Apart from in Shillong, I had had no exposure to audience Q&A in India. I started enjoying it a bit now, but I also felt extremely jittery before the screenings. Let me talk about one small incident just before the screening got over as that sums up the feeling that evening left us with.

Ten minutes before the film ended, a young girl walked out of the theatre. Both Sanjay and I felt disheartened that someone from the audience was walking out. She went to the restroom, then came out and walked up to us and said that she was sorry that she had walked out of the screening. Her brother was seventeen when he came out to his parents as gay and HIV-positive, and her parents didn't accept him. He had shot himself. She was overwhelmed with memories and could not bear to watch till the end. She hugged us tight before leaving.

Our next New York screening was on 1 July at the New York Asian Film Festival—Imagine Asia. I think I will quote critic Robert Urban to sum up the entire experience.

So when is the last time you attended a film where the entire audience wept, applauded and stood in spontaneous ovation? Such heartfelt reactions occurred on July 1 at the New York Asian Film Festival's screening of the groundbreaking movie

*My Brother Nikhil.* It is, hands down, one of the finest gay/
AIDS-themed films I've ever seen . . .

A high point at the film's New York Asian Film Festival
screening was when its handsome star Sanjay Suri (Nikhil)
appeared onstage in person at the movie's end to speak to the
audience. To suddenly see him in the flesh, alive and well, after
the torture of watching his slow wasting death onscreen was an
emotional shock to all. It was like seeing a loved one come back
from death, and the audience let out a simultaneous gasp and
sigh of relief as he took the stage . . .

Viewing *My Brother Nikhil* can be an emotionally
exhausting experience because it reminds us of our own recent
history, much of which we perhaps hoped we'd never have to
deal with again. But when we see the same things occurring
in India today that Americans went through ourselves only
a short time ago, the term "never forget" has never seemed
more relevant.[*]

The other high was that our film was written about in the
*New York Times.*

Quietly, gently, *My Brother Nikhil* has tested the limits of the
Indian cinemagoer's sensibility.

Commercially, it is no runaway Bollywood blockbuster; nor
is it meant to be. Rather, its impact lies in having served up a
story about love and loss—sentimental staples of contemporary
Indian cinema—with a gay man at its center, and having done
so without kicking up the slightest fuss from India's cultural
conservatives. As one review published in the latest issue of

---

[*]  See https://www.sanjaysuri.com/news-and-media/online-media-articles/
review-of-my-brother-nikhil-robert-urban.

Outlook, a mainstream newsweekly, put it, 'The two lovers seem just like any other couple.'[*]

The next day we were flying back—Ambika and Sanjay to India, while I was going to take a few days' break in Berlin with my friends Philip and Merle. We were happy that we had flown thousands of kilometres to be in the US. We had been anxious about how another culture would react to our creation, and we were returning with a lot of love. The journey of *My Brother Nikhil* had just begun, and I feel happy that even fifteen years later, it is watched on various online platforms.

A funny incident from my Berlin trip comes to mind. My friends had coordinated a screening at the Indian Embassy in Berlin. It was an extremely emotional moment for me to come back to the city where I learnt the craft, with Dr Grote sitting in the audience. Philip and Merle were glowing with pride. Tina and Jorge too were there along with Dorothy (she used to curate the Indian films for Berlinale). The screening was a success and it was followed by an engaging Q&A session. I would keep looking at Philip and Merle for reassurance that I was doing fine. There was this very attractive Latin American guy sitting in the audience. He raised his hand and proceeded to ask me, 'Are you married?' I thought it was an odd and irrelevant question and also knew where he was headed. My first thought was to snub him, but he was just too gorgeous. So I looked at him and replied, 'I will answer the question if it is a proposition.' The crowd roared with laughter and clapped. He was now red-faced and soon disappeared. There were many in the audience who wanted to click photographs or chat, and by the time I could get out, Dr Grote had left. I was disappointed and wondered if he had not liked the film. Philip

---

[*] Somini Sengupta, 'Gay themed film tests sensibilities in India', *The New York Times*, 6 April 2005, https://www.nytimes.com/2005/04/06/movies/gaythemed-film-tests-sensibilities-in-india.html.

and Merle had organized dinner with all our friends at a 'Henne' in Kreuzberg known for its chicken delicacy. We drank ourselves merry till the wee hours of the morning.

The next day, I got a call from Dr Grote, and he told me how proud he was of me and that he wanted to cook dinner for me. That indeed felt special.

Early in 2006, *My Brother Nikhil* was screened at the Milan Gay and Lesbian Film Festival, where it won the Audience Choice award. After the screening, a group of young Italian men surrounded me and tried to sing '*Le chalein*'. I have lost count of the number of cities where I have had screenings: Montreal, London, Hamburg, Venice, Florence, Bremen, Frankfurt, Paris, Bangkok, Seattle, Durban, Rabat (Morocco), Chicago, Washington DC, Austin, Candy (Sri Lanka), Syracuse, Michigan, among others.

Sometimes I am amazed at how caring humans can be in spite of seeing so much of the hate narrative all around. After the Indian Army's refusal to give an NOC to my script for *We Are*, I received an email from Yuri Guaiana, who was my driver during my trip to Milan. He now works with allout.org and offered to generate international support for me.

I must add here that our film, the music director, singers, Sanjay, Purab and I were not nominated for any of the main industry awards in India. Juhi was nominated as Best Supporting Actor Female at Filmfare, Zee Cine and IIFA Awards. I wonder why she was nominated in that category when she was the female lead. But we all know the story of awards. There has recently been a lot of discussion about outsiders and nepotism in the industry. Looking back at my journey with *My Brother Nikhil* and *I Am* in the Bollywood/Hindi film industry, I feel it does have some answers to what I try to pretend does not exist. But in my case, I am sure homophobia too raises its head.

Let me end this chapter with one special event. In May 2005, the Saathi Rainbow Gay and Lesbian Film Festival, Calcutta, awarded me the Best Director award for *My Brother Nikhil*. I couldn't attend the ceremony as we were at Frameline. What was special is that Baba attended the ceremony, accepted the award on my behalf and also spoke to the audience. He said that it was amazing that they were giving me the award, but more people should make an effort to go and watch the film in the theatres.

Somewhere, many oceans away,
They are celebrating our love today.
Love wins,
While you and I in the shadows wait,
Our love enchained in our homeland
By lies about our history and by hate,
Longing for the sunshine.
We wait.
Maybe many centuries later,
We will walk hand in hand in this land,
And claim what should have been ours.
Till then, my love,
Let us in the shadows kiss.

# 20

# *Bas Ek Pal* (2006)

In spite of the critical success of *My Brother Nikhil* and the YRF distribution, I wasn't flooded with work offers. There was radio silence. When I look back now, I know what it meant—homophobia. At that time I was too busy enjoying the journey to be able to analyse.

Shailesh Singh, who used to be a production assistant on *Abhay Charan*, connected with me upon my return from Berlin. He was very insistent that I direct a film for him and help him become a producer. He said he would arrange all the finances.

I now resumed work on the script of *Bas Ek Pal*, roping in my sister, Irene, to develop the screenplay.

I was happy to team up again with Juhi and Sanjay. With *Bas Ek Pal* also started a long association with DOP Sachin Krishn whom I had first met at FTII and with whom I also shot a corporate film. While designing the look for *Bas Ek Pal*, we discussed in detail how we would work on different colour schemes for lighting up each character's space. The colour palette became an intense coordination between the camera department, costumes and production design. I enjoy working with Sachin. He has a certain calmness about him that suits the overwhelming atmosphere on the set.

*Bas Ek Pal* brought up many new challenges for me. It was the first time I was working in sets with a much larger crew and shooting for many more days. I know it would be still considered rather economical, but forty-five days was a lot for me after having shot *My Brother Nikhil* in twenty-seven days. This was the first time I was working with a professional action director, Sham Kaushal, and a choreographer, Remo D'Souza.

My luck ran out with the production designers I was working with. It was not their fault at times, but the bottom line was that things would keep going wrong with that department, and I ended up working with three different production designers. The other department I ended up having three different heads for was music. It was, in a way, the end of a relationship and the beginning of another beautiful working relationship.

When I started putting together the team of *Bas Ek Pal*, Pritam was signed on as music director. I was excited since we had such a long history of producing music together. I like to have my songs ready way before the shoot as I like to use most of my songs as a part of the storytelling. The first song recorded was '*Aah zara*' with my favourites KK and Sunidhi. Remo choreographed the song on Sanjay and Urmila Matondkar. Did I mention that I have nicknames for some people? By now, Sanjay was saved on my phone as 'Imp'. Some people who didn't know about our friendship thought it meant 'important', but for me he was an imp because he was always teasing me in wicked (but not evil) ways. I later added Ambika as 'Impess'. I know this may sound sexist, but I liked the sound of 'Impess'. Urmila Matondkar, who was a part of the cast along with Jimmy Sheirgill, Sanjay and Juhi, wasn't very comfortable with on-screen kissing. It wasn't that commonplace in mainstream Hindi cinema back then, and I didn't really try hard to convince her as I (rather stupidly) had felt too embarrassed to do that. Since then, her name is saved on my phone as 'Kiss me not'. Jimmy was someone I already knew and he was also friends with Sanjay. We became very good friends during the shoot. Generous, kind and always smiling, Jimmy was a party man who would constantly take me out to party. Just before the shoot, he told me that he had been thinking about his character, and he thought that the character should have a tattoo saying 'sex maniac' as that was the essence of Sameer's character. That suggestion did not work for me, but he became 'sex maniac' on my phone! Many years later, I was bathing when my housekeeper screamed from outside the bathroom door that 'sex maniac' was calling!

Coming back to Pritam, the second song that we recorded at Spectral Harmony was '*Alvida alvida*', a song that many film-makers had been eyeing, but I had told Pritam when he was still in FTII that I wanted to use it for my film. When he first recorded the song, it was in his voice, and as it wasn't working for me, I wanted KK to sing it instead. My shoot schedule was coming closer and closer, but somehow Pritam would keep cancelling recording dates with different excuses. Finally, on one of the days that he had cancelled the recording saying he was ill, my producer Shailesh told me that he was actually recording at YRF Studio for one of their productions. Pritam later told me that I had misunderstood, but by then the damage was done. The lack of communication did not help and I felt very let down. I know it was important for him to do bigger productions and I am happy that he has achieved incredible success, but I had felt very hurt back then.

This is when I decided to bring in Mithoon, who was just nineteen at that point. Mithoon composed the wonderful title track of *Bas Ek Pal* sung by KK and Sunidhi. '*Tere pyaar mein*', written by Amitabh Varma, is another of my favourite songs from the film. Then he played the scratch of '*Tere bin*' and that song was like magic. I just couldn't get the tune out of my head, and though I didn't really have a place for it in the film, I wanted the song. Mithoon too was keen that I use it. I'll admit that I could never do justice to the song in the film, but we made a video for the song featuring Atif Aslam with the music company. The song was one of the biggest hits of that year. I always wondered why this song never got nominated for the Filmfare awards that year, be it for Atif or this wonderful debut music composer.

More recently, I was in Srinagar on 13 December 2020 attending a live event, and I had a goosebump-inducing moment when singer Junaid Ahmad, without knowing that the song was from my film, sang *'Tere bin'* and the crowd went wild. When I was in Karachi in 2018 for the Karachi International Film Festival, I spoke with Atif, who was in Lahore. He told me, *'Bas Ek Pal* was the turning point of my life, and if you are in Lahore, please be my guest. And if you ever need my voice for a song, please do not worry about money.' I felt proud and happy.

*Bas Ek Pal* was the beginning of a long association with Mithoon. I have seen him grow as a music composer with each passing year, but the person has remained the same when it comes to his relationship with me. He always assures me that whenever I am making a film, I should reach out to him without thinking about budgets. He stood by me when I was making *Shab* (2017) and composed the entire album. The first time he played the scratch of *'Oh saathi'* in the recording studio, I started to cry and couldn't talk for a while, thinking about a relationship that I had just come out of. Later, Arijit sang the song and brought in a tenderness that no one else could have. Sadly, this song too did not receive its due from the industry. With Mithoon, I feel respected as a film-maker; he reads the script thoroughly and does not play stock songs to me. He makes them for the film. After the screening of *Kuch Bheege Alfaaz* (2018), he came to me and said, 'Not fair that you make a romantic film and I did not get to make a song.' I know we will work together many more times.

As of now, I am looking forward to working with Pritam again for my upcoming film *We Are*. I have very fond memories of the amazing days and nights that we spent making music, and it would be good to revive that. Pritam and I have had a rather complicated relationship, and it saddened me a lot that when we finally got down to working on my film, it ended in disappointment and bitterness. Strangely, though, we've never lost touch. He comes for my film screenings, and I have followed his musical journey with happiness. Our mothers remain very close friends. After all these years, Pritam and I are taking baby steps towards working together again.

While shooting *Bas Ek Pal*, I learnt about the specific role played by each person on a film set. I used to get involved in everything, constantly briefing each assistant director and production person about what to do. My first AD was the super-efficient Vinay Waikul, who at one point during the first schedule came up to me and said he needed me to function in a certain way so that he could function efficiently! Vinay said, 'You tell me everything, and I will brief my team. You will not instruct anyone from the direction team individually, as this causes confusion. It's my job to get the work done according to your vision. You please be with the actors and your DOP.' That was very good advice, which I didn't follow completely at the time, but I have learnt over films that a film-maker needs to spend as much time as possible with the actors before a shot. Practical considerations aside, I actually love interacting directly with my direction team and having a personal equation not just with my AD but every member of my team. I feel happy to see them grow—Vinay Waikul, Amar Kaushik, Mitakshara Kumar and Prashant Singh are all independent film-makers now, creating beautiful moving images for cinema, the web and TV.

During the making of *Bas Ek Pal*, Shailesh remained in the background, always telling everyone what a pleasure it was working with me and how I had made everything easy for him as a producer. But as soon as the film was ready, his demeanour changed. He was suddenly taking all business decisions without divulging details to me. *Bas Ek Pal* had a terribly planned release, and despite the music being such a huge success, it was a big setback for me. I feel that the film never got a fair chance. The number of prints and the show timings were both terrible. Shailesh claimed that he had lost money and came to meet me in an auto, though I later learnt that he had already bought a new car. I had felt responsible for the losses and let go of the balance remuneration due to me. Whenever we meet, he still talks about how much he wants to make another film with me, but I know there is no truth in that.

# 21

## *Sorry Bhai!* (2008)

After *Bas Ek Pal*, I was signed up for a film by Studio 18. This was supposed to be a remake of Sai Paranjpye's *Chashme Buddoor*, and I was a little nervous as I had loved the original and knew I would rather shoot an adaptation than a remake. Anyway, I was excited that I would be trying my hand at a new genre, that of romantic comedy. I started working with Ashwini Malik as my writer. It was decided that the film would be set in Australia and in 2007, Ashwini and I went for a script recce to Australia. That is where I met the lovely Mitu Bhowmik who over the years has become a very precious friend and a strong supporter. We travelled across Victoria, Sydney and the Gold Coast over twelve days. It was all very exciting, and I was thrilled at the prospect of shooting in Australia; the story was going to be set organically there, and it wouldn't just be a backdrop, like in many Bollywood films.

During this trip, I also met another beautiful person—Jas, aka Juspreet Singh Walia. He was one of the other producers on that trip looking at possibilities of shooting in Australia. Jas became a good friend during the trip and an important part of my life.

We returned to India and started working on the script. We were constantly interacting with the studio team and everything seemed perfect. The nightmare began during the casting process—the only actors who were interested in working with me were not 'big enough' for the studio. After a few months of trying various combinations, I was suddenly told that the studio would not like to continue with me for the project as they wanted stars, and since I was not capable of bringing in the names they wanted, they decided to drop me as director. Studio 18 signed on David Dhawan to direct the film instead.

When something like this happens, what hurts you the most is that the time and effort you put into doing something is dismissed for reasons not in your control. I realized that I wouldn't be getting the kind of support I had expected from a studio and would have to continue my journey independently. The studios were there not to support new talent; they were there to piggyback on established people. The system empowered those who were already empowered, a system where the industry at large remained under the control of a few, be it finance, production, distribution and exhibition.

During the lockdown in 2020, due to a sad series of events, everyone was finally talking about the 'mafia', the control freaks that do not let 'outsiders' find space easily. I have experienced that in various ways, be it in the exclusion from mainstream awards or the struggle to get the desired number of shows and the correct show timings for my films at the time of release. The multiplexes, which were meant to give life to independent cinema, soon became our death. High ticket pricing and preferential treatment to films from big production houses made it impossible for independent cinema to compete. I have always thought that ours were 'word-of-mouth' kind of films. But how would that ever happen if my films got pulled out of the theatre during the first weekend because 'it didn't perform well'? How would 'word of mouth' happen when we could not match the spending power of the biggies on paid media? Everything is streamlined for the big films to flourish. Giving us space is always projected as doing us a favour. We are supposed to feel grateful. I have never understood why a 100 crore film's ticket should be priced the same as a 1.5 crore film's. Surely something is wrong with the system. Big star-driven films are important, but a healthy industry also supports some content-driven films, even if the box office does not make huge profits. I strongly believe cinema exists for entertainment but also as a creative medium and a powerful tool for social change. Why does entertainment have to only be regressive and populist? I can go on and on, but let me stop this rant. Nothing much has changed over the years, and challenges keep taking new forms just when you think there is some hope. Once again, I am learning to negotiate new challenges. That's what one gets for remaining on the fringes.

I was told to develop another script. Ashwini wrote the script of *Sorry Bhai!*

When Ashwini started work on *Sorry Bhai!* we decided to primarily set it in Melbourne as we had done such an extensive recce there. But we soon realized that we were not getting any studio to back the project any more. Apart from Studio 18, I also went to YRF (who made *Mere Brother Ki Dulhan* a year later) who thought that the subject was not in a space that excited them. I was very sure I wanted to make the film, so I started to explore possibilities of actors, thinking that the cast might help me get the finances. The first person we roped in was Sharman Joshi. I had always wanted to work with Shabana Azmi and was thrilled when she said yes to the film. Shabana put me on to Boman Irani. They were a fun duo at the shoot; they would sing songs, crack jokes and keep the mood light. By then, my friend Jas had decided to help us out with the film by putting in the initial funds needed. He suggested that we could shift the film to Mauritius. Sanjay, Ashwini and I went for a script recce, and we reworked the script to set the film in Mauritius.

The film was slowly taking shape, though we still didn't have our lead actress and enough finances. And then a friend told me that Chitrangda Singh was probably thinking of getting back to acting in films. I had loved Sudhir Mishra's *Hazaaron Khwaishein Aisi* and I had also loved her performance in it. I sent her the script, which she enjoyed reading, but she was still unsure about saying yes. I flew down to Delhi to meet her and talk in detail about her character. In real life, she looked even more breathtaking. We started shooting the first schedule in Bombay with the funds Jas had organized. I remember we shot a sequence with Chitrangda and Sharman at Whistling Woods on the first day of our shoot. I was especially excited because this was the first time and probably the only time that Ma and Baba visited me during a shoot. I loved that proud look on their faces.

I was shooting, but there was this constant nagging stress— what would happen after the first schedule? We had booked flight tickets to Mauritius and I was kidding myself that everything would work out, but things weren't getting sorted. I had borrowed the money for the first schedule from Jas, but we still didn't have any financing options for schedule two. Finally, two weeks before we were supposed to fly off to Mauritius, Sanjay had a meeting with Vashu Bhagnani and convinced him to come on board as financier. One of the conditions was that we give up our credits as producers and become co-producers. It was such a big relief at that point that it honestly didn't matter, and soon we were on our way to Mauritius for the shoot.

There was a lot in *Sorry Bhai!* that was like our family. Shabana's character was a bit like Ma, and in our family, Bhai was always the mama's boy. Bhai is a physicist and a little absent-minded too. Ma used to tell us stories about how she used to swim in the village pond and how she always beat her brothers. We used these stories while fleshing out Shabana's character.

Shooting in Mauritius is a memory that I'll always cherish. On off days, we would all go to Banana Beach Club and let our hair down. Once, Amar Kaushik, who was my third AD at that time, was pretty drunk on beer and he took over the dance floor. He pretended to bowl while a French lady there pretended to be the wicket. After a point, everyone stopped dancing just to watch this unique performance! From that day onwards, Amar became 'Disco Dancer' in my contacts list.

There were a lot of people in the crew with whom I had worked before. Shubha, who had come as continuity supervisor, realized that the first AD was not really being able to handle things, so on the third day of shoot, she announced that she would take over as first AD. I always feel touched about how she treated the films that we have worked on together as her own, and her concern for me makes her do much more than her official job description entails. There was also Azaan and Juhi Shekhar in the direction team, apart from Nikit Doshi, who was a film student from Australia and had come as an intern. And there was the ever-smiling and warm Ravneet Goraya handling production. My favourite Arun Nambiar was doing the sound, and I was once again working with Sachin Krishn on the camera. Sachin needed to take a fifteen-minute snooze after lunch, so he would find some quiet corner and just go off to sleep. Sachin is listed in my phone as 'Noon Siesta'. I missed Ambika in the team, but it had been only a few months since Aryan, Sanjay and Ambika's first child, was born. She joined us later in Mauritius, and for me it was a stress buster to return from the shoot and go to their room and pick up little Arry, to walk around and play with him. It was fun to make his tiny fingers touch the leaves of plants, to let him walk barefoot on the grass. Now he stands at least five inches taller than me, a gentle and kind teenager. I love that Sanjay's sons call me 'dada' and not 'uncle', and during their pre-teen years, they used to consider me their property and promptly drag me to their room to chat while the adults talked in the living room.

I cook fish for Arry sometimes (Sanjay has turned vegetarian), and I recently asked him when he would like me to cook fish for him next and was touched when he replied, 'I'll ask Dashmi didi (the housekeeper) when she wants as she also loves fish, so you can cook for both of us.' Incidentally, Ambika tells everyone that she used to be totally averse to eating fish till she tried fish cooked by me. Even Ma likes fish cooked by me, saying that with others' cooking, there's a strong fish smell that she can't stand. Sanjay's younger son Adi is more the momo boy. He doesn't enjoy fish, and I have to make momos for him.

I think I may have mentioned before that I have this terrible habit of forgetting names. I was shooting a scene with Sharman and at some point I needed to tell him to turn to face the camera. We started rolling and I suddenly went blank about Sharman's name. Those were days of shooting on film stock, and as the camera was rolling, Sachin nudged me, 'Give your instruction.' I asked him, 'What's his name? I can't remember.' Sharman overheard this, and Sachin burst out laughing. It was really awkward.

One important lesson from this shoot was how to handle actors. The first day that I was shooting a scene with Chitrangda and Shabana, there was a bit of nervous energy on set. It was also the first scene I was shooting with Shabana, and being a big admirer of her work, I wanted to impress her. And Chitrangda was edgy because of the endless comparisons with Smita Patil. The scene required Chitrangda to get emotional and hug Shabana. When we were preparing for the shot, Chitrangda (who I used to call Aliyah during the shoot) told me that she felt that Aliyah doesn't need to hug the mother. As I was explaining why I wanted it, Shabana intervened and said, 'Why do you want to insist when your actors don't feel the need for it organically?' I realized that maybe she had a point, and I shouldn't be so closed. I wasn't happy, but I went along with it and told them to do it the way they felt was right. After I saw the way the shot was progressing, I wasn't happy at all. So I told Chitrangda that I wasn't happy with the shot, and now I wanted her to do it the way I wanted it. We did the scene again, and it was what I wanted. The minute I said cut, Shabana commented, 'You were right, this is better.'

Over the next weeks, I think all of us developed very healthy relationships where ideas and suggestions were welcome and either I got convinced or I convinced the others. I feel it's important for a director to be secure and humble enough to accept a good idea. It will only enrich the film. And if you don't believe in something, do not go ahead with it to please anyone. Your ultimate loyalty has to be to the film and the film alone. When you are working for a platform or producer, you are constantly working for more eyeballs and cannot necessarily be true to the content. I admire those film-makers who can navigate this space and create the amazing content that they do. I fail miserably.

When we were shooting, Sharman would often tease me that I was so mesmerized by 'Aliyah' that I was not paying enough attention to the others. One day, we were shooting a song sequence in an open red jeep with Sharman and Chitrangda. I needed to take Chitrangda's shots, so Amar volunteered to drive the jeep while Chitrangda gave her reactions. While doing the shot, Chitrangda suddenly burst out laughing. Amar was so immersed in the situation that he was giving her romantic looks!

I must also add that Vashu Bhagnani was the ideal financier during the shoot. The money always came on time, and he never came to the set or interfered.

After a thirty-five-day schedule in Mauritius, we returned to Bombay for the last two days of the shoot. Many of my friends, including Sanjay, told me during the shoot and also later that 'this film was not me'. I sincerely don't believe that. I believe that I can celebrate romance and smiles, and that every film I make does not have to be dark, heavy or sad. To me, *Sorry Bhai!* is an empowering and progressive film. Yes, I faltered in some places, but I do that in every film I make and I learn a little more each time. If there is a kind of film that is not me, I would say it would be a complete action film, a slapstick comedy or horror.

Once the edit was complete, our producer suddenly wanted to make rather strange changes. To my complete horror, he said, 'Let's do something like this, that the scientist boy is trying to make the dog fly, when the girl sees this and is charmed. She comes running and he runs up to her, they hug, and let's have a song there. This will lift the romance, which is too subtle now.' I thought these things only happened in the realm of industry gossip, but it was now happening to my film. We had to think fast as I wouldn't let anyone do this to our film. Thankfully, most of my actors stood by the film and didn't have free dates immediately for any additional shoot. Meanwhile, we were in talks with Mumbai Mantra for the acquisition of the film. The Mumbai Mantra team of Minnie Vaid, Vikramjeet and Saurabh Prabhkar had already watched and loved the film and were keen to acquire and distribute it. I thought that our producer would perhaps no longer want me to make those changes, but he now became even more insistent. I called up Anand Mahindra, who had not yet seen the film. He asked me to send him the script so that he could read it during a flight and take a call. He read the script and enjoyed it thoroughly and communicated that Mumbai Mantra would acquire the film if we changed nothing. Finally, the film was safe!

The next challenge came days before the film's release. This was a huge lesson I learned about how unfair the entire system is towards the producer. A singer/composer filed a case for Rs 1 crore in damages, claiming that one of the songs in the film was similar to a song he had composed. There were two aspects to this: one, that our music composer and the singer were close associates once upon a time and had worked on many albums together. The second was that our music director had indemnified us in the music agreement that the songs were his original compositions. How was a producer supposed to be aware of every song ever composed and whether a song is original or not? Why should the producer be the one to suffer when the fault is someone else's? The hearing was in Delhi one day before the release. The fact is that we didn't have huge amounts of money, and the release date couldn't be pushed either. So it was decided that I would edit out the song from the film. This was a heartbreaking process, not only because it was my favourite song in the film but also because songs in my films are mostly a very integral part of the storytelling, and so the disruption in the narrative was obvious. But there was nothing I could do at the time. The prints were already dispatched, so we had to send instructions to every theatre across the country so that the print could be edited in the projection room. The song was a part of the background score thrice in the film, and we hoped that they would edit it out properly. My sister and I, both being editors, went from theatre to theatre in Bombay on 24 November 2008, deleting the scenes. It was like mutilating your own baby. The next day, 25 November, we went along with the actors to Delhi for the film promotions and also to attend the court hearing scheduled for 27 November. The scheduled release was 28 November.

They say it never rains, but it pours.

The next day, the team was doing a live session at a studio in Delhi when the show was suddenly interrupted.

26/11 happened.

We went back to the hotel, switched on the TV and watched the horror unfold in the city we call our home, the city that has given us so much. I was crying because of what was unfolding on the television screen and also because I know that this was the end for our film. The film wouldn't get a chance to be discovered by the audience. For the next few days, everyone was glued to their television sets, and there was also the fear of more terrorists being around, and theatres were not being considered safe spaces. It took a *Ghajini* at the end of December to bring the audience back to the cinemas.

The next day, Vikramjeet and I went to the court for the hearing. I was already devastated and also nervous as I had never been to a courtroom before. Though the box office verdict for the film was decided the previous night, what happened here was a small consolation. After being taunted by the singer that I was a 'good actor' since I had worn my T-shirt inside out (I had obviously not noticed), the verdict was in our favour. My music composer played the original Middle Eastern song from which both he and the singer had got 'inspired'. It was no one's original composition! We were told to pay Rs 50,000 to a gurudwara as charity. My music composer rightly offered to pay the amount.

We immediately called up as many theatres as we could to ask them to put back the deleted scenes. Very few did it and most of the prints remained mutilated. In Bombay, Ashwini and Irene went to some halls to put back the removed bits, and I did the same in Delhi. It didn't really matter, as no one was watching films. It was sadly too late to stop the release as the prints had already left for different theatres and overseas. If we stalled the release now, the film would probably be out online illegally. Moreover, a lot of money had been put into film promotions before the release. Three months of promotions would have been wasted, and one would need a significant amount of money to release the film at a later date. But the biggest fear was piracy.

The box office disaster of *Sorry Bhai!* became a big setback for me. I had done one film after another, and now there was nothing coming my way.

# 22

# *I Am* (2009–2012)

I was raring to go and had so many stories I wanted to tell, but somehow nothing seemed to move. The kind of stories I wanted to tell had no takers. There are a lot of film-makers who claim that they have found the wings of freedom with OTT. I have not; I am old-fashioned and like my cinema to be watched on the big screen. I don't want my stories to fit into a structure prescribed by platforms. I don't want to be told how to make my story more audience-friendly. I still pride myself as an artist. I have nothing against those who find their freedom there—I'm happy for them. But I hate it when they generalize and almost try to appropriate you into that narrative. I hate it when they almost want to dismiss cinema. I took flight there, and I will find ways to keep doing what I love to do.

Sanjay and I discussed trying out the crowdfunding route via Facebook. Sanjay was initially a little sceptical but then agreed that we should try it out. He also thought it would be easier if I could work on four or five shorts instead of one feature film so that we could raise finances for each short separately. With a short film, I wouldn't be able to reach out to an audience in the theatre and, like I mentioned before, I am old-fashioned about this. I decided to connect the stories thematically and through characters, so that it could come together as one film.

I went off to Berlin to visit my friends Philip and Merle and start the writing process. The first story I wrote was *Abhimanyu*. A few months earlier, I had come to know designer Ganesh Nallari from Hyderabad. He had told me about how a relative of his abused him as a child and how when that person was finally dying, he went up to the dying man and said, 'I forgive you.' That story had shaken me, but for Ganesh it had been therapeutic to talk to an outsider for the first time about the abuse that had hurt him so deeply as a child.* He had been in tears while talking to me, and I knew I wanted to make a film about what he and many others have experienced—abuse at the hands of people closest to them. One thing I wanted to change was to make the abuser a stepfather, and in the film Abhimanyu never forgave him or the mother who kept silent throughout the period of abuse. I wanted to make these changes because complicity should not be forgiven, for even when one learns to deal with the scars, they remain.

I wrote the first draft over two days, and then Merle read it and guided me through the next draft. She then took over when I started writing *Omar*, for which we followed the same process. *Omar* was personal because of my acute awareness of my identity as a gay man and how vulnerable we are as a community. For me, the story was kind of oracular: I felt the pain and fear of the character at that time, little knowing that in 2011, I would go through a similar nightmarish experience.

A guy I knew from the gym where I had worked out for nearly five years wanted to meet me and show me his work. I found him attractive, and both of us had flirted many times over messages.

---

* 'I Was Sexually Abused until I was 17: Ganesh Nallari', *The Indian Express*, 3 December 2016, https://indianexpress.com/article/entertainment/entertainment-others/i-was-sexually-abused-until-i-was-17-ganesh-nallari-4408742/. Accessed on 14 March 2022.

I was also aware that he was gay, though I didn't know if he was actually seeing someone. We met one evening over wine and dinner and chatted a lot. I saw his work, and since he had wanted me to be honest with him, I told him that it was very bad. We flirted and got a little physical with each other. It was refreshing for me as he never talked about work or any favour he needed from me; he was, in fact, affectionate and promised to take me to his home town. We parted as friends, promising to meet more often, and the next morning he even sent me some sweet messages.

Then came the shock, and my world collapsed. I got a call from a journalist that the fellow had reached out to her and told her that I had molested him. I would never ever deny that we had gotten physical with each other, but it was not true that I had molested him. I did get intimate with him, but it was consensual. I told her that it was unfair that she should make news out of this as there was no case against me, and that she was just doing it on the basis of a false claim. But then, yellow journalism is what it is . . .

The headlines of the publication, circulated all over the country, had my photograph alongside his, saying that I had allegedly molested him. I was alone in my flat, feeling numb, crying, blaming myself for seeking love and desire, confused about why he did what he did. I had never felt that anything happened that evening to make either of us uncomfortable. I was worried how my friends, my crew, Baba and Ma in Calcutta, my sister and her family, Sanjay and his family, Bhai would take it.

I received a call from Baba and Ma. I cried on the phone, and they said that they loved and trusted me and told me to fight it. Soon, all my assistants came to tell me how much they loved me. My friends Sanjay, Mukesh Sawlani and Amar Kaushik were there, discussing how to handle the situation. My friend from Humsafar Trust, Vivek Anand, immediately offered legal help. Writing about the incident brings back the pain, even after ten years. My landlady called me up and told me that she knew me well enough and not to worry, that truth would prevail. Didi was initially very angry with me and told me that I should think a little about the repercussion that my family would face, that my niece in school might face. I was broken—did it mean that I stop living my life because someone else was trying to malign me? Just because I am gay, do I not have the right to love, to flirt, to desire, to make mistakes and learn? Some people told me that I should never have anything to do with someone from the industry. How unfair is that, since actors will date actresses, directors and producers date others from the industry from the opposite sex, doctors and nurses fall in love and marry people from the same profession, as do teachers and sundry others? Am I not supposed to do the same because I am gay? As long as I do not misuse my position, make false promises or force myself on anyone, why should I be denied the right everyone else has?

I think Didi's initial reaction was out of confusion and a sense of helplessness and not knowing what to do. The next day, she started an online campaign to gather support for me. She called up and wrote to people from the industry who knew her or me and got them to endorse me on social media. She believed me totally when I told her that I had not molested this guy.

It was decided that I should file a police complaint, and for the first time in my life, I went to a police station. I will be forever grateful to Amar for accompanying me, shielding me from the humiliation and harassment and dealing with the police. On my own, I would have broken down or collapsed. Though I was the one making the complaint, I was asked all kinds of insulting questions and was told that my parents hadn't brought me up properly and I had grown up behaving like an animal, like a buffalo. They suggested that I should ideally be kept in a lock-up since I indulge in such sinful activity. All this while they were looking at me and laughing, saying they could tell that I could never have molested that guy! It was Amar who, while feeling furious at how I was being treated, laughed and joked with the cops and handled the entire process of registering our complaint. I guess I was kind of lucky as this happened during the brief period when the Delhi High Court had decriminalized homosexuality (2009–2013), and though I was not under Delhi jurisdiction, I was still spared the worst treatment.

The next day, my lawyer Usha Andelwal advised that we should file a defamation case for Re 1. I was also touched that the person with whom I was having an on-and-off relationship at the time came to meet me and gave me a hug with reassurance, love and warmth. He decided to spend the next few nights with me so that I wouldn't be too depressed. That was a kind gesture.

What moved me the most is when Ambika came with the two boys and told me that she needed me to babysit them for a couple of hours—her love and trust meant the world to me. Sanjay and Amar were constantly at work figuring out what to do. Most mainstream television networks kept away from this as they thought it was more gossip than fact. The case did not hold beyond a week, but it left me scarred for a very, very long time. Healing was not easy.

I think I couldn't step out of the house for nearly a month. I felt as though everyone was judging me. I didn't go to the park for at least three months. I was going for a meeting one afternoon, and as I was walking outside City Mall, a young girl stopped me and said, 'I have seen your photograph.' I felt numb; I had never thought that this would become my identity. The girl then said, 'I just wanted to tell you that you don't look like that kind of person, and I trust you.' I don't think that girl ever knew how much her words meant to me, but after that, I started going out once again.

When after this extremely painful incident I received the National Award for *I Am* in 2012, I felt vindicated.

When I was working on *Omar*, I had reached out to Humsafar Trust for help with research and data of how the LGBTQIA community was being targeted through Section 377. The truth is that there were very few actual arrests and sentencing because most people who were blackmailed paid huge sums of money to protect themselves. The police also abused many, both sexually and financially—it was not uncommon for people who were caught cruising or making out in public places.

Blackmail is something the community still has to deal with. Though the law no longer criminalizes us, many are not open about their sexuality. Our society is still far from being inclusive. There are many fake accounts of men on Grindr and Tinder who hook up and then get violent and blackmail their victims; sometimes they use force, and with closeted men, the trick that works is the threat of exposure.

Going back to 2009, after returning from Berlin, I had put up a post on my Facebook page about why I wanted to make *Abhimanyu*. I think the campaign was rather innovative, and 'WHY ABHIMANYU' spoke about how the story touched me and why I felt the film should be made. Anyone who felt the way we did could become a part of the film by becoming a co-producer/co-owner, by contributing with finances or by volunteering in various departments during production.

The first cheque that came in was for Rs 2,000, and both Amar and I were thrilled. We felt that the film would get made and that we should open a bank account for it. What was more touching was the message with the cheque: 'I feel that with this film, my story will be finally told. I am a student in Pune and this is all I can contribute. I cannot reveal my name, I prefer to remain as D.' Over the next few months, before we started shooting the film, I met many survivors. There were men and women who came to our office; some of them wept as they shared their stories of surviving sexual abuse and remaining silent for so many years. For some, it was cathartic to be able to speak to someone without the fear of being judged. To get so much trust was an overpowering feeling—all I did was lend a ear.

One of those days, Harish Iyer, a CSA survivor and human rights activist, came over to our office. He narrated to me the horrific story of his sexual abuse as a child.* I feel outraged whenever I hear about children being sexually abused, very often by family members and trusted friends. Harish gave me a lot of insight into the mindset of a survivor. I included a pet cat in the film because he explained to me how he had found refuge and comfort in his pet dog. That was a space of unconditional love. Merle thought that the cat would be interesting, and we drew parallels to the way Abhimanyu developed as a character—someone who seeks attention and isn't 'loyal'.

The process of making *I Am* again affirmed my belief that film-making is not a one-man show. There was a collective energy driving us in making this film. There were activists like Pooja Taparia from Arpana and Vidya from Tulir who came forward with not just contributions but also reached out to others to join us in making this film possible. We were also forming precious bonds through the process. Similarly, when we put out the post seeking crowdfunding for *Omar*, a new set of associations formed. Humsafar Trust came in as one of the major producers for this story. The entire team of Vivek, Ashok, Pallav and Sohail have always been supportive of the work I did. Then there was Pawan from SAATHII, and of course the lovely Anjali Gopalan, whom I met in her Delhi office. I still remember her saying with a chuckle that the problem with the 'boys' was that they were all ready to party but not to contribute when it came to films like this, be it through funding or by going to the theatre. It is true that there are so many financially powerful gay men and women. If they

---

* Anjali Bisaria, 'Activist Harish Iyer Shares His Gutwrenching Story of Being Raped for 11 Years as a Kid', It News, 13 January 2016, https://www.indiatimes.com/news/india/activist-harish-iyer-shares-his-gutwrenching-story-of-being-raped-for-11-years-as-a-kid-249359. html. Accessed on 14 March 2022.

contributed to the making of films narrating our stories, it would help the community a lot, but . . .

Many started to offer their services for the film as volunteers. Arches, a young journalist from the *Times of India*, interviewed me in Goa. He had done his research well, and I enjoyed being interviewed by him. After the interview, he asked me if he could assist me. That was a smart move, since I was already convinced that he would be an asset, and he joined as assistant. There was Sandeep Malani from Bangalore, who volunteered as assistant for two stories, and Aarambh Singh from Whistling Woods, who made the first fundraising promo for *Omar*. Nalini Ratnam volunteered to do the casting in Bangalore and Archana Balan did the line production for *Abhimanyu*. Fashion designer Aki Narula offered to style for *Abhimanyu*.

There were a lot of people from overseas who became a part of making *I Am*. There was Sonia from Germany, who regularly sent me funds throughout the production and later even invited Juhi, Sanjay and me to a special screening of *My Brother Nikhil* and *I Am* in Frankfurt. She lovingly called it the 'Onir Film Festival'. There was Rahul Dutta from Dubai, who also became a co-producer along with his wife, Karishma. When Juhi and I went to Dubai for the Asia Vision Awards, he was there in the audience with Karishma, cheering for our film. There were people from different countries who volunteered and did subtitles in German, French, Italian, Spanish and Chinese.

The celebrated Karachi-based film-maker Nabeel Qureshi and producer Fizza Ali Meerza also came on board as co-producers, and Nabeel also cut a promo for *Omar*. We used the promos on social media to raise more funds. I finally met Nabeel and Fizza during my first trip to Karachi in 2012, and we remain close friends. I feel it's a huge loss for both our industries and for the artists that there is an embargo on collaborations and showing our films in each other's countries. But thanks to OTT platforms, a lot of those barriers are now broken. I never understood why people should have problems when every collaborative effort will contribute towards building peace so that one day our soldiers do not have to sacrifice their lives at the border.

I remember my first trip to Karachi. We were a group of twelve from India going for the Indo–Pak media mela. I was supposed to screen *I Am Omar* there. We were all a little apprehensive because of the stereotypes the media has created. What seemed ridiculous is that we had to take a flight via Dubai to reach a place that's much closer to Bombay. At Dubai Airport, I ran into Urmi, who was on her way to Baghdad. We hugged tightly as we bid each other goodbye. After all, who knew what fate had in store for us!

When we landed at Karachi Airport, there was a loudspeaker announcing, '*Sab Hindustani uss taraf*'(All Indians to one side). That was intimidating, and it was only when we landed back in Bombay that we realized that a similar welcome lay in store for visitors from Pakistan at our airport. We met our hosts soon enough, and the minute we were in the bus, we forgot any hostility along with the fact that we were in a foreign country and needed to look out and take in the sights! From the airport to the hotel, we chatted like long-lost friends. At the end of our week-long stay there, I felt that some of us had formed bonds for life. There is the ever-smiling Chuck Lala (Raheel Nabi), who keeps teasing me about me being a 'celeb', and then there is the warm and kind Yusra Askari and the naughty crime journalist Norbert Almeida (his in-laws live in Goa), journalist Shiraz Hassan, Samra Muslim. And of course there was the beautiful and brave Sabeen Mahmud. She was shot a few years later for being who she was. I remember how she faced criticism during the conference as a lot of the Pakistani women wore saris and bindis, reclaiming it as a part of their identity. Bindis and a sari were considered by some as symbols of Hindu identity and hence not approved of.

I was very careful about how I behaved with the women in Pakistan because of my stereotyped notions of what would be considered appropriate in an Islamic state. I soon realized that my beliefs were misplaced and my interactions there were no different from my interactions with women friends here. Though the atmosphere during the official events was different, the common element throughout was the warmth. We used to party every night, and it was amazing. I remember being pampered with gifts and treated to delicious food every day. I remember nights at Biryani of the Seas (BOTS) and all the food I ate there. I have always wondered if I could ever match the hospitality and love I received there if my friends were to visit Bombay.

I said it then, and I will say it now, that when I went for my first trip to Karachi, the warmth that I experienced was such that I have never felt so loved and at home anywhere else in the world. It also made me immensely sad to see how brutally we were divided and how the communal forces still continue to thrive by dividing us at every opportunity they get. Sometimes I wish there was nothing like religion, and I hate how it's always pitting people against people instead of talking about love. Who is better, whose God is more powerful . . . instead of helping spread love, empathy, peace and kindness, religion manifests itself as one of the main reasons for violence and hate.

We went for the Bangalore recce for *Abhimanyu* when we had just Rs 7 lakh, and we needed another Rs 25 lakh to be able to complete the six-day shoot. You have to remember that this was before digital shooting became the norm. The biggest advantage of shooting in digital is that you do not need to restrict how much you shoot the way you had to while using expensive stock. Digital film-making has, in a way, democratized film-making—the tools of shooting and editing are much more easily accessible now. The best example is a film made by film-maker Rima Das, *The Village Rockstar*, which was shot digitally with a miniscule budget. She

wrote, produced, shot, edited and directed the film and it went on
to being selected as India's entry at the Oscars in 2019. You can
even make a film on an iPhone now if you really wanted to. We
shot *Abhimanyu* on 16 mm to save money. We got the lighting
unit from Madras as the transport would cost less and the crew
from Madras was cheaper than the Bombay crew.

Once we were back from Bangalore, it was hectic for Sanjay
and me to reach out to every possible person we knew through
social media and otherwise. We were posting testimonials of people
who had joined in as crew, of our cast and of people who were
contributing. Another reason we chose to start with *Abhimanyu*
was that I could take Sanjay for granted. I knew he would be
comfortable playing a damaged, bisexual CSA survivor. I wanted
the vulnerability element and the player bit in the character, and
I knew that Sanjay would be great in bringing out each of these
elements. The role most difficult to cast was that of the father.
Some actors didn't feel comfortable playing the abuser while
others didn't find the length of the role tempting enough. I finally
reached out to Anurag Kashyap. I knew that many theatre artists
approached him for work and thought that he could perhaps help
me find someone. I sent him the script and he called up and asked
if we could meet. When we met, he told me that he was abused as
a child* and that he would like to do the role himself. That meant
a lot to me because I could see that it was something that had hurt
him deeply, and he was moved by our script and wanted to be a

---

* 'When Anurag Kashyap Revealed of Getting Abused as a Child by a
22-Year-Old', Koimoi.com, 28 September 2020, https://www.koimoi.
com/bollywood-news/when-anurag-kashyap-revealed-of-getting-
abused-as-a-child-by-a-22-year-old/. Accessed on 18 March 2022;
'Anurag Kashyap Was a Victim of Sexual Abuse? - TOI', YouTube,
17 May 2015, https://www.youtube.com/watch?v=XsHevjP2Pmo.
Accessed on 18 March 2022; 'Child abuse: Battling the stigma',
YouTube: NDTV, 16 July 2008. Accessed on 18 March 2022.

part of the film. Shernaz Patel and Radhika Apte were both kind enough to say yes because the script stirred them.[*]

I was once again working with Arvind Kannabiran as DOP and Arun Nambiar for sound. We introduced a new music composer, Rajiv Bhalla, with the song '*Bojhhal si lamho ki saye*'. Amitabh Varma was writing the lyrics once more. Elton Fernandez came in to do the make-up for the entire film—another new friendship that I cherish. I have seen very few make-up artists who take so much pride in what they do. He read the script, understood the characters and worked on the look that was needed for the film and not necessarily what the actor wanted. He was deeply invested in the film. We started shooting for *Abhimanyu* in July 2009. One of my favourite scenes is when Abhimanyu tells Natasha that he was abused as a child. Sanjay was powerful in the scene, and it was difficult for me to control my tears during the shoot. After the shot, I went to the balcony and had a good cry. I felt Elton's arms on my shoulder comforting me. 'It's okay, it has happened to many of us.' I told him that I had never been sexually abused as a child; I was moved because the performance was so real and that I knew that Abhimanyu represented multiple men and women who had faced this.

I made a conscious decision to have a man as the survivor. There were two reasons. One, the number of boys who get abused is more or less the same as the number of girls, and it's only shame that prevents them from speaking out. Also, many accept it as a part of growing up. A girl child is at times a little more conscious of and protected by the family against unsafe touch. Boys don't get told about this concept. Two, I felt that many men in the audience wouldn't empathize the way I wanted them to if the survivor was a

[*] 'Anurag Kashyap Was a Victim of Sexual Abuse? - TOI', YouTube, 17 May 2015, https://www.youtube.com/watch?v=XsHevjP2Pmo. Accessed on 18 March 2022.

girl child. I wanted them to feel uncomfortable and accept that it could be a boy child too.

During the shoot, one of the contributors sent lunch for the entire unit one day, another person let us use his car. It was amazing to experience this love and trust.

By the time we started shooting for *Abhimanyu*, I had also started to cast for *Omar* as there were overlapping scenes to be shot. The character of Jai from *Omar* was Abhimanyu's friend. Rahul Bose read the script and called me immediately with a yes. He had lots of questions about how far I wanted to push the narrative and my approach to the characters. It is always energizing for a film-maker when your actor is so invested in the character.

After the shoot of *Abhimanyu*, we put in all our energy to raise funds for *Omar*. *Omar* was to be shot in Bombay, which automatically made it more expensive. By now, Arjun Mathur had agreed to be a part of the film, but casting the abusive police officer was not easy as many were not comfortable with the idea of the character forcing another man to give a blowjob. I had seen *Rakta Charitra* and loved Abhimanyu Singh. I was a little apprehensive about whether he would agree, but I really wanted him as the cop had to be physically intimidating. Luckily for us, he looked at the role as a challenge he wanted to take up.

We started shooting *Omar* in August 2009. We started ideating on the third story in between the two shoots. I had wanted to do something in Kashmir ever since my first trip in 2008. Sanjay's story as a person who had lost his home always touched me deeply. I've always felt connected to his loss, having myself lost my childhood home, Thimphu. The first time I went to Kashmir to research a story, I lived with my friend Azaan and his family. It had been lovely to sit with the family every night, chatting for hours while holding a *kangri* (a cane basket with live coals) under the blanket. During that visit, I had gone to what used to be Sanjay's home; he gave me directions over the mobile, and I finally found the house and the tree which he had said would be outside the gate. Sanjay hadn't been back home for seventeen years, ever since the fateful night in 1990 when Uncle was shot, and I wept for his loss. I wanted to know if Sanjay was open to us doing something inspired from his experience of leaving home.

The first two stories were co-written by Merle and me and had male protagonists. I wanted the next two stories to have women as the central characters and, as with the first two, have one Hindu lead character and a Muslim one. I spoke to my friend and writer Urmi Juvekar to come on board as I knew that she could give the concept the texture that it needed. It was not an easy topic. She thought that it would be good to see the story from the perspective of two women as we hardly get to see conflict from the point of view of women. She also thought it could be a poignant story of loss—the loss of a Pandit woman's home and identity and the loss of her Muslim friend who is stuck in a space of conflict where her life has stagnated. Urmi brought in a certain tenderness and poignancy to the story that made it my favourite in the anthology.

Sanjay, Urmi and I went to Kashmir for a location recce and research trip. It was an emotional journey for Sanjay, but he was also happy to be back in the place of his birth. That's when we discovered Ahdoos, which has become my go-to restaurant whenever I am in Srinagar. I love the *gostaba, ristaa, methi maaz* and the *ahdoos pulao.* The waiters there recognize me and welcome me with warmth every time I go back. We were staying at Hotel Heevan Resort at Nishat Bagh; the owner, Faizan Burza, offered to host us during the shoot and also became a co-producer for the film.

We returned to Bombay and got busy with the *Omar* pre-production while Urmi started developing the script of *Megha.* Even before the story was developed, I had told Juhi that she would have to do a story and also be a co-producer. She always jokes, 'Onir made me pay to get a role in his film.' I feel Juhi sensed the character's anguish when we were finally in Srinagar in October 2009, shooting amongst the deserted Pandit homes in Karan Nagar.

Having Manisha Koirala in the film to star alongside Juhi was like a dream come true. She is 'Kuch na Kaho' in my contacts list. That's the effect her effervescent beauty has. I loved how she surrendered herself to the role and was happy that she didn't really have to put on make-up and get her hair done for the shoot every morning. It was lovely when on some evenings we sat with her by the fireplace at Heevan Resort and, over a glass of wine, talked about life and art. She's a beautiful soul. Later, when I went to Kathmandu for a screening of *I Am* for the Blue Diamond Society, Manisha came over for the screening. The audience was overjoyed when I spoke to them in Nepali.

Shooting in Srinagar was not easy. There was always the danger that someone from the crowd could be planning an attack. We would shoot in three to four different locations each day, the idea being that we would not be in any one place for long. Only Sanjay, AD Amar, line producer Faizal Burza, the security head and I would know the next day's plan. The minute we commenced shooting, a crowd would start gathering. We had to be extra careful as telling the 'Pandit' story was not going to be popular with a majority of the local populace. There would be a lot of security needed whenever we were shooting outdoors to control the press as well as the civilians.

In 2009, it wasn't easy to get junior artists for a shoot in Srinagar, and getting women to come in front of the camera was even tougher. There are exceptions, but even now in 2020, as I tried to get a girl to agree to do some shots for a music video, I realized how reluctant they were. Patriarchy, in the guise of religious morals, dictates the space allocated to women in Kashmir. Men will mostly deny that there is any such problem, but over the years I have met some amazingly brave women from Kashmir working in a hostile atmosphere of conflict. They face even more challenges than their male counterparts, having to deal with patriarchy in the form of religion as well as tradition, and the presence of the armed forces doesn't make things easier. The gaze of the forces has also driven many to seek the comfort of the hijab.

In 2022, as I plan to shoot the sequel to *I Am* called *We Are*, I'm finding it difficult to cast a Kashmiri woman for a certain role. And casting a Kashmiri boy to play a gay character is challenging.

My friend and assistant Azaan and his family helped us a lot during the shoot. Ambika went to their home and to the homes of some other friends to source items we could use for production design. Azaan's brother volunteered to act in a scene and also gathered all his friends to be there as background faces. We were shooting a scene in Karan Nagar, where the character played by Faheem asks Megha if she is a tourist and she replies that she is a Kashmiri Pandit. When he comments, 'Oh, the ones who had fled?', she shouts angrily in Kashmiri, 'Fled or made to leave?' We knew that this was a sensitive dialogue and people could possibly react, so I told Juhi that she should act as if she was shouting, but her voice shouldn't be audible.

Later that same day, while shooting in a narrow lane near Habba Kadal, someone threw a stone at the camera. It missed the camera but hit one of my assistants. We left immediately. We were told that we couldn't shoot with Juhi and Manisha at Habba Kadal, downtown, as that was the epicentre of stone throwing. So we shifted our actors and crew to a safer lane, and Arvind and I, along with two more people, went to Habba Kadal and pretended to be a Doordarshan team shooting some documentary. That's how we managed to have enough shots of the area to be able to recreate the atmosphere in the edit.

We had hired two little girls for two days of shoot, and on the second day, the father suddenly doubled the rate. When questioned, he resorted to the horrible tactic of screaming loudly in a bid to instigate the crowd: 'You guys come from outside and misuse the locals.' Thankfully, our local team handled the situation immediately. Similarly, the owner of the building we were showing as Juhi's house decided after the second day of shoot that he wouldn't allow us to shoot the third day as he wanted to start dismantling the house. It was ironic because the house had once actually belonged to a Pandit and the present owner was a ex-militant who wanted to dismantle this beautiful house and make a modern cement structure. Yes, I know I'm sounding like those nostalgic, unrealistic outsiders who want time to stand still. The truth is that the old has to make way for the new till the old eventually disappears. What comes up in place of the old is unfortunately very ugly most of the time. Juhi finally came to our rescue as she had become friends with the ladies of the house, and they convinced the men that we should be allowed to complete the shoot. After so many years, I find it kind of sweet that his son messages me on Instagram. He has memories from the shoot and wants to be a part of the film industry.

I knew that with *Megha*, we would perhaps not make everyone happy. We didn't want to unfold a narrative of hate but wanted it to be about loss. After *Megha* was shot came the difficult part. The first three stories had happened relatively fast, probably because many people identified with the stories and wanted to be a part of our journey. *Afia* wasn't easy, partly because we had to change the story because of a rather unfortunate reason. Like *Megha*, Merle and I had started developing the story for *Afia* around July. I wanted to tell a story inspired by Merle's journey to discover her father. We thought it would be interesting to see how a twenty-five-year-old German girl deals with the discovery that she is actually half-Indian and her coming to India in search of her biological father. I had found an actor who I thought would be a perfect fit, and we met in our office. She seemed very excited, and I introduced her to Merle over e-mail so that they could exchange ideas. We started working on the script, and then in August, *That Girl in Yellow Boots* was announced. The premise was too close to our story and I had to drop the idea. So, after the *Megha* shoot, we started thinking of various possible stories. Among them was a story about NGO corruption, which turned out to be really powerful but somehow did not fit with the theme. That is when Urmi came up with the concept of single motherhood and sperm donation. She had seen an advertisement of a sperm donation clinic in the newspaper that amused her, and now it seemed to be the perfect fit. (This was written three years before *Vicky Donor* released in 2012.)

When we spoke to Nandita Das, she was excited not only by the script, but also because there was a lot of talk in the media about the unique way in which we were making this film. Purab had to be a part of this film in some way, and having him as the donor seemed just perfect. I always associate KK's version of the song '*Ek ajnabi hasina*' with Purab and Nandita. The story behind casting Anurag Basu is funny. I was at Juhu Marriott for a meeting. Suddenly, Anurag Basu comes walking to me and asks for Rs 500 to pay the cab. He had forgotten his wallet. I gave him the money and told him that it was his signing amount and I wanted him as the Bengali doctor. He not only readily agreed but also bought his own flight ticket.

Once the script was developed, we decided that it would be best to start the anthology with *Afia* as it was the gentlest of the four. Till then, the sequence had been *Omar, Abhimanyu, Megha*. I had earlier planned how we would transition from one story to another; *Afia* ended with Afia in the cab and a long shot of the Calcutta street, *Omar* began with a night shot of Marine Drive with Jai in the car and *Omar* ended with Jai driving off into the night. I had wanted to cut from that close-up wipe to *Abhimanyu* on his bike in a Bangalore street at night. *Abhimanyu* ends with the girl in the dream doing the flying gesture, and the next shot was to be clouds through the plane window from Megha's point of view. The shikara going away was supposed to be the last shot of the film. We later realized that there would be a lot of people who would get so shocked by *Omar* that they wouldn't watch the next two stories, so we made *Megha* the second story and *Omar* the last one.

I think I never mentioned why Abhimanyu sees himself as a girl in his dream. I had written this down when I was studying in Jadavpur University—the images were from a childhood dream. In my dream, I had seen myself as a young girl, and I thought it would be beautiful to use that image for Abhimanyu. It also added another dimension to his bisexuality.

The *Afia* shoot was special for me because it was the first time I was shooting fiction in Calcutta. The funding took time, and we finally managed to start shooting in February 2010. Satyajit Ray Film & Television Institute (SRFTI) was sporting enough to provide stay for the crew at discounted rates. I shared a room with one of my assistants, Akhil, whom I had nicknamed 'Gunda'. After the shoot, we would often stand in the balcony, having a drink and chatting about various things. Designers Dev and Nil volunteered to do the styling; Mallika Jalan offered to do our line production.

By the time we were ready to shoot *Afia*, my associate Amar Kaushik had gotten busy with *No One Killed Jessica*. He had asked my permission and I knew that though I would miss him, it was important for him to do a bigger film and also get paid. Instead of me paying Amar, his wife Nalini had ended up contributing to the funds and becoming a co-producer for *I Am*. When I told him that he should go ahead for the other film, he had tears in his eyes as he had not expected it to be so easy. He came back as my associate when I was shooting for *Shab* in 2015–16.

I reached out to Vinay Waikul, who had been my first AD during *Bas Ek Pal*. He was free and immediately offered to join us. He refused whatever little money I offered him and said that it was his contribution to the film. Vinay was supposed to be my first AD for *Sorry Bhai!*, and just before the shoot he had been offered Aamir Khan's *Ghajini*. Of course, I had told him to take that up. I feel you need to celebrate the growth of everyone who works with you.

The craziest shoot was on the Calcutta metro. We just had permission to shoot during the first two hours of the services. It was extremely difficult for Nandita to change costumes twice during those two hours. When budgets are small and yet you manage to shoot what you want, the satisfaction is immense. Shooting with Juhi at Gariahat and at Flury's was a nightmare in terms of crowd control. The sari shopkeeper in Gariahat was so overwhelmed that he gifted Juhi a beautiful sari. She posed for a photograph with the sari and returned it to him saying that it was a beautiful sari, but she hardly ever wore one and he should not waste it on her. I love her grace. When we were shooting at Flury's, three little girls broke through the cordon, rushed up to Juhi and just screamed in their excitement.

*Afia* was the only story we shot on 35 mm film as we hadn't been able to afford 35 mm for the rest, shooting them on 16 mm. Calcutta had no flicker-free light available at that time, and we had wanted the clinic sequences to have a cold look, which was not achievable with 16 mm. My friends teased me that I was being biased as it was my city. Of course, my writer Urmi was happy at the special attention given to her script. One of the practices I like to follow is to always call up and check with the writer if I am making a change in the script during the shoot. It is someone's work, and it's important for a film-maker to respect that.

After the shoot, other challenges came up. Mithoon, who had composed two songs, was in contract with a music company. None of us had expected that there would be a problem as their relationship was great and I was totally open to taking our music to the music company. The music company honcho we were dealing with was an arrogant man who thought he could treat us according to his whims. He is one of those high-handed Bollywood personalities who exploit talent, and the industry is finally speaking up against this. He not only refused to offer any upfront MG (minimum guarantee) for our music, but he also berated our film for being 'non-commercial' and said that we would need to pay them Rs 75 lakh to promote the music and that we could not do the promotions of the film through anyone else. Sanjay and I have this one policy: whatever the challenges are, we will not allow anyone to blackmail us. We walked out, and the music company said they wouldn't let us use Mithoon's songs for the film. I reached out to Amit Trivedi, who was a darling and made two extra songs for us at a very, very discounted rate. The irony is that the song '*Issi baat pe*' composed by Amit Trivedi and written by Amitabh Bhattacharya later won the National Award for best lyrics.

I had to wait another seven years before we could use Mithoon's songs for *Shab*, of course reprogrammed. But this experience was not nice—this is what I call the industry bully, one who squeezes the independent artist as much as they can.

Sanjay and I believed that with the wonderful ensemble cast of talented actors, we would get a studio to take up our film for distribution. The OTT platforms were not there yet, even though I'm no longer sure how they would have reacted to the film. But at that time, even before the fight with the film certification board began, the journey of rejection had started. No one wanted to touch a 'serious', 'dark' film. It's okay to deal with dark and serious themes as long as it's 'entertaining', we were told. How you make 'child sexual abuse' entertaining, I really don't know. I was working on stories that had moved me and I believed would move my viewers. Months passed and nothing was on the horizon. I think I have survived this repeated rejection only because of the constant and unwavering strength and support I have received

from my friend Sanjay. He never made me regret what we were
doing. Yes, we did at times wistfully think that if would be nice to
make some money while pursuing creative happiness, but that was
not what drove us. Otherwise, we wouldn't have made *Chauranga*
after *I Am*.

The next big challenge that we faced was the CBFC. After
the first screening, we were told that the film would get an 'A'
certificate and we needed to cut about twenty-one minutes from
the *Omar* section of *I Am* and another couple of minutes from
*Abhimanyu*, and some dialogues were to be muted in *Megha*. I
was shocked that the board members evaluating my film were
so LGBTQIA illiterate and had equally messed-up ideas about
women's rights.

For *Omar*, their observation began with, 'You have shown two
men looking at each other romantically, this is not acceptable . . .'
You can imagine what they thought about the police assault on the
gay couple. What helped me fight this was the Delhi High Court
judgment that decriminalized homosexuality in 2009, just before
we shot the film. I had incorporated this in the film, but it was still
not applicable to the rest of the country.

For *Abhimanyu*, they remarked, 'How can a mother be shown
as someone who is aware of the abuse the child is facing?' These
illiterate people were not aware that most child abuse happens within
the family, and that very often parents know and either overlook it
or pretend it never happened. Different CSA organizations were
funders of the film and I had checked the script with them as I
didn't want to communicate anything wrong. But . . .

The third ridiculous remark that I remember was for *Megha*.
They wanted the slogan 'We want the Pandit men to leave at
once but leave their women behind' removed. They said this
was derogatory towards women, clearly not understanding the
dynamics of war/conflict where women are targeted to demoralize
and weaken the men.

We spent six months trying to get the film certified. And finally, I had to edit out about three minutes of the film, mostly from *Omar*, but also those two crucial dialogues in *Abhimanyu* and *Megha*. While this drama was happening, Sanjay was trying his best to get us a distributor or production house. This time, we were not as lucky. Finally, Juhi said that she would help us release the film. She introduced us to her friend Anish Modi, and together they provided the release funds. The film was released in 2011, nearly a year after we had completed the post-production work.

The film went on to win two National Awards. It was a high—a moment of vindication. But the awards didn't make the journey any easier. Six months later, my bags were packed and I was ready to leave Bombay, unable to find the funds to continue to make films or sustain myself. Sanjay and Juhi convinced me to not give up. I unpacked the bags.

As we celebrate ten years of the release of *I Am*, I feel sad that I have not been able to recover enough of the investment to be able to return the release money or the amounts put in by my various co-producers. The system does not allow you to tell these stories. The film travelled to various film festivals all over the world and won many awards. But I did not have any work after that. A few months later, while returning from Hyderabad, I switched on my phone upon landing in Bombay and found scores of new messages. The phone rang before I could read any of them. Sanjay was on the line, telling me that *I Am* had just won the National Award for Best Hindi Film, 2011. As I was speaking with him, we realized that Amitabh Bhattacharya had also received the National Award for best lyrics for our film. I was there at the airport, weeping with all kinds of mixed emotions. The film's commercial failure, the inability to find any TV channel willing to buy our film, the absence of work opportunities and the fake scandal against me had left me exhausted. And then this happened. It gave me back my confidence, in a way, to continue fighting. Though the euphoria did not translate into work, nor did it mean that our film got sold, but I got back my faith in my work.

Now when I am making *We Are*, I don't have the energy to go the *I Am* route, not because I am sceptical about getting support, but because I am disheartened. When we were making the film and it turned out to have such an incredible cast, I had hoped that we would make enough money to pay everyone back. I used to dream about how we would maybe make some extra money as well, and how I would be able to share that with all those who made this dream happen. But years passed and no sales happened. When the platforms came in, they too offered next to nothing. This is what crushed me. But today more than ever, I feel the need to push myself to find ways to make my movies. I need to talk about queer lives from the subcontinent. Our stories are still as precious.

The awards gave me the courage to sacrifice the possibility of NFDC part-funding *Shab* so that they part-funded *Chauranga* instead. This was our first production that I did not direct. Bikas Mishra, whom I had met in Locarno, directed the film. Both Bikas and I were in the NFDC Binge Lab script workshop in Locarno, and he had told me about his script. I read it and loved it. I knew I could never direct a film like this, yet I could feel for the characters and the script fascinated me. I told Bikas, 'I don't know how, but I want to try and produce this film.' We started shooting the film in 2013, with Mohan Mulani from Singapore as co-producer. A kind man whose love for cinema made him want to support us, he is also co-producer of *Shab*. We didn't realize that times were unfortunately becoming tougher for indie films, and neither film did well at the box office or manage to recover costs from OTT platforms. The world of big players was marginalizing us day by day. This experience made me decide to stop producing films after 2017. I cannot bear the burden of failing to recover someone's investment. Film-making is a very unpredictable business and that is what makes it most stressful.

With every film, one makes some beautiful connections. I remember going to meet actor Prosenjit Chatterjee for some work when I saw this beautiful lady in jeans and a white shirt come down the stairs. I was totally smitten by Arpita Chatterjee. Prosenjit always reminds me that I had come to cast him and ended up casting Arpita not only for *Chauranga* but also for *Shab*. She has not only become my dear friend, but also my mother's favourite.

During *Chauranga*, I learnt how to be a producer and not try and step into the director's shoes. Except when Bikas wanted some creative advice, I avoided giving him any suggestions. It had to be, and is, his vision. He had a team of young assistants apart from his first AD Sandip—Suraj, Chakshu, Siddharth, Nikunj and . . . Two of the boys fell in love with the same girl and that was some drama, indeed. For nearly a month before the shoot, the team lived in our Calcutta house. The first schedule was shot in Bolpur.

Because of my Bengal connection, we managed to rope in many amazing Bengali artists. The two boys who were the lead were the very talented Soham and Riddhi Sen. Soham's love interest was Ena Shah. My friend and talented actor Tannistha Chatterjee was the Dalit woman, and Dhritiman Chatterjee the slimy blind priest. Unfortunately, I think we cast Swatilekha Chatterjee for a role that could not do her talent justice. Sanjay played the zamindar, apart from handling the production with Rahul Bhanja.

The labour laws of the Calcutta film industry were tough, and the monsoon made the shoot even more difficult. We lost a lot of precious time and finally decided to shift the second schedule to the Keonjhar district in Odisha.

*Chauranga* later won the award for best film in the India Gold competition at MAMI 2014 and the best feature film award at the Los Angeles Indian Film Festival (IFFLA) 2015.

It was around this time that I met my 'Little Buddha', but I will talk about it elsewhere.

You,
Who choose oblivion,
And left me with ashes as memento,
You too will adorn my canvas,
The fire and the smoke.

And you,
Whose smile floats into my slumber,
Who I am yet to meet,
Your kiss too will find its way,
Tapping on my keyboard.

I do not live to experience the end
But to discover new beginnings.

# 23

# Pakistan Stories

After the shoot of *Chauranga*, I was again invited to Karachi to attend the Sindh Festival with Shabana Azmi. We were supposed to be Bilawal Bhutto's guests. I was very excited as I would meet my friends once again. Moreover, I couldn't meet Nabeel on my last trip, and this time I knew we would finally meet. I asked my assistant, Chakshu, to come along. We planned to fly into Lahore and return via Wagah. The first time I visited, I realized that one needs to mention the cities one plans to visit on the visa and also stick to the return route mentioned therein.

There's one funny episode that I forgot to mention from the earlier Karachi trip. When an Indian goes to Pakistan and vice versa, you have to report to the police station every day or every few days or while entering or leaving the country, depending on your visa status. Among the delegates who were supposed to report to the police were journalist Karuna John, comedian Sanjay Rajoura and me. One of the Pakistani hosts came along with us, and the experience was right out of a bad Hindi film.

The police officer had his feet on the table and started asking us all kinds of strange questions about why we were in Karachi, when the fact was that we had been invited for an official event and not a private one. At some point, the officer offered Karuna an egg that was laid in the police station by a hen that was around. I do not know why he did it, but he insisted that it be consumed and Pakistani hospitality remembered. The Indian SIM card does not work in Pakistan, and we weren't supposed to have local SIM cards, but I had arranged for one. When the police guy asked me if I had a mobile, I said yes and received a kick under the table from our Pakistani host. I quickly added that it was the Indian mobile that was not functional here. Somehow, the man seemed too interested in me for my comfort. The questioning went on for nearly three hours, and he even wanted the details of my Facebook page. That was when I got the second kick under the table. Revealing my Facebook ID might not have been a great idea as my profile at that point proclaimed, 'I am Gay and I refuse to be Invisible'. Of course, at that point, I rather craved invisibility. Luckily, there was a power cut. The police officer noted my name 'Anirban Dhar' and said he would check my profile later. As we were allowed to leave, I was chuckling . . . he wouldn't find me as 'Anirban Dhar' on Facebook for there I was just 'Onir'! Later, we were endlessly teased that one Christian and two Hindus were picked on for reporting to the cops. We experienced so much love otherwise that this experience never merited anything more than some laughter.

I had never seen so many people with guns in my entire life as I did on the streets of Karachi. Every house with high walls had armed guards, and the newspapers, along with the weather report, horoscope and films, had a map of crimes committed. I remember there being as many as 103 shootings or killings in one day during our stay.

Shabana and I, along with Chakshu, were put up at the Karachi Marriott. There was a lot of security around us, unlike the 2012 trip when I could just roam around with my friends. But my friends would now land up at the hotel and we would go out after the event every day. I finally met Nabeel, who drove me around Karachi and showed me his city while narrating many fascinating stories. When he visited Bombay and sang Mohit Chauhan's 'Guncha koi' in my house, my mother commented, 'But you are not a foreigner.' He laughed and replied, 'Aunty, I am not.'

Being Bilawal Bhutto's guest meant more security. The second night, someone knocked on my door at 2 a.m. and wanted to know if he had left his pants in my room. Before you start imagining things, he was NOT one of my Grindr dates. I panicked and called Chakshu, who was in the next room. By the time the security guys came up, the man had disappeared. One of the questions he had was if we were from Gujarat. When I told Shabana about the scare, she immediately spoke to the authorities. The entire floor was vacated, and we were now the only guests on that floor. Security was also increased further.

When Bilawal heard how Shabana and I loved mutton *nihari*, he sent hot *nihari* and naan to the hotel early one morning. It was truly delicious, but the quantity could have fed ten people.

One day, Shabana and I casually walked across to the other side of the road, where stood an art museum. Within ten minutes, a convoy of security men descended upon us, admonishing us for not informing them. They told us that walking around like that was not safe. We dismissed their warning, thinking they were being paranoid, but we realized how stupid we were being just two days later. There was a bomb attack on the bus that brought the security personnel to the hotel every morning. Thirteen lives were lost; it was a very sad day for all of us. The screening of my film *I Am* was cancelled too as there was a bomb scare at the multiplex. I had to wait till 2018 before I could screen a film of mine in Pakistan. That was when *Kuchh Bheege Alfaaz* was screened at the Karachi International Film Festival.

Now for some fun Grindr facts. On my second visit to Pakistan, I knew that I could connect to the hotel Wi-Fi and use

WhatsApp, etc. I had no idea if anyone used Grindr here, but the first time I opened the app, I was glad that piracy exists. Piracy doesn't believe in borders and bans, and many from the queer community knew about my films and were keen to meet me. The next few days were rather interesting.

Now that we are no longer criminalized by law in India after the Supreme Court ruling on Article 377, I feel very sad at the state of the LGBTQIA communities in many other countries where you can be imprisoned, tortured and hanged for being queer. After the Taliban recently took over Afghanistan, so many people from the community have reached out to me to help them escape. Unfortunately, there is little I can do, and there is no special provision for queer Muslims who are persecuted in their countries to seek refugee in India. I have friends in Iran who are forced into living a life of duplicity, as the consequence of being discovered is a cruel death penalty.

Lahore was a short but memorable visit. The food street next to the music street . . . and the red light area was such a fascinating place. Walking across the border, I felt a rush of tears . . . Why were we divided, and why do we keep increasing the divide? We are actually, for all practical purposes, one.

# 24

## *Shab* (2017)

Immediately after my Pakistan visit, I started shooting *Shab*. My first script, written way back in 2000, was finally going to see the light of the day. I had never discarded the script; I had kept revisiting it for fourteen years, modifying it as the world around me changed. The film had got populated with more gay characters who were just living their lives—they were no longer merely 'issues'. Later, after the CBFC screening, I was told by a member, 'But you have shown them as normal.' I got so angry at that. He had actually called me 'not normal' through that one sentence. The entire process to get a 'UA' rating took nearly a year, and we had to go to the now-abolished Appellate Tribunal in Delhi, give references of my earlier film *My Brother Nikhil*, which had got a 'U' certificate in 2005, and *I Am*, which got 'U/A' in 2011. I remember my rage when an important member of the CBFC tried to reason with me saying, 'I understand you, Onir, and I respect you and your work, but try to understand that this will be seen by kids. What's the message? Can't you do something where these boys seem more like brothers?' I could not believe that someone could actually say something so sick. Lovers as brothers! But this was before the Supreme Court verdict decriminalized homosexuality, and this form of humiliation was common. I had to listen and keep arguing, keep trying to bend the 'rules' where I could. This is what has changed with the 2018 verdict. No one can dare say this to me again. I will not listen to such bullshit.

I shot *Shab* in Delhi over four different seasons. I did not want to cheat, so despite a low budget, we actually went and shot four separate times. And that is when I found You one evening, as my lover in a Lajpat Nagar *barsati* (small rooftop apartment). More on this later.

*Shab* brought a few more beautiful people into my life—my lead actor Ashish Bisht and French actor Simon Frenay. And though Arpita was already a friend when we shot *Chauranga*, *Shab* brought us really close. Also my DAs (director's assistants) Siddharth and Surya (I call him 'Fragile'), and Tanvi. Mitakshara, whom I call 'Paapi Pet' and who had worked as the third AD for *Bas Ek Pal*, came in as first AD. I remember when she had first approached me for a job as an AD, she had used this terrible line, 'Sir, *paapi pet ka sawaal hai* (I have to feed myself).' Of course, that was not the reason why I hired her. Ambika was the script supervisor and also the overall creative producer. She supervised the casting, acting workshops, art and costumes. This was Sachin's third film with me.

Ashish had come for an audition for a role in *I Am Afia* in 2010. We thought he had a spark and was very charming, but he was also too raw and needed to train and learn. He shifted to Bombay in 2011 and was under my guidance. Finally in 2014, we shot with him. I love his dedication and hard work, and his innocent look also worked for the role. It was not an instant choice—we had shortlisted many, among them the now-famous Kartik Aaryan. I had loved his audition, but the reason we didn't cast him was that he looked naughty and I needed innocence, a face that has not experienced the world, never fallen in love and probably has sex for the first time in his life as a character in the film.

I did a lot of workshops with my actors for *Shab*—with Ashish, Arpita, Areesz, Simon and Shray. I needed the gay characters to feel comfortable with the male touch and relax with each other as friends so that there would be no discomfort during the shoot. I told each actor to write their story before and after the film. Then I gave them situations that were not from the film but what the characters might face and get them to enact those. I like this process, as the actor starts owning the character. He/she/they start imagining the house, the clothes, food etc. Then I take bits and pieces of that and add it to the script. So the script has memories of the actors. I remember it's from Ashish's note that I made the character come from Dhanaulti, and I shot the zigzag road in the mountains the way he described it. With Ashish, the most difficult part was to get him to look with love at Arpita. So, Arpita used to tell me to show him how to do it and tell Ashish to imitate me. I love Arpita for how loving and mischievous she is. Later during the shoot, she would constantly tease me and embarrass me whenever there was any intimate scene to shoot by insisting that I act it out. It reminded me of a prank Juhi played on me during *Bas Ek Pal*.

There was a small, intimate moment in a song between her and Jimmy. Jimmy was lying shirtless on the bed, and she had to caress his face. It was simple, but she insisted that I should show her exactly what to do. Every time I pulled the bedsheet down, Jimmy pulled it up again, and then I showed Juhi how to caress him but without touching him. When the shot started, she did the same and did not touch him. She kept insisting that I do the scene as I wanted her to do it. So, finally, I made one of my assistants lie down in bed and I caressed his face, much to his embarrassment. While I was doing that, Juhi asked Sachin to roll the camera!

I had met Simon Frenay in Paris when I had gone for the screening of *My Brother Nikhil* and *I Am* at Forum des images in 2013. We spoke and met over the next few days. What really struck me about Simon, apart from him being a good actor, was the kindness that was a part of his personality. He was curious, interested and very much aware of the colonial discourse and fights fiercely for migrants in France. We were meant to be friends, and over the years he has become very special. He stayed in my house when he visited Bombay and Calcutta after the *Shab* shoot and has a special equation with my mother. Sometimes I feel that he FaceTimes with her more than with me. My mother feels excited about his Instagram and Facebook updates and never forgets to tell me the details. We had planned that he would come down with his mother to Bombay in 2020, but then the pandemic happened. When I first met him, I did not know he was gay. I am glad that his sexuality had nothing to do with him being cast as Benoit. 'Benoit', incidentally, was the name of a French volunteer at the Rabat International Author Film Festival I had attended and had a crush on.

I love the way Simon calls me and starts his conversation with, 'Hello, my Onir.' His use of 'my' makes me feel like I belong. Simon was definitely the favourite with the crew because of the kindness with which he treated everyone. Later in 2015, when Amar, Zain, Ashish and I were travelling in Europe after the first schedule of *Veda* in Manchester, we stayed with Simon in Paris and he took us around the city. We went to a gay strip club one night, and after a point Ashish and Zain asked why we couldn't go to a female strip club! I love how Simon handled this with dignity and told them that this was his city and he was showing his friends the places he loved, just like in India we had taken him to places we wanted him to see. After Paris, we travelled to Berlin, and then Ashish and Zain returned to India while Amar and I travelled to Spain. Amar is a great travel companion as he likes to experiment with food and loves to walk around, exploring places.

I remember spending my birthday in London—Ashish was very sleepy and went back to the hotel at 11.45 p.m. Amar, Zain and I were at a night club, and we didn't have enough money to keep buying as much booze as we wanted. Soon Amar made friends with an Arab who was sponsoring everyone's drinks! Another Saturday, when we were not shooting, all my ADs said that they wanted to visit a gay nightclub in Manchester, but the club was only for members. Being the smart one, Amar told the bouncer about my work for the community in India and even showed him my Wikipedia page! Soon we were all inside, dancing. At the end of the night, the boys were exchanging notes about whose bum got pinched how many times.

In 2021, after the pandemic restrictions had eased somewhat, I was in Delhi and caught up with my former DA, Surya. He wanted to take me out for a drink and we went to a joint in Connaught Place. The bouncer said, 'Stags not allowed.' I don't know what came over me, but I looked at Surya and, much to his shock and amazement, said, 'But we are partners.' The bouncer hesitated, asked my permission to go in and check, came back and escorted us in. Surya was smiling ear to ear. Later, a girl who probably recognized me, came up to us and said, 'Hi, I just wanted to tell you guys that I have been watching you, and you both look so cute together.' I am sure Surya has vowed to himself to never again come out drinking with me.

Coming back to the *Shab* shoot, there are so many memories of that one year. We had hired two flats for the assistants to live in. I would very often go in the morning when they were still waking up and cook lunch for them. And then, at times we all would go to the Lajpat Nagar Afghan restaurants to eat. I loved the food there.

When we were shooting in Rishikesh, I wanted Ashish and Arpita to climb up a small cliff. Ashish was rather sceptical about the safety, so I climbed up and helped Arpita too. I also stepped into the freezing river to encourage them to do the same. I feel I now understand better what the term 'captain of the ship' means.

The character of Neil, played by Areesz Gandhi, is very close to me. I feel that, in many ways, Nigel, Neil and Benoit had a lot of me in them. Neil's constant search for love, his lonely nights at bars, his getting mugged are all inspired by real life. The sequence when his lover says that he will get married but they can continue and 'father *ka toh death hi ho jayega* (this would kill my father)' are what my lovers had told me. Benoit's line to Neil, 'For how long will you hide yourself?' is an unspoken question to my lovers. I had cast a young boy for the role that Shray finally did, and a week before the shoot he called Ambika, saying that he wanted to opt out as his widowed mother had threatened to commit suicide if he did the role.

It was amazing how friends in Delhi went all out to help. Deepak Bharadwaj let us use all his expensive carpets and Kashmiri art for doing up one room of Raveena's house. Myna Mukherjee, who helped hugely in the art department, let us use invaluable original artwork from her gallery to design another room, while Winnie Singh let me pick up all *thankas* and Buddha artefacts from her house for the third room. This time too I was not lucky with the art department, but my friends saved the day. Ambika's dad, Ashok da, let us use his luxury cars as it would have cost us a lot to hire them. Similarly, Ambika's mom, Boudi, let us borrow a lot of her cutlery to set up the kitchen where we were staying. Ambika also borrowed real jewellery from her family for the shoot. My friend Varun Bahl was a sport to do a cameo in the modelling competition sequence, as was Deepak. Sanjay's brother, Raj Suri, flew down all the way from Australia to do the role of the flamboyant, gay designer. He was brilliant.

*Shab* had its share of other problems. The café in Hauz Khas Village where we shot Neil's Café in the first season outright refused to let us shoot in the same place in the second season. No amount of persuasion helped. Finally, we found Diggin and incorporated a bit in the script that explained that the prick of a landlord did not renew the lease for the earlier place.

There was also a kissing scene between Simon and Areesz that I wanted to shoot in the bungalow. Very soon, a crowd gathered and the minute the kiss happened, they started making crude and threatening comments. We shifted inside and shot the rest of the lovemaking scene in the bedroom. But again, what really impressed me is how the entire unit did not give a damn every time two men kissed. We just went on and shot the next scene.

I cannot not talk about the costumes of *Shab* when I am discussing the film. My friend Wendell Rodricks offered to style the character of Mohan, rechristened Azaffar (after my Pakistani actor friend), for free. He was so sweet that he sent his personal aviators and jackets for the shoot. Later, he even did a cameo as himself in the film. His passing away is a huge loss for the community and for me as a friend. I once spent an entire week in Goa with him and his beautiful partner Jerome, and the love and hospitality I experienced is something that I'll cherish forever. When I was leaving, he packed a lot of Goan sausages for me. Much after he left us, I kept having them, trying to extend the connection as long as I could. I want to see his dream project of a museum of costumes in India come true soon.

Mohan Mulani, who was part-producer for *Chauranga*, had rightly been disappointed with the financial outcome of the film. It's one thing to be told that there are risks and a totally different thing to face financial loss. He backed out for the last schedule of *Shab*, and I was (once again) desperately looking for a financier. This is when Sheetal, who was the producer of *Veda*, came in with the gap funds. The nightmarish experience of being unable to generate revenue, the pressure from different financiers and the unscrupulous agents who exploited my film and refused to pay what was due to me for years finally broke me. I decided to stop producing films.

Every bit of the journey from completing the film, to censor board certification, to releasing it in 2017 was a nightmare that I am still dealing with.

After struggling for a year, we decided to release the film independently. My friend Jas once again pitched in with the print and publicity money. But things were more difficult than the days of *My Brother Nikhil* as I did not have a powerful studio like YRF backing me, and the media would no longer write about your film because of the content alone. Welcome to a time when your YouTube/Facebook/Instagram/Twitter post will not reach enough viewers unless you spend money to boost viewership. There is very little that happens organically, and it was impossible to make the kind of noise required for a film like this. The concept of word of mouth wouldn't work here as I could just release the film in less than seventy screens. The show timings were miserable, and by the time the audience got to know about the film, the theatres were too far off, the show timings inconvenient or the film taken off the screen by Monday. I felt disheartened after having had the film premiere in New York and then travelled to film festivals in Melbourne, Sydney, Stuttgart and Florence, among a few others.

When the film was being released, some journalists who specialize in gossip said stuff like '*Nirmata Onir ko pyaar ho gaya hai*' (Film director Onir is in love). I was worried about how Ashish would deal with this when he called me. He said a leading publication had called him about it. He told me, 'I don't really care, people normally gossip about heavyweights. I am lucky they think I deserve to be gossiped about.' He laughed his carefree laugh, and I was relieved. He called a little later saying that it was on TV and he had got worried and called his parents. He had told his parents that maybe he should not display any signs of affection for me in public. I was very touched when I heard their reply: They knew me and had met my family, and he should not change anything in our equation because of some silly gossip.

# 25

# *Kuchh Bheege Alfaaz* (2019)

In 2018, I started shooting for what was a truly memorable experience; it was also the film that I shot the quickest. *Kuchh Bheege Alfaaz* was with the highly talented and wonderful human being Geetanjali Thapa and the very talented but much-flawed Zain Khan Durrani. The film also had the energetic and earnest Shray Rai Tiwari, who had done a small role in *Shab*. I also worked with the legendary Barun Chanda (I wonder what makes these people so humble and kind), the talented Chandrayee, the spirited Mona Ambegaonkar and the very friendly Saheb Bhattacharya, who loved to take us all partying to GRID. We also cast the extremely talented Shefali Chauhan, sister of my DA Siddharth Chauhan from Shimla, who played a small role in the film.

How the script came to me is in itself a story. I was evaluating scripts that had come for the Sundance-Dhrishyam script lab and came across the script of *Kuchh Bheege Alfaaz* by writer-director Abhishek Chatterjee. I loved the script and hesitantly wrote to him, asking if he would be open to the idea of my directing it. He replied that he had once come to meet me, seeking to be an intern. I had politely refused him, saying that it would be stupid to give up his well-paying job to intern with me. He said if I would let him intern, he would be happy to give me the script. I asked him to come over the next day.

My friend Saurabh Prabhakar, who had also helped us in the marketing of *Chauranga* and *Shab*, introduced me to Yoodlee Films. I knew Sid (Siddharth Anand Kumar) from before and I thought their attempt to nurture indie films was commendable, though I must add that they too could not really survive for long enough to create a new ecosystem in the industry. The entire Yoodlee team was excited about the film, and we started on a beautiful journey of mutual respect and trust. There were a lot of script discussions, but the final creative call was mine in all aspects. And all the discussions were healthy.

The casting took some time as we were looking for someone with a good voice and Urdu diction. Zain, who had joined me as an assistant during *Shab* and had also been training with me to be an actor, was finally chosen. I was happy that Yoodlee was willing to go ahead with a new actor and had not insisted on an experienced person instead. Closer to the shoot, we arranged for Zain to go to a radio studio and learn the nuances of the profession from a few RJs.

I found a new friend in Geetanjali Thapa—I think the Nepali in me felt like I had found a long-lost connection. I love her genuine, no-nonsense attitude and absolutely transparent friendship. And I love, love her as an actor. She just lights up the screen with her smile. Meeting her reminded me of the Nepali girl who was my first crush, Paro. We then lived in Kalikhola, and one day we kids had dressed up as bride and groom and exchanged garlands. I think Ma was so young a mother that she also treated us like dolls that she played with. I wonder what happened to Paro.

During *KBA*, apart from making my three lead characters write their stories, I tried another experiment. I gave them the clothes they would wear in the film a month before the shoot so that they could start owning them. They carried the clothes to Calcutta and decided what the character would wear each day. The assistants would keep track of continuity and laundry. I felt this exercise helped the actors own their characters a little bit more. Working on the artist wardrobes was stylist Pooja Sethi, a person with an infectious laugh.

*KBA* was shot by Nusrat Jafri, with whom I had earlier worked on some fashion documentaries and it had been fun. I was working with a female DOP for the first time, and I think she brought in a certain gentleness to the film that I loved. And it was the fastest that I ever shot a film. We were done in nineteen days, in Calcutta and Shimla. What I love about Nusrat is that she never refuses any shot I want, however difficult it may be logistically. She always tries to make it happen.

My niece Trisha, then sixteen, wrote the poems for the flashback scenes. I felt so proud when she won the Promising Young Writer award at the London Asian Film Festival.

*KBA* is again a very special film because of the overwhelming messages I have received from the time the film released on Netflix. I'll pick two of them from Instagram.

In all honesty, I was aware of my pull to you but I didn't expect I'd keep loving you similarly even after two years. You're still my favourite visual poet. And no matter how many times I see you, you always make me equal parts emotional. You make me accept myself just a bit more. To be me more. To thrive harder to reach my goal which I had given up on around a decade ago. You inspire me. To love. To accept. To heal. To move on. To forgive, myself and others. To be courageous when there seems none. To believe in my randomness, the whole package. All of it. Most of all you make me like my flaws. I have never liked my scars before but now I can't imagine being without them. It's the flaws that make me who I am. But most of all you helped meet someone I can call an amazing friend.

I am perfect because of my imperfections. That perhaps is the first step towards meeting love; to love yourself first. (Shumayla/@cluelessconundrum)

Love . . . is weird. On rainy days it's the ring of a wrong number. It looks very much like a question mark up until the day—out of nowhere, the right answer just walks onto your street.

When that happens, falling in love becomes as easy as your head touching the pillow. It's a late night radio show. It's the hum of poetry in your earbuds. It's your laughter. Love is a good night's sleep.

But when the lovers are not around, is love unemployed? No. It is constantly opening doors and shelves inside you. It's noisy. The cling clang of cutlery can travel across oceans. And if you think there are no doors left to open, that the last time was the last time you loved someone—give it time. Wait a while and you'll see love is capable of opening the windows that weren't there before.

Where does it live? Love owns a small house inside the forest. It's a magic house. It becomes invisible if you try to search for it. The key into that house is acceptance. So call off the search party and forgive your little imperfections. Sit back and relax. Love is on its way. Love is already here. (@barelyswati)

Chakshu was my first AD this time and it's been great to see his growth from when he was an intern in 2012. Ashish, who joined me in 2016, is now my DA. He has been one of the luckier interns because a few days after he joined, I shot an ad with Kareena Kapoor for AND, followed by an ad for Star in Austria. I had named Ashish 'Lost Bist' as he used to be so nervous in the beginning that he always looked lost, and it took a lot of effort getting him to talk. He's now an expert at blackmailing me, and each time I scold him, he goes and complains to Ma, who has declared to all the assistants that she is the ultimate boss because she is the director's mom.

My Baba and Ma live with me and Ma loves to chat with my team. Currently, Ashu is her favourite. Any time Ma has a problem with her Facebook or Instagram, Ashish has to stop all work and attend to her. I like how after lunch every day, she steps into the office and offers everyone a clove. I am happy to see how quickly Ashish has mastered various editing software and also the camera. He shot two documentaries for me along with Nikunj—*Widows of Vrindavan* and *Raising the Bar* and more recently shot sections of *SAMA*, an Indo-Italian collaboration. He also sportingly models for my poems and in one of them, he even had to have his arms around me romantically. Raj Suri clicked the photo. Of course, Ashu is questioned by his girlfriends, but I am proud to see how secure he is about himself and hence us.

~

Over the last three years, I have been working a lot in Kashmir. I have organized workshops for students through the Indian Army there. The research for the Pulwama series and another series on inspiring stories of army–civilian interactions makes me travel across Kashmir, meeting all kinds of interesting people. People from the army, civilians, activists, journalists, students, former militants, separatist leaders—I meet all kinds of people. I feel sad for the unending sorrow and violence the people have experienced. There are many narratives and many points of view, and I have no idea what the road to peace is. I do try in my little way to take what I believe is a small step towards peace, and I try and include all voices in my narrative.

While working in Kashmir, I make sure that I have Kashmiri assistants working with me. Moin and Saleem Reshi feel like family. Saleem has been teaching me Kashmiri, but the most difficult part of learning the language is that when I try to speak with anyone, they reply in Hindi or English and laugh at my attempts. But I am not going to give up. Some of my Kashmiri friends jokingly call me 'half Kashmiri' and tell me that I have probably travelled across the state more than most of them. For me, going to Kashmir now at times means not letting anyone know, like I sometimes do when I go to Calcutta. There are too many people I know who would feel hurt if I didn't visit them. The family of one of my first Kashmiri assistants, Azaan, always insists that I should come and stay with them like I did the first time I visited Kashmir. I feel guilty that I don't manage to make it happen enough. I feel blessed that my Kashmiri assistants like Saleem sometimes come to Bombay and take care of my parents when I am away travelling. When I witness the love I receive from their families and the love my parents give them, I wonder why this can't be the overall narrative in the country. Why can't the narrative of love and acceptance defeat the narrative of hate? I think we will defeat hate . . . some day soon . . .

It rained all night,
I woke up,
To your glance,
I blinked my eyes,
You were still there,
Smiling gently.
I reached out to touch you,
The thin air embraced me,
Drowning me with the fragrance of the mountains.
The rain continues to fall,
Indifferent to my anguish,

Refusing to find answers for me,
To give me strength,
To not seek asylum in the mirage.
For the infinite universe awaits . . .
Somewhere there is a shooting star for me.

# BITTERSWEET

# 26

# Park Street

It was 30 August 2020. I was taking a post-dinner walk when I bumped into him; it had been a while since I last saw him. I will call him 'Park Street'. You'll soon know why.

December 2018. Times LitFest Kolkata, Tollygunge Club.

Winter evenings in Calcutta are usually lovely, with just that slight nip in the air that brings a spring to the step. I was in a panel discussion about queer representation. This was probably the festival's first edition and things were kind of disorganized, with multiple sessions happening simultaneously in very non-intimate spaces. Plus, because of the venue, a lot of people thought that it was not open for all. As I started speaking, my eyes travelled across the room since I like to keep evaluating the audience interest level so that, if necessary, I can change track.

As my gaze travelled from right to left across the room, it stopped midway, at the door. He was standing there—light-skinned, oval face, brownish hair, tall. He was an attractive man. All through my talk, my eyes kept finding their way back to him. He was with a couple of foreigners, and I assumed that he was one of the international guests.

Once the session was over, the doorway stood empty—he was no longer there. I had planned on hanging around for some time as I wanted to attend some of the other sessions, and went to the writers' lounge for some coffee. As I switched on my mobile, there was a message on my Grindr. The profile pic of the man looked similar to the man at the door. The message read, 'Nice talk. Btw I liked your pants.' It seemed like my evening in Calcutta was going to get more exciting. I texted back.

I: Were you the man standing at the door, constantly texting?
He: Yes.
I: I was wondering who's this attractive man.
He: You're flattering me.
I: Why didn't you come up and meet me after the talk?
He: Your fans had surrounded you and I felt intimidated.
I: Am I so scary? I don't bite.
He: Haha
I: I'm at the lounge having coffee, why don't you join me?
He: Well, I have already left the venue and am on my way back to the hotel.
I: What a pity. Where are you from?
He: I'll be flying back to Delhi tomorrow.
I: I'm flying back to Mumbai tomorrow. And I have nothing to do this evening.
He: I too will be in my hotel room in Park Street. Don't know anyone here.
I: Maybe you should turn back.
He: Are you serious? I'm half-an-hour away.
I: I can wait for the beautiful man.
He: It'll take me 45 minutes.
I: I'm waiting.

It took him about an hour to come back. He was smartly dressed in jeans and a black polo T-shirt with a thin red line running around the collar. He walked into the lounge with a chuckle—he had this irresistible chuckle that was difficult not to fall in love with.

We had coffee and spoke for an hour, each of us probably checking if the other wanted to take this forward. I told him that I wanted to go back to my hotel to change my pants as they were inviting too much attention and I already had all the attention that I needed (I was wearing maroon pyjama pants from Anaam, a designer who pushes me to wear stuff beyond my comfort zone). He laughed loudly.

We spoke non-stop during the drive from Tollygunge Club to Marriott. At the lobby, I asked him if he would prefer to wait downstairs or come up to my room. He said he would come up since he wanted to use the restroom.

We went up, he used the restroom and I changed into a black T-shirt and jeans. We kept talking, and he told me that as a teenager, he had the biggest crush on my friend Sanjay Suri. So I told him that we should click a selfie together and send Sanjay a hi. He held the phone and I put my arms around his neck as he clicked the photo. Then he turned around and started kissing me.

During the next hour, we kissed a lot, laughed a lot and kept debating about how far we should go. He kept saying that he didn't like going all the way the first time, yet he was the one constantly trying to undress me and then teasing me saying, 'You Bombay guys are so shameless.' Our banter in between the kisses and laughter was a Delhi versus Bombay thing.

I took him out for dinner to Peter Cat, a restaurant on Park Street. Later that night, we sat on the steps of an adjoining shop and looked at the moon. I decided I would nickname him 'Park Street'.

Over the next seven months, we met each time I was in Delhi or when PS (Park Street) came to Bombay on any official work. I believed we enjoyed each other's company, and having met him on Grindr, I was not worried about him suddenly getting married. The only thing I found odd about him was that he was somehow very reluctant to come home or meet any of my friends. I thought that he perhaps felt like that would seem like a commitment, and he didn't want to commit. It didn't bother me too much. I liked his company but wasn't thinking beyond that.

I was planning to go to Australia for an event in August. I made a nervous offer to him—nervous because we were in a 'no strings attached' relationship—that I could give up my business class travel and opt for two economy class tickets if he would like to come along and spend some time with me. I told him that it would be fun to get to know each other beyond hotel room lovemaking. It made me really happy when he chuckled and agreed readily.

Australia was magical. I told him about how You had hurt me, but I mostly didn't remember You at all for those ten days. He was one person who helped me love my body, for he gave it so much love. He made me shun shame, and we could be naked in each other's presence without switching off the lights. Sometimes we made love three times a day.

We walked around, exploring parks and streets, driving to different destinations. We kissed in the middle of the streets and parks . . . it was all so special.

I seek you,
Amidst neon nights,
At the Playboy club,
Among a multitude of bodies,
Swaying to the monotonous beats,
I find you.

I seek you,
Amidst the city crowd,
Strolling down Marine Drive,
Hands clasping transform,
Into yours and mine,
I find you.

I seek you,
Across many coffee tables,
Engulfing my presence,
In the scent on his collar,
My colleagues wondering,
Why I am smiling,
They can't see who holds my gaze,
I find you.

I see you,
When the moon is bloody red,
And the night raining mangoes,
The air restlessly panting,
And all I see,
Is the tranquillity in your eyes,
You find me.

One night, I had to go to a party where I thought he might get bored. So, I told him that maybe he should explore the gay clubs in Melbourne. I was back in my hotel room around 1 a.m. and went off to sleep not expecting him to be back before the morning. He returned at 3 a.m. and woke me up to tell me how he thought I was just perfect. We ended up making love.

I was a little taken aback the next day when he asked me if he could go to Sydney as his parents wanted him to meet a prospective bride. I knew he was closeted with his family, but I hadn't seen this coming. I made it very clear that I wouldn't stop him. After all, we weren't formally seeing each other. But I did tell him that I would be really disappointed if he went ahead with this and that he needed to talk to his family soon. Messing up a girl's life is just not okay. He agreed with me that he needed to make that move soon, and maybe moving from Delhi to Bombay would help.

He went to Sydney the following day, and to my dismay, I found myself thinking about him and missing him much more than I had expected. When he came back after a day, he seemed relieved that the Sydney trip was over and said that he wished we could just run away somewhere.

Our host threw a party the next evening and many from my industry were in attendance. PS came along with me. He was wearing a suit and looking dapper. I could see many of the people present were dying of curiosity. What was his equation with me? Were we just friends? Was he my lover? Was he an aspiring actor? I could hear all the unspoken questions. I had warned him about this, and he had come prepared; in fact, he now seemed to be enjoying the attention. After the party, a few of us were invited to continue partying at a colleague's hotel room.

PS and I changed into more casual attire and joined the after-party. It was a warm and intimate circle of people, and though I felt a little out of place, the kind host made sure that PS and I were comfortable. This is when I noticed that one of my fellow film-makers seemed to have taken a fancy to PS.

The next morning, when PS told me that the film-maker had added him on Insta, I wasn't surprised since I found that I too had been added. Now, let me make it clear that although PS was introduced to everyone as my friend, many from the circle knew that he was my lover. I joked with PS that I wouldn't be surprised if he got a message from the film-maker during the day.

By the afternoon, the gentleman had started messaging PS, who was giggling like an overwhelmed little boy, laughing and sharing the content with me. Though it was very obvious to me that the film-maker was trying to flirt with PS, when PS asked me whether he should reply, I told him that he should, since messages do need replying to! The film-maker told him that they should definitely catch up in Bombay or Delhi. I hid my irritation with the film-maker for being so unethical and shameless. And PS for being what I thought was naive.

Another couple days of bliss, and it was time to return. Him to Delhi, and me to Bombay. But we had started to talk seriously about his shifting to Bombay.

Once in Delhi, PS put in his papers and started to apply for jobs in Bombay. I forwarded his CV to a few people I knew. I think he came down to Bombay for an interview some time in October 2019. He had earlier promised to stay over at my place this time, and we had planned to cook together. I was excited and had told my friends that they would get to meet him. It seemed as though we were on the brink of taking the relationship one step further.

The first disappointment was when he told me that he was flying back to Delhi the same day and we should meet for lunch at a restaurant. I was genuinely upset but went to meet him for lunch, which is when I found him gushing and excited like a little boy. When I asked him what he was so excited about, he told me that I should not get judgmental or be mad at him. I told him I would not.

He had gone for coffee to the film-maker's office, where they had chatted for two hours. About how lonely a person the film-maker was and about how PS seemed to be such a wonderful man . . . The film-maker had also asked him about the job profile and salary he was looking for and said that they should keep in touch, etc., etc.

At that moment, something had just not seemed right . . . Well, that was the last time we met, until 30 August 2020. He had shifted to Bombay and was living with his brother and sister-in-law very close to where I live. But, apparently, he had been too busy to call, forget about meeting me.

Week 1: He was busy house-hunting and fitting in at his new job.

Week 2: He was still trying to fit into the rhythm of the new job. I had wanted him to come with me to watch some films at MAMI, but he had said that it would be difficult as he was living with a family, house-hunting and also had a new job. I waited, but there were no calls or meetings. Just WhatsApp texts.

Week 3, on WhatsApp:

I: Hey.

PS: Hey, what's up?

I: When are we meeting?

PS: Weekdays are hectic, it's just crazy. But will meet you soon.

I: I was thinking we could go and watch 'The Sky Is Pink' together.

PS: Oh, I watched it at the premiere.

I: Oh.

PS: The entire office was invited.

It was strange that he had not bothered to tell me which organization he had joined.

Week 4: No communication from him unless I messaged asking something. I asked him what his plans were for the weekend. He said he was going to Alibaug for the weekend with his office team.

Week 5: He had still not made a single attempt to meet me. This, after the time we spent together in Australia.

I decided that I couldn't let myself be treated like this. I wouldn't be kept waiting. I sent him a message.

I: I want you to be honest with me. I find it strange that you've been here for 5 weeks, live 15 minutes away, and yet do not have the time to meet me. What is it?

PS: No . . . It's nothing like that, I am just caught up . . .

I: Tell me honestly, it's okay. I'd rather you are honest. Are you seeing that film-maker?

PS: How can you even suggest that? I haven't even spoken to him after shifting.

I: Honestly, I don't give a f\*\*\* whether you're seeing him or not. But I'd be a fool to not understand that you're avoiding me. You're hurting me by making no effort to meet. I can't be treated like an afterthought, and if this is what I mean to you, I think we should forget it.

PS: So, what is it? Just like that, you want to end it?

I: What is it that you want? That I keep waiting? You knew how hurt I was when you walked into my life. And yet you hurt me too with your dishonesty. I'm done.

Had I been mistaken, he would have called me up, tried to talk to me, made an effort. But he did not. I was also angry that my fellow film-maker hadn't hesitated for a moment before starting to flirt with my love interest just moments after meeting him at a party.

I had just started healing when PS walked into my life, healing from what is probably the most intense and also the most traumatic of all the relationships I've had. PS knew about it, and he still went ahead and hurt me.

# 27

# Thinking of You

How do I talk about You and yet not talk about You. You, who for me, will never become 'he'. Now that all the anger and bitterness is spent, all that remains is hurt; but more than the hurt still is the love. Should I be mortified that after all that happened, love still remains? I don't know; but yes, it is still love.

And maybe that is why I need to end with You.

Delhi, 2013. My friend Deepak Bharadwaj's living room. A small party, maybe ten or twelve people, me sitting in one corner of the room as I watch You walk in through the door. From that moment on, no one else in the room exists for me. I am so aware of your presence that although You are sitting far away, near the living room door, I feel ready to dissolve when your eyes occasionally acknowledge my presence.

You finally walk up to where I am and we are introduced. We speak for a long time, but I don't remember anything except that my throat goes dry. And then, as I am gazing into your eyes, You promise to keep in touch and meet me in Bombay.

Even now, my thoughts feel somehow incoherent when I think of You or try to put into words what we were. Even now,

I can feel my ears go red, and I'm almost feeling anxious, as if You are watching over my fingers as I type this.

I have no recollection of our interactions over the next few months, but one evening You stood outside my door with your bag. I remember that night. While you slept beside me, I was sleepless and my fingers longed to feel your skin. But I didn't dare touch You as I did not want to make a mistake and lose You. It was probably a hot night as I remember you taking off your T-shirt sometime during the night and turning away from me. The moonlight that leaked through the curtains outlined your contour and your skin glistened. I lay awake all night, steeped in desire.

And then, there is that night from January 2017, when You again lay beside me, your back to me. The glow of WhatsApp messages on your phone lit up your face and You occasionally stepped outside the room to talk to someone. That night had felt desolate.

We lay naked,
Side by side.
I had laid naked my soul,
You had laid naked your body.

The night desolate,
A cacophony of silence,
As the unspoken disseminate.

We lay naked,
Cloaked by words
That did not find their way
To your lips.
We lay naked,
Drenched in tears
That did not escape
My eyes.

You had told me once about how much You wanted to go paragliding, and I had planned that we would celebrate the new year with a weekend of paragliding. The day had been beautiful—we had walked to some Buddhist caves and felt at peace. I had even managed to overcome my fear of paragliding because You were there, urging me on.

But that night I had known that what I had been refusing to accept was true. That You had, for some time now, left me. I needed to tell You that You were being cruel in not talking to me about it, in keeping me in the dark.

The next day, we walked in the forest and lay down on the grass by the pond, side by side, yet not touching each other. You did not pull me close and place my head on your chest like You had done innumerable times in the past.

WTF Versova, 8 January 2017. We were back in Bombay and I asked You to join me for a drink. WTF was the place where we had spent countless evenings drinking beer and chatting about life and art. I told You that I wanted us to stop meeting as it made it tougher for me, that it was evident to me that You had moved on and that You were hiding something from me. Of course, You denied everything vehemently, insisted that You still loved me and said I was imagining the distance. How did You expect me not to know the difference when your lover has not made love to you for months, has suddenly shifted the love to a platonic space? There was so much dishonesty, behaving like so much of our past had never existed, that we had not spent countless nights loving one another.

I remember those nights when, after we made love, You would draw me close to your chest, and I would often feel uncontrollable sorrow. I would tell you that lying in your arms, I had this foreboding that I would soon lose You. And You would look at me with your indolent eyes and promise that You would stay. I would then sleep peacefully, though that sadness would come back to me later. You had promised to be the one to light my pyre. Now, we don't even talk.

2014. I was in Delhi for work. We had become good friends by then and we could chat for hours about literature, cinema, music and life. I would look forward to your smile every day, and when one day You mentioned that you were house-hunting, I hesitantly suggested that You move in with me. You readily agreed.

Smoke-filled evenings, sometimes accompanied by beer or wine as we would chat into the night. I soon felt that You knew everything about me and understood me like no one ever had before. You always listened with so much interest and affection, and I too began to feel like I knew You well. I don't know if my eyes betrayed the fact that I was in love with You. For me, your proximity was beautiful, and yet I was always anxious that if You guessed my secret, you would perhaps be uncomfortable with our closeness.

One night in Delhi, as we stood smoking our cigarettes in the balcony of my Lajpat Nagar *barsati*, you asked me about the incident that has traumatized me the most in life: the false charge of molestation against me in 2011. As I told You about the incident that had shaken me to the core, I saw tears roll down your eyes. That night, You kissed me and told me that You loved me, that you would never hurt me.

I believed You, and from that night on, what started with gentle kisses became the most intimate, intense, emotional and physical relationship I've ever had. You told me that I was the second man You had been physically intimate with. The first was as a teenager with one of your friends, which had been a purely physical act. You said that you loved me and didn't want me to be with any other man. I accepted your bisexuality and also your being polyamorous. I have never been too possessive, loving my own space and giving others theirs. But what does matter to me is honesty. I feel I am capable of loving more than one person at the same time, and that love for different people does not need to be compared or lead to exclusiveness. So, I accepted that You could have relationships with women while being in a relationship with me. As long as I felt loved, it didn't matter to me. But though I didn't ask it of You, You did promise that there would be no other men in your life.

This was the time when someone with whom I had an undefined relationship between 2013 to 2014 decided to end things. I still think of him with a lot of affection and love. And he too treats me with love.

My short story with him was pretty funny.

He had messaged me on Instagram for an event. I had readily agreed as I loved his doe-shaped eyes (I have a thing for eyes and lips). My secret name for him was 'Little Buddha'. Soon, I was walking around with him, discovering a Himalayan hill station. The event was hectic and we hardly had any alone time, except one momo dinner at a Chinese restaurant over which we bonded. When we met again some months later, I still had no idea about his orientation. We were supposed to share a room and he told me, 'Listen, I want to tell you that I am straight.' I told him that it was okay, but I thought that he was beautiful. He blushed and we went to sleep.

The second night he told me, 'Listen, I'm sorry I lied to you. I am actually bisexual.' I laughed and I said it's okay. We held hands, and I stroked his eyebrows and went to sleep.

The third night he said, 'I'm sorry, I lied. I'm actually gay.' We kissed and made love.

I don't know if he was what I would call a lover. I think he was somewhere between a close friend and lover. It is an affair I'll always cherish.

We were at a Lajpat Nagar coffee shop when he told me that he was going away. We were sipping coffee, both of us weeping. We didn't fight—he just knew that there was someone special waiting for him, that it was someplace else where he would be happier. He suddenly got up and sat on my lap, hugging me. I loved this about him—how he didn't care if others were shocked; he expressed his affection without any fear.

He was the first man with whom I had a romantic dance in a nightclub (I don't consider my wild nights at Voodoo as romantic). His arms around my neck, we had danced to a slow number until a moron seeking my attention started trying to get in between.

I woke up
To find you gone.
On the bedsheet lay
A baby pine cone,
A bit of the distant mountain,
That took you away.

But then I will always have this.

Coming back to You, he was the first person to tell me that You would hurt me. I didn't believe him, thinking that he was jealous even at the time of parting. I was foolish; he truly cared for me. Maybe losing him didn't cause me much distress because I had just found You, and I was experiencing one of the happiest phases of my life.

It's odd that whenever I think of You I can't think linearly. Sometimes I find us in Paris—holding hands and walking, the quick stolen kiss at the top of the Eiffel Tower, making love in my friend's guest bedroom in Berlin. Sometimes we are in a tiny hotel bathroom in London or in my room in our Calcutta house—we had promised to travel the world together and make love in every city. I remember how, while in transit at airports, we would run around looking for the smoking room to have a quick smoke before the next flight. And how we would later hold hands beneath the blanket on flights.

I no longer go to airport smoking rooms. You left your imprints all over my world, and some of those I now avoid.

In 2018, I was talking about You to a friend as we walked by the river Salzach in Salzburg. I showed her the ring You had given me when we had exchanged rings, and she asked me to throw it into the river, that the act would help me break free. The next day, I told her that I was feeling truly liberated after having flung away the ring. But here I am in 2022, writing about You while a finger of each hand sports a ring that You gave me—one from the time we bought each other rings at a flea market in Paris and the other from the Kalighat temple in Calcutta.

How do I just erase all of that . . . does life have an erase button so powerful?

When You moved to Bombay in 2015, You started spending your weekends with me. I would take You to all those pubs and eateries that I used to visit during my initial years in Bombay—Toto's Garage, Hawaiian Shack, Pal's Fish Corner, Mohammed Ali Street during Eid. If Ma and Baba weren't close by, You would kiss me while I was in the kitchen, cooking. Then there were those nights with pitchers at WTF. You too were never afraid of displaying a certain amount of affection and, strangely, it was me who always discouraged You because I didn't want You to be judged. Thinking of it now, I feel that wasn't a nice thing to have done. In a way, I had perhaps nurtured deceit.

There were also evenings of music as I was learning to play the guitar. We would sing (out of tune) old Hindi songs into the night or just listen to '*Aaj jaane ki zidd na karo*' (Don't insist on leaving tonight). I think You were the only lover I have had who insisted on holding my hand while watching movies. We waited till the lights went off and then You would take my hand in yours. I guess this is what society does to us—even a simple act like holding hands can be subjected to so much hatred and condemnation that one hides it. By the time that draconian law changed, we had already parted ways. But I wonder, how many of us would openly hold hands even now? The world around us is changing at a very slow pace and these small gestures still remain absent in our public spaces.

Imagine growing up in a world where you never heard stories about yourself, where you were never present in a history or a biology class. Never present in cinema or TV apart from being ridiculed with over-the-top caricatures that you could not and did not identify with. Your sense of identity was absent since your childhood. And then, one day you realized that you are the 'other'. You have to learn to accept yourself. You also have the task of making the world accept you and your love. I always wonder why it is so difficult for the heteronormative world to accept me; I accepted the heteronormative world without any effort. But I suppose I was never given a choice, and they were not aware of me.

I was very happy when You shifted to my flat sometime in 2015, and this was the first time I actually lived with someone I loved. It has remained the only time. The following months were the most beautiful ones and yet, at the same time, those months were also the beginning of the end of our relationship.

At some point, I realized that my acceptance of your right to be polyamorous did not give You the right to hurt me. You started returning late night after night—at 4 a.m. or 5 a.m.—drunk and trying to make up by being extra affectionate. I used to pretend to be asleep whenever I heard You at the door, but I was actually awake, waiting. When You slipped into bed and hugged me, I no longer felt the affection that I earlier used to. I started writing poems about a feeling of absence, and You wrote poems of love. You made me believe that they were for me and I would be moved, as though we were having a dialogue through poetry. At that time, I didn't know that there were others too who were being made to feel that the poems were for them.

The night stares blankly,
The anxious breeze murmurs
Cravings of the desolate skin.

The moist glance on the fecund sand,
Anticipating your shadow,
To merge into mine . . .

Sprawled side by side,
Beneath the void,
The lake whispered
Stories disparate.

Grab me by the hand
And set me off
To the other bank,
Where I need not breathe you . . .

At one point, I realized that I couldn't continue to let my work suffer as a result of the constant unhappiness I felt at being taken for granted. I told You that maybe it would be better for both of us if we lived separately. I remember the day You packed your bags and stood at my door with tears in your eyes. You said, 'I'm leaving, but my heart remains in this room and I'll come running back every second day.'

You showed me the flat you were renting, saying I was the first person to see it, and I helped You set up the place. A few days later, I had a minor accident when a car ran over my foot. It wasn't a serious injury, but my foot had to be put in a cast and I was in a lot of pain. Since You had lived with me for so many months, I was hoping You would volunteer to be with me at a time when I was finding it tough to manage alone. But you had disappeared, perhaps busy celebrating the new flat. Much later, I came to know that your girlfriend—whose existence I hadn't even known of—had moved in with You. Of course, she didn't know that I was your lover.

In 2016, I constantly felt traumatized, questioning myself for staying on in a relationship that seemed to be more hurtful than comforting. And yet, I kept holding on to those fleeting moments of togetherness. I would push back the thought that, barring once, You had never asked me over to your place. I didn't realize that You couldn't call me home as your girlfriend was staying there, and even the weekends when You would come over kept getting fewer, I presume because You had to figure out what excuses to give her. Yet I was never totally sure about what I meant to you because there still would be moments of intense love. We travelled together to Australia in August 2016. We held hands on the flight, stole a kiss and dared each other to steal an airline blanket.

But once in Melbourne, I sensed the distance once again, something that your newfound interest in religion made more pronounced. There would be the odd evening when You would suddenly hold my hands under the table in the middle of dinner or even kiss me. But it was the space between us that I was constantly aware of. I could feel the effort You were making to make me feel loved.

Melbourne was one city that we travelled to and did not make love in. That was also the last time we travelled together out of the country. The plan to visit the Seven Wonders together disintegrated, and I wrote the series of poems, 'Diary of a cigarette butt'.

It'd been raining,
The sky overcast.

I sat by the window,
Where you used to sit,
And smoked a cigarette.
I missed your wet lips
On the cigarette butt.

Remember how we walked
With our hands on the walls
Of Neruda's Macchu Picchu,
Listening to the voices
Silenced centuries ago,
Yet speaking to you and me
As we sat by the window,
Continents away,
Smoking into the night.

I miss those voices,
That spoke to me,
As I felt your wet lips,
On the cigarette butt.

I was in New York—1 May 2017. I had not met or spoken with You since the night of 8 January at WTF when I told You that I didn't feel loved any more and that you were hiding something from me. You could have told me that You were in love with someone else and living with that person. But you chose to vehemently deny everything and, while parting that night, insisted that You wouldn't let me walk away from your life. For the next four-and-a-half months, You made no attempt to connect with me.

I was in New York attending the NY Indian Film Festival when I received your voice mail saying that You loved me to the moon and back, telling me how much You missed me and that You wished me happiness. Hearing your voice made all my defences collapse. I called You, and we promised to meet once I was back.

There You stood outside the door, and it felt as if You had never gone away. We hugged and kissed and wept. You were back in my life, but somewhere deep down, I was aware that it could never be the same again.

Autumn 2017. You told me that You had fallen in love with a poetess from Canada. I pretended to be unaffected and happy for you, although I was struggling to accept the fact that You were no longer present in my life as a lover. You introduced me to her over a video call, and I actually ended up becoming friends with her over the next few months. Even though our relationship had changed drastically, You pretended that it was the same. Sometimes I wonder whether You thought I was a naïve, trusting fool. I remember one night when we had gone to a pub with a group of friends and You were so drunk that you picked me up and danced. I didn't know whether to feel happy or sad or to perhaps keep feeding myself the lie that You actually loved me and that it was society and your new-found religiosity that stopped You from being in a relationship with me.

Why do I still try and find justifications for your behaviour?

I remember the only time I spent a night at your house, which was also when I met your father. That night was one of the saddest of my life. You dragged a mattress from the other room and laid it on the floor for me. This was not just for the benefit of the family, not just for appearances. We didn't share a bed.

May 2018. I was in Vrindavan shooting for the documentary *Widows of Vrindavan*. I was tired after the shoot and happened to be checking the Insta stories of friends. I came across an article about a girl speaking about her experience of physical and mental abuse by her ex-boyfriend. Reading the article shook me as it seemed like the abusive ex-boyfriend was You. It was 11 p.m. when I called her. I think we spoke till 1 a.m.

I didn't sleep that night.

The months that followed unfolded like a horror story. I got to meet and know various women whom You had hurt emotionally and physically during the time we were together, some whose existence I didn't even know of. I came to know about the women You brought to my flat when I wasn't home. Lies . . . so many lies.

I almost feel like I don't know that person. For me, You weren't a person capable of such aggression. None of us are perfect—You have your weaknesses and I have mine—but this wasn't what I could have ever imagined as possible. I remembered that You were the only person Baba had ever warned me about. He never interferes about my lovers or friends, yet about You he had once told me, 'There is something not right about this boy.' I had argued with Baba, saying that he was prejudiced.

The poetess from Canada called me. Apparently, she had discontinued the long-distance relationship when she found out that You were making the same promises to other girls and that You were supposed to be getting married in a couple of months.

Last night I had an apparition.
I lay beside him,
Bruised within . . .
The light from the mobile,
Lit up his face.
His eyes restless, searching,
As messages flew across . . .
Professing love.
And then I saw her,
Lying on his other side.
As she wept silently,
She, who was violated,
Emotionally and physically.
I reached out to her,

And she gave me her hand,
And we walked towards the door,
Where you stood,
Brave woman,
And hugged her and me.
As we walked towards the sunrise,
His face was lit up,
And his fingers continued to type vigorously.
He did not see us leave.

You, who, on that 2017 evening at WTF, when I told You it was over, had told me that I was the one closest to You after your mom and dad, hadn't even informed me that You were getting engaged in a week's time.

Perhaps I always knew how it was, and so I had saved your name on my phone as 'Mirage'.

I recall how jealous You had pretended to be when you once met 'Rondu', the name I used for one of my love interests.

One night in 2009, 10 p.m. I was chatting with this boy on Facebook. He lived in South Bombay. By 1 a.m., he had driven down to meet me. We chatted for three hours. He was a very cute and attractive boy. Tall, with long eyelashes. He spent three hours trying to convince me how it would be perfect if we were in each other's lives. For three hours, I tried to convince him, over cigarettes, that he was much too young and immature, and I didn't understand why he wanted to be in my life. This continued every weekend. He would come over and try to convince me, and I would not be convinced. I was constantly thinking that there had to be some other motive; I was not ready to trust him. I used to enjoy talking to him, but his earnestness also made me hesitate to just have a casual affair with him. We would chat; he was always so fascinated by my work, and I loved to listen to stories of his world. He was from a business background; he knew money talk, which I have never understood. He would laugh at how completely stupid I was about money matters.

Six months later, I was in the UK for an event, and he called to check how I was doing. As we spoke, there was a knock on my hotel room door, and I opened the door to find him standing there. He had travelled all the way, still trying to convince me that I should seriously consider letting him into my life.

I did. That was the first time we made love.

We travelled together a lot. To Spain, Paris, Berlin, Melbourne, Calcutta, Delhi, Goa and Kashmir. Wherever we travelled, he too, like me, enjoyed walking for hours exploring the city. He would care about what I wore and ate and would be there, looking at me proudly from the audience whenever I went up on stage.

He did have one habit that I found difficult to get used to. He loved gambling and would disappear for hours at night to go to casinos. But I tried accepting that this was how he was, and he made up for those absent hours all through the day.

I used to often fight with him, though. About his vacillating approach to work and his addiction to gambling, which would at times make him borrow money from people. I could see that he wanted to get out of the vicious circle, but he wasn't succeeding and it was affecting our relationship.

Cut to 2012. We had won the National Award for our 2011 film, *I Am*. Sanjay and Ambika were at the airport with me, going to Delhi to receive it. Sanjay kept insisting that we wait a little before checking in, and then I suddenly saw him walking up to us, grinning ear to ear. He had connected with Sanjay to find out when we were leaving and booked himself on the same flight. He told me that he had to be there with me on such an important day of my life. He was there, cheering me from the audience. I knew this was true affection and love . . . however imperfect it was.

That night, after the party, the four of us were chatting over wine in Sanjay's room, and he said he was sleepy and went off to the room we were sharing. Sanjay and Ambika started to tease me, and after a while, I went back to my room. He had bathed and was waiting for me wrapped in a white towel, his hair still wet, his perfumed skin damp.

A few months later, he told me that he would have to get married but wanted our relationship to continue. I told him I was okay with that as long as he was willing to tell his wife what I meant to him. I didn't want to, consciously, ever be a part of causing another person hurt because my lover was being dishonest.

But You, whom I had loved more than anyone, used our relationship as an excuse and tool to hurt people.

I never understood what your fiancée meant by saying that she knew how important I was in your life and that she wanted me to forgive You and the three of us could have a happy future as friends. I really did not know what that was . . .

By the way, I still have one of your T-shirts that I sometimes wear at night and sleep. I can still smell You.

My palm remembers—
The eyeballs quivering,
The shape of your nose,
The warmth of your cheek,
The silken touch of your lips,
The soft earlobes,
The arched eyebrows,
The perspiring forehead.
As sleepless nights engulf me,
These palms bring forth memories,
Of sensations divine . . .
Stories of love,
Tenderness,
Caring,
Hurt,

And farewell.
The contour of your face,
Engraved in my palm,
I drown my face in it,
No time,
No distance,
Nothing can take that away from me.
It's forever mine
You . . . locked in the memory of my palm.

~

Late 2020. The COVID-19 virus had engulfed our lives. It gave me a lot of time to think about life, about You. It made me, for the first time, think about what You had once told me and I hadn't listened to properly. You had told me that you were having problems and seeing a counsellor or a psychiatrist; that you were taking medicines, and that that was the reason for your sudden fits of anger, fainting, crying and memory loss. Though I had never personally experienced your anger and had only seen the tears, I now feel guilty that I perhaps did not listen closely enough and that maybe You were telling me the truth. Maybe somewhere in the labyrinth of lies, You were also fighting your own demons. I'll probably never find out.

I remember us sitting inside Love & Latte after one of our last big fights. You were telling me that you were sorry, that I was your only friend in Bombay, that You loved me immensely, that You were seeing a counsellor . . . And this will sound like a 'filmy' coincidence, but at that very moment, a young boy walked up to You and said, 'Hey buddy, it was a lot of fun at the party last night, na . . .' Just when I was ready to believe You, everything came crumbling down yet again.

The mountain
Was aflame all night.
The dawn
Gifted an ocean of ashes.

Buried in the ocean bed,
Not lost forever,
The ashes preserve
His touch,
His voice,
His taste,
His colour,
His scent,
My dreams.

The ashes remain to remind me,
When the air is still,
The night forlorn,
That once,
Many doleful moons ago,
The mountain was in flames.

~

In spite of all the anguish, I'm living a life of love, lust, loss, and I
love the journey.

I continue to nurture the idea of falling in love. Every year, I
tell myself that next year I will get married. So, as of now, I think
I will find my partner this year and marry him next year. Not that
I am a big fan of the institution of marriage. But maybe we can
redefine the rules. I just want to have all the fun, mind you, not the
fanfare. No, I do not want a Big Fat Gay Indian Wedding. But an

intimate one with people I love, and, of course, I am going to ask Anita Dongre to dress me . . . See, I am dreaming yet again . . .

I started writing poems because of You and nearly all my poems are about You. I used to love reading your poems, imagining that they were in response to mine. And then I stopped . . .

Your toothbrush,
Worn out,
Standing next to mine,
Refuses to find its way,
Into the dustbin.